T0304785

# Stitching Governance for Labour Rights

Transnational labour governance is in urgent need of a new paradigm of democratic participation, with those who are most affected – typically workers – placed at the centre. To achieve this, principles of industrial democracy and transnational governance must come together to inform institutions within global supply chains. This book traces the development of 'transnational industrial democracy', using responses to the 2013 Rana Plaza disaster as the empirical context. A particular focus is placed on the Bangladesh Accord and the JETI Workplace Social Dialogue programme. Drawing on longitudinal field research from 2013–2020, the authors argue that the reality of modern-day supply chain capitalism has neither optimal institutional frameworks nor effective structures of industrial relations. Informed by principles of industrial democracy, the book aims at enhancing emerging forms of private transnational governance as 'second-best' institutions.

JULIANE REINECKE is Professor of Management at Saïd Business School, University of Oxford. She is a Fellow at the Cambridge Institute for Sustainability Leadership and Research Fellow at Cambridge Judge Business School, from where she received her PhD. Juliane's research focuses on transnational governance, collective action and multi-stakeholder collaboration, sustainability in organizations and in global value chains. She serves as Associate Editor of *Academy of Management Journal* and as a trustee of the Society for the Advancement of Management Studies (SAMS).

JIMMY DONAGHEY is Professor of Human Resource Management at the University of South Australia, Australia. His main research interests focus on the effects of internationalisation on the employment relationship. He is an editor of the journal *Work, Employment and Society*. Aside from his academic interest in employment relations, Jimmy has been an active participant in industrial relations in both the UK, where he was a branch officer and national executive member of UCU for over 15 years, and Australia, where he is currently branch secretary of the UniSA NTEU branch.

# Business, Value Creation, and Society

SERIES EDITORS

R. Edward Freeman, *University of Virginia*
Jeremy Moon, *Copenhagen Business School*
Mette Morsing, *Copenhagen Business School*

The purpose of this innovative series is to examine, from an international standpoint, the interaction of business and capitalism with society. In the twenty-first century it is more important than ever that business and capitalism come to be seen as social institutions that have a great impact on the welfare of human society around the world. Issues such as globalization, environmentalism, information technology, the triumph of liberalism, corporate governance, and business ethics all have the potential to have major effects on our current models of the corporation and the methods by which value is created, distributed and sustained among all stakeholder–customers, suppliers, employees, communities, and financiers.

# Stitching Governance for Labour Rights

Towards Transnational Industrial Democracy?

**JULIANE REINECKE**
*University of Oxford*

**JIMMY DONAGHEY**
*University of South Australia*

CAMBRIDGE
UNIVERSITY PRESS

# CAMBRIDGE
UNIVERSITY PRESS

Shaftesbury Road, Cambridge CB2 8EA, United Kingdom

One Liberty Plaza, 20th Floor, New York, NY 10006, USA

477 Williamstown Road, Port Melbourne, VIC 3207, Australia

314–321, 3rd Floor, Plot 3, Splendor Forum, Jasola District Centre,
New Delhi – 110025, India

103 Penang Road, #05–06/07, Visioncrest Commercial, Singapore 238467

Cambridge University Press is part of Cambridge University Press & Assessment,
a department of the University of Cambridge.

We share the University's mission to contribute to society through the pursuit of
education, learning and research at the highest international levels of excellence.

www.cambridge.org
Information on this title: www.cambridge.org/9781108486873

DOI: 10.1017/9781108764421

First published 2023

*A catalogue record for this publication is available from the British Library.*

*Library of Congress Cataloging-in-Publication Data*
Names: Reinecke, Juliane, author. | Donaghey, Jimmy, author.
Title: Stitching governance for labour rights : towards transnational industrial
    democracy? / Juliane Reinecke, Jimmy Donaghey.
Other titles: Stitching governance for labor rights
Description: Cambridge, United Kingdom ; New York, NY : Cambridge University Press,
    2023. | Series: Business, value creation, and society | Includes bibliographical references
    and index.
Identifiers: LCCN 2022052232 (print) | LCCN 2022052233 (ebook) |
    ISBN 9781108486873 (hardback) | ISBN 9781108708388 (paperback) |
    ISBN 9781108764421 (epub)
Subjects: LCSH: Labor laws and legislation, International. | Labor laws and legislation. |
    Employee rights. | Labor and globalization. | Labor–Standards. | Business logistics.
Classification: LCC K1705 .R455 2023 (print) | LCC K1705 (ebook) |
    DDC 344.01–dc23/eng/20230103
LC record available at https://lccn.loc.gov/2022052232
LC ebook record available at https://lccn.loc.gov/2022052233

ISBN 978-1-108-48687-3 Hardback

# Contents

Contents                                                        vii

# Figures and Tables

# Foreword

In 2014, I was honoured to deliver the annual Sir Patrick Lowry lecture at Warwick University. It was early in my tenure as Director General at the ILO, and my topic was the relevance of tripartism in a world of work challenged to adapt to the realities of new technologies and innovative business models.

It was evident at the time that the traditional checks and balances of regulation, industrial relations and the social contract itself were not keeping pace with new work modalities; the troubling consequences included growing informality, inequality and weaker social protection in some cases. Yet there was also evidence of the enduring capacity of democratic and representative institutions to evolve in the ways they protect workers and regulate and resolve conflicts at work. My argument was that as these functions are vital to the development of prosperous, democratic, inclusive and peaceful societies, a central role of the ILO must be to support them to meet the challenges posed by our changing realities.

It was in the vibrant discussion that followed that I first met Juliane Reinecke and Jimmy Donaghey and learned of their research into new forms of industrial democracy in Bangladesh. It was less than a year after the catastrophic collapse of the Rana Plaza building in which over 1,100 workers died and many more were injured. The tragedy broadcast to the world the human cost of weak regulations and protections at work and raised complex questions about the responsibilities of global garment brands to ensure the safety of the workers in the supply chains that make the clothes they sell.

The ILO had been instrumental in supporting the government and employers' and workers' organisations in Bangladesh to develop and implement a programme of reforms aimed at ensuring stronger governance, high standards of industrial safety and proper compensation for victims of the accident. I therefore took the opportunity to introduce the authors to colleagues at the ILO in order to support their research.

Their book is valuable as it looks in some detail at two interventions in Bangladesh that were designed to increase the role of workers and their representatives in initiatives that improved their safety at work. It assesses their effectiveness and, while the authors conclude the interventions fell short of perfect, it is clear that they made significant contributions to the dramatic improvement in industrial safety that has taken place in the Bangladesh garment sector since 2013. Understanding how and why is important.

The authors further pose the question of what we can learn for other sectors and other locations by putting democratic values at the centre of workplace institutions and supporting them to adapt and strengthen. Answers to this question are even more pertinent than in 2014 when we first met. The COVID-19 pandemic has led to further informalisation of work and inequality between peoples; and globally, women, youth and vulnerable communities have been the biggest losers.

The recovery and indeed the future of work must be human-centred and socially just. Restoring democratic institutions to the heart of the workplace is part of the solution.

Guy Ryder
*Director-General, ILO, 2012–2022*

# Foreword

In the wake of the 2013 Rana Plaza disaster in Bangladesh, one of the world's worst instances of the abuse of workers' rights in global supply chains, Juliane Reinecke and Jimmy Donaghey build a case for transnational labour democracy in global supply chains central to so much of social and economic life. In the absence of effective nation-states, they propose an approach in which workers and their representatives can participate in international supply chain governance to secure labour rights.

This approach is founded upon two emerging trends. First, there is the emergence of collaborative private governance between business and civil society organisations *on behalf* of workers who are otherwise unrepresented in rule-making, specifically for their own working conditions. Second, there are systems of international industrial democracy in which workers' rights are secured and defended by *their own* representatives.

The beauty of the book is in combining two sorts of insights on which Reinecke and Donaghey substantiate and illustrate their case for transnational industrial democracy. The first are from their research in post–Rana Plaza Bangladesh, a laboratory for combinations of public and private, national and international initiatives directed at working conditions in the apparel industry. The second is from their theorisation of the problem of the abuse of labour rights and the possibilities of democratic innovation drawing on a wealth of relevant private and public governance literature.

As they readily admit, Reinecke and Donaghey's vision of market-driven transnational industrial democracy is far from perfect and even far from sure. But *Stitching Governance for Labour Rights: Towards Transnational Industrial Democracy?* illumines, first, how emerging initiatives recognise the importance of representing workers' interests and that these interests should be balanced against those of business and, second, how these initiatives can have positive impacts on industrial safety and on wider institutional attitudes to worker representation.

More broadly, *Stitching Governance* provides a fine platform for further research, practice and policy-making for new forms of democratic transnational governance.

Jeremy Moon
*Series Co-Editor*
*Copenhagen Business School*

# Acknowledgements

It is difficult to acknowledge everyone whom we have discussed this project with over the past nine years. In addition, the need for anonymity of interviewees prevents us from naming them. On that note, we thank all those 100 plus people who were interviewed or allowed us to observe meetings to conduct the research. Without their time, research like ours would be impossible. In addition, we know many of our interviewees met with multiple other research teams and while one one-hour interview may not seem like much, they quickly add up in time. There are some people, though, who do deserve singling out: Polly Jones who suggested the Accord as an initiative to research; Rob Wayss at the Bangladesh Accord; Peter McAllister, Martin Buttle, Jamil Ansar and particularly Debbie Coulter at the ETI; Guy Ryder for both writing the Foreword to this book and opening doors for us with the ILO in Geneva and Dhaka; Laura Gutierrez of the WRC for linking us to labour actors in Dhaka and being such a vivacious person in such a challenging context; Liz Kwast for her excellent and rapid transcription skills as well as our driver Jangahir who showed unbelievable patience in navigating the complexities of Dhaka.

Building on the theme of the book, our funding sources were many and certainly 'stitched' together! We acknowledge funding from British Academy/Society for the Advancement of Management Studies Small Grant (SG141754, 'Developing Innovative International Labour Governance: The Response to the Rana Plaza Disaster'); Andy Lockett, who as dean of Warwick Business School provided internal funding; the ESRC Impact Acceleration Account, which enabled us to work with the Ethical Trading Initiative; and the Warwick-Monash Alliance. Juliane Reinecke acknowledges the support of the British Academy Mid-Career Fellowship (MD20/200043), which helped her in writing up the research. We also acknowledge the research assistance of Davinia Hoggarth on our ETI Workplace Social Dialogue research. In addition, we thank the following academics who commented on drafts at various points or with whom we had detailed conversations about our research, including Guido Palazzo, Niklas Egels-Zanden, Ed Heery, Pete Turnbull, Sean Buchanan, Ian Greer, John Kelly, Paul Marginson, Dirk Matten, Paul Edwards, Michael Saward, Steve Frenkel, Elke Schuessler and Matt Amengual, Marek Korczynski, Andreas Rasche, Mike Saward, Gregory Jackson and Jennifer Bair.

A number of chapters draw upon parts of journal articles that were previously published, though all have substantial updates and changes. We acknowledge the editors and reviewers of these articles who certainly helped to sharpen the contributions in the book. In this regard, the relevant chapters and linked articles are Chapter 2, which draws on parts of Donaghey, J., Reinecke, J., Niforou, C., and Lawson, B. 2014. From employment relations to consumption relations: Balancing labor governance in global supply chains. *Human Resource Management*, 53(2): 229–252; and Reinecke, J., and Donaghey, J. 2021. Towards worker-driven supply chain governance: Developing decent work through democratic worker participation. *Journal of Supply Chain Management*, 57(2): 14–28; Chapters 3–5, which draw partially on Reinecke, J., and Donaghey, J. 2015. After Rana Plaza: Building coalitional power for labour rights between unions and (consumption-based) social movement organisations. *Organization*, 22(5): 720–740; and Reinecke, J., and Donaghey, J. (2022). Transnational representation in global labour governance and the politics of input legitimacy. *Business Ethics Quarterly*, 32(3), 438–474. Chapter 6, which draws on Donaghey, J., and Reinecke, J. 2018. When industrial democracy meets corporate social responsibility: A comparison of the Bangladesh Accord and Alliance as responses to the Rana Plaza disaster. *British Journal of Industrial Relations*, 56(1): 14–42; and Chapter 8, which draws on Reinecke, J., and Donaghey, J. 2021. Political CSR at the coalface: The roles and contradictions of multinational corporations in developing workplace dialogue. *Journal of Management Studies*, 58(2), 457–486.

# Abbreviations

| | |
|---|---|
| ACT | Action, Collaboration, Transformation. |
| AFL-CIO | American Federation of Labor and Congress of Industrial Organizations |
| BGMEA | Bangladesh Garments Manufacturers and Exporters Association |
| BKMEA | Bangladesh Knitwear Manufacturers and Exporters Association |
| BSCI | Business Social Compliance Initiative |
| BUET | Bangladesh University of Engineering and Technology |
| CAP | corrective action plan |
| CCC | Clean Clothes Campaign |
| CSR | corporate social responsibility |
| DIFE | Department of Inspection for Factories and Establishments (Bangladesh) |
| EPZ | export processing zone |
| ETI | Ethical Trading Initiative |
| EU | European Union |
| FDI | foreign direct investment |
| GDP | gross domestic product |
| GIZ | Gesellschaft für Internationale Zusammenarbeit |
| GSP | Generalized System of Preferences |
| GUF | global union federation |
| IFA | international framework agreement |
| ILO | International Labour Organization |
| ITUC | International Trade Union Confederation |
| JETI | Joint Ethical Trading Initiatives |
| MFA | Multi-Fibre Arrangement |
| MNC | multinational corporation |
| MOLE | Ministry of Labour and Employment (Bangladesh) |
| MoU | memorandum of understanding |

| NGO | non-governmental organisation |
| NGWF | National Garment Workers Federation |
| OSH | occupational safety and health |
| PC | participation committee |
| RCC | Remediation Coordination Cell |
| RMG | ready-made garment |
| RSC | Ready-Made-Garment Sustainability Council |
| TUC | Trades Union Congress (UK) |
| UCU | University and College Union (UK) |
| UNGPs | UN Guiding Principles on Business and Human Rights |
| WRC | Worker Rights Consortium |
| WTO | World Trade Organization |

# 1 | Introduction

**Vignette 1:** Large cracks started to appear in the Rana Plaza building complex in the Savar district of Dhaka, Bangladesh. The next day (23 April 2013), a bank, shops and offices, located in the lower floors of the building, closed due to safety concerns. However, several thousand garment workers, who lacked collective representation, were made to enter the building for fear of losing their jobs or worse. The building collapsed, killing over 1,100 workers.

**Vignette 2:** Having been sitting in heavy Dhaka rush-hour traffic for four hours en route to a meeting with the National Garment Workers Federation, a Bangladeshi union federation, we finally arrive at their small, ground floor office that is tucked away in one of the small side streets of Dhaka. A trade union meeting is taking place. Inside, about twenty-five mainly young women trade unionists from a factory squeeze around a large table in the main room. Hours earlier, a number of them had been dismissed by factory management for speaking out on safety grounds. A mass walk out had ensued. Responding to our question about what we can do to help, the immediate request is for us to write to the American brands for which the factory has been producing. They say it is only through the power of the brand over the employer that the workers will be reinstated.

**Vignette 3:** The UK Trades Union Congress (TUC) and Labour Behind the Label, the UK arm of the international Clean Clothes Campaign, had planned joint action outside a number of Edinburgh Woollen Mills stores across the United Kingdom to protest against its refusal to sign the Accord on Fire and Building Safety in Bangladesh and failure to pay into the victims' compensation fund. The UK high street retailer signed the Accord just a few days before the planned action. The TUC called off the day of action and commended Edinburgh Woollen Mills for signing the Accord. Labour Behind the Label, in contrast, was frustrated that the TUC had called off the protest since the retailer had not yet agreed to make compensation payments to victims of previous factory disasters.

In contrast, the trade unionists were frustrated that, right up to the last minute, campaigners were making what they saw as unreasonable demands, thereby jeopardising the progress made.

As these three vignettes demonstrate, globalisation has blurred the lines of responsibility, accountability and representation in global supply chains.[1] This is tragically highlighted by the Rana Plaza disaster, outlined in Vignette 1, which shunted labour issues in the garment industry into the global spotlight. In the simplest terms, the Rana Plaza disaster was an engineering failure: the building was unable to support the weight load necessary for the factories. At another level, this and other tragedies that have bedevilled garment production in Bangladesh and other developing economies also demonstrate the abject failure of corporate-driven labour governance and the consequences of a lack of workers' power to refuse unsafe work. The prevailing model of social auditing, where external assessors carry out checks against company or multistakeholder standards, had failed to protect its alleged beneficiaries: workers at the hard end of global supply chains. Part of the problem is that these private governance institutions show little concern with the democratic representation of those affected: workers and their representatives are not involved in social auditing in any meaningful way, nor have there been any substantive means developed by which such involvement can be leveraged.

Could more democratic involvement of workers have prevented tragedies such as Rana Plaza? The central premise of this book is that the democratic involvement of workers is central to effective and fair governance. Health and safety is one area where research has shown repeatedly that governance is indeed more effective when workers are involved (Gunningham, 2008). Notwithstanding debates about the relationship between democracy and effectiveness of governance, the argument about democratic representation and participation goes beyond instrumental effectiveness. Human dignity and the right to self-determination are integral elements of basic human rights, which extend into the workplace and the mechanisms governing it.

---

[1] There has been considerable academic debate about terminologies such as global commodity chains, global value chains, global production networks and global supply chains. The nuances of this debate are beyond this book, and we use the generic terminology of global supply chains, as used by the International Labour Organization.

Questions about democratic representation have become pertinent since global supply chains have emerged as the dominant form of value creation in the global economy. By their very nature, global supply chains cross national boundaries and thus are challenging for democracy: labour rights are no longer an issue solely between employers and workers but involve actors at different levels of the supply chain. As Vignette 2 demonstrates, workers and their representatives increasingly target action against Western brands rather than their actual employer to improve workplace conditions. As a result, Western brands have become implicated in the governance of labour and human rights, especially when public governments fail in their responsibilities (Scherer and Palazzo, 2011). Whether this democratises corporations by re-embedding them into democratic processes or instead privatises governance is subject to debate. It is clear, though, that global governance goes beyond representative politics by public actors. It certainly raises questions about who can legitimately represent workers at different points in the supply chain: trade unions in production countries, elected worker representatives in consumer economies in the West or unelected labour activists? While these can be complementary, they also give rise to competing claims to democratic representation. This is illustrated in Vignette 3, where non-government organisations (NGOs) seek to represent workers alongside trade unions. With private claims to participation in global governance processes on the rise, it is time to investigate the conditions for democratic private governance.

The purpose of this book is to explore the questions raised above about whether meaningful private transnational labour governance can emerge in a way that is underpinned by the democratic representation of those affected. This requires bringing to the forefront of the debate worker representation and who can legitimately represent workers. For proponents of industrial democracy, the answer is clear: it means governance of workers by workers for workers. At the transnational level, however, the issue arises of whether and how other forms of representation have some validity, such as that provided by labour rights NGOs, who may not be democratically elected but have the power to influence corporate actors. Thus, empirically, the question posed is: What kind of institutions might promote more deliberative, representative and inclusive decision-making processes within private governance arrangements? To respond to this, we draw on seven years of extensive empirical research that we conducted into the global governance response to the Rana Plaza disaster. Ultimately, we will argue that what is needed is a new paradigm of global labour rights, rooted in transnational industrial democracy, as a prerequisite for a more just and sustainable globalisation.

## 1.1 The Supply Chain Model and National Democratic Regulation

At the turn of the millennium, there was much activity by those labelled by the popular press as 'anti-globalisation' activists. Most famously, this was brought into focus by the Battle of Seattle in 1999, when protests were held at the World Trade Organization (WTO) Ministerial Council meetings in the United States. Yet, while often labelled as 'anti-globalisation', the protests were focused on the highly pro-capital and socially unjust form that globalisation was taking (Wright, 2010). At the heart of such criticisms is the triumph of private corporations over national institutions of democracy. In the twenty or so years since the Battle of Seattle, while attention has been drawn to this shift through activism such as the Occupy movement during the Global Financial Crisis, globalisation has not slowed down. This has led to troubling times for democracy globally. This manifests itself in different ways at opposite ends of the supply chain.

Advanced economies, often at the consumption end of supply chains, have witnessed an increase in populism and nationalism to curb global trade and supply chains. This was exemplified by the US abandonment of international treaties under a populist right-wing President Trump but also the rise of both right- and left-wing anti-European Union (EU) groups in Italy, France and the United Kingdom, which have dented the vision of a democratically governed global polity. At the other end of the supply chain – typically to where production has been outsourced – the concerns about democracy are of a different nature but have attracted much less attention. Global supply chains have added hugely to global wealth in bringing economic growth and employment to developing countries. However, this is not without a price, with the development of democratic participation in the workplace in emerging economies often being the victim of such development alongside increasing income inequality. We seek to address questions over democratic participation at the point of production. Globalisation is in need of democratisation to ensure wealth and prosperity are not created to the detriment of worker welfare. Thus, instead of curbing global supply chains, the question we seek to address is: How can more meaningful democratic participation and input into the governance of global supply chains be developed in order to advance a more just and equitable form of globalisation?

As a key part of globalisation, the global supply chain has become the dominant form of value creation in the world economy. Global supply chains made up 80 per cent of global trade and 60 per cent of global production in 2016 (UNCTAD, 2016). These supply chains are dominated by global corporations, which are becoming increasingly powerful. According to Global Justice Now (2016), 69 out of 100 of the world's biggest economic entities were corporations in 2015, based on turnover and gross domestic product (GDP). The first implication of this concentration of economic activity within supply chains is that how value is created, sustained and distributed among stakeholders can no longer be approached from the standpoint of the individual organisation but has to focus on the intertwining of social and economic relations within and across global supply chains (Reinecke et al., 2018). While existing theories of institutions are based on closed entities with clearly defined boundaries, such as organisations, nation-states, municipalities or corporations, we are no longer dealing with individual companies with clearly defined boundaries. Instead, boundaries have become fluid and overlapping and we are faced with complex and globally stretching networks, linkages and relationships (Gereffi et al., 2005). The second implication of this is that, by their very nature, global supply chains cross national boundaries, which almost immediately raises questions about transnational democracy. Production is distributed among global buyers and myriad suppliers across multiple countries. Hence, authority and control over the employment relationship and labour conditions are dispersed among various national and international regimes and actors in the supply chain. It is clear, however, that the persistent human, labour and environmental rights violations we are seeing are a result of the lack of democratic oversight – whether that is states that actively suppress rights (Anner, 2015) or those that are administratively weak (Dobbin and Sutton, 1998). In these circumstances, the ability to hold global corporations to account is diminished. While scholars have talked about transnational governance as a possibility to re-embed the corporation into democratic relationships and become responsible corporate citizens of a world polity (Crane et al., 2008), a key dimension of this has yet to be fully addressed: the need to infuse the complex intertwining of global production and trade relationships with democratic representation.

By its very nature, the global supply chain model undermines democratic oversight and binding state regulation as well as workplace-level democratic participation. The political economist Dani Rodrik (2013) argues that globalisation, state governance and transnational democracy are part of an incompatible trilemma. First, at the workplace level, globalisation creates immense downwards pressures on labour standards in manufacturing due to the reduction in trade barriers. Globalisation has witnessed much outsourcing of labour-intensive production to particular geographic locations where direct labour costs such as wages are low or more indirect costs such as workforce flexibility offer advantages. In these sites, there is often an immature structure of industrial relations, typified by low levels of trade unionism and little factory-level worker participation, meaning workers are not in a strong position to resist downward pressures. In addition, for many, a manufacturing job with stable income may be preferable to working in primary industries.

Second, at the national level, governments who may otherwise be inclined to legislate to prevent the effects of these pressures being pushed onto workers face the risk of being viewed as inhospitable to multinational corporations (MNCs), which could cost jobs and exports. Developing nations are incentivised to drive down standards and become what Philip Cerny (1997) labels 'competition states', competing to attract inward investments. At this level, national systems of tripartite industrial relations are under pressure, being transformed from distribution systems to those maintaining competitiveness in global markets (Regini, 2000): unions are incorporated into systems of national competitiveness, with wage shares being the price of the maintenance of employment.

Third, achieving meaningful transnational public governance to prevent a race to the bottom falls into the trap of opening up space for free-riding from countries that refuse to sign up to any global rules. For example, the ILO, whose structures were developed for the age of nation-state capitalism, has been challenged by globalisation as fewer states ratify conventions and fewer conventions are agreed (Standing, 2008; Baccaro and Mele, 2012), though there has been a significant effort in recent years to adapt to the new world of supply chains (Ryder, 2015; Thomas and Turnbull, 2018). In terms of union actors, even though global union federations (GUFs) are present, they are a relatively weak actor with little power. Building solidarity across countries has generally proved to be an elusive goal.

The implications of this trilemma for workers are stark. Studies suggest that, rather than improvements in average labour rights performance, most regions appear to be deteriorating further (Levi et al., 2013). This has been the case particularly in the garments sector, where there has been severe downwards pressure on worker rights and labour standards. In addition, not only are outcomes worse, but democratic representation of workers is often sacrificed in the name of economic development.

## 1.2 Transnational Democracy and Private Labour Governance

Democratic representation is typically seen as the main legitimating principle of government (e.g., Cohen, 1989; Benhabib, 1996; Dryzek, 1999). At a broad level, democracy is defined as 'self-determination, a system of decision-making in which those affected by decisions participate in decision-making instead of being ruled by others' (Bryde, 2011: 214). Democracy also concerns questions about basic human rights such as autonomy, self-determination and self-development (Werhane, 1985). Traditionally, democracy is seen as being realised when citizens can choose freely by whom and how they are governed, a process that is circumscribed by geographical boundaries at the nation-state level or membership in associational structures. By this account, democratic representation should be proportional to the extent that people are affected by collective decisions. Democratic theorists have called this the 'all affected interests principle' (Goodin, 2007).

Can existing governance structures in the international system be democratised in line with this principle or do we need a different conception of democratic representation? In a globalised economy and world society, people are increasingly being affected by economic and social processes, as well as by decisions at the other side of the globe. The boundaries of who is impacted by decisions are redrawn by globalising economic and social relations. At the same time, supply chains create new forms of social connectedness (Young, 2006), which have prompted consumers to start raising questions about how geographically distant workers are treated. As a result, working conditions in South and South-East Asian factories are often shaped more strongly by Western corporate policies and consumer sentiment than by state oversight or local union negotiations with local employers (Reinecke et al., 2018). This has led to private efforts to establish labour standards in global supply chains. Our focus in this book is on the question of representation beyond national geographical boundaries and the possibility of democratic input into these private governance processes.

The rise of private, transnational labour governance has been well documented (Bartley, 2007; Hassel, 2008; Locke, 2013). Under sustained pressure from labour activists, consumer groups and increasingly public bodies, global buyers have come to acknowledge a degree of moral responsibility for labour conditions in their supply chains. As a result, a substantial element of labour governance has shifted from public authorities to private bodies, who set labour standards and, at least in principle, enforce them through the potential sanction of terminating existing or future commercial contracts. Typically, scholars have seen this as a pragmatic, second-best response that developed in the absence of a system of global justice and the inadequacy of the ability of nation-states and international organisations to reach across the multiple countries in which production is located (Locke, 2013). A more optimistic approach suggests that private governance is illustrative of an alternative model of democratic politics that embeds corporate political activities in decentralised processes of democratic will-formation (Crane et al., 2008; Scherer and Palazzo, 2011). These processes involve an array of non-state actors, including global NGOs, activists, social movements, civil society actors, multi-stakeholder initiatives, brands and industry associations in decision-making processes. Increasingly, such mechanisms of private governance also intersect with, or are actively supported, enabled or even mandated by Western governments (Knudsen and Moon, 2017).

According to this account, firms become embedded in processes of democratic deliberation and fill the regulatory vacuum in global governance, perhaps even assuming a state-like role to fulfil governance roles where state systems fail (Scherer and Palazzo, 2011). As corporate citizens, firms pledge to protect, enable and implement citizenship rights (Crane et al., 2008). In their codes of conduct, they promise to ensure that workers can exercise their democratic human and labour rights. Based on the ILO's Core Labour Standards, codes of conduct typically have provisions for guaranteeing freedom of association or collective bargaining. In principle, there is a commitment to respect and even enable citizenship rights: however, studies of code enforcement have shown consistently that outcome rights that may lead to reputational risks, such as health and safety violations, are more rigorously enforced than process rights that may conflict with managerial control (Barrientos and Smith, 2007; Anner, 2012; Bartley and Egels-Zanden, 2016). Similarly, Locke et al. (2013) highlight that private standards are a poor substitute for public regulation in highly contentious areas such as freedom of association.

Private regulatory initiatives are thus highly ambiguous in terms of democratic legitimacy. Private actors have no democratic mandate for engaging in labour governance, are not subjected to democratic control and cannot be held properly accountable except by the court of public opinion. Arguably, corporations have positioned themselves purposefully within a legal grey area, if not a vacuum, where they escape legal liability for workplace conditions in supplier factories. While corporations participate in and increasingly develop governance standards aimed at protecting labour rights, exposure to competitive market pressures undermines not only their ability, but also their motivation, to enforce these standards. This leads to the problem of weak enforcement due to voluntary contributions and absence of effective sanctioning systems. Studying various private initiatives to improve labour standards in the global footwear and electronics industry, Richard Locke (2013) and Locke and colleagues (2013) argue that while private governance may lead to an initial improvement in labour standards in supply chains, ultimately this levels off when these standards threaten the competitive nature of the supply chain model itself. Rather than a form of democratic embedding, critics therefore view private governance initiatives as protecting brand reputations and limiting the legal liability of global corporations (O'Rourke, 2006).

Amidst these debates about the process of democratic representation and participation, trade unions have largely been overlooked as a structural mechanism for worker representation. Instead of acknowledging claims to greater representation, there is a tendency towards paternalistic benevolence. Workers are often treated as passive recipients of global buyers' corporate social responsibility (CSR) programmes, which points to a core weakness of such approaches (Donaghey and Reinecke, 2018). If democracy demands that all those who are affected by economic and social processes are included in deliberative processes, then it is surprising that workers – the core beneficiaries – have been excluded from the debate about global governance. This raises the important question of how democratic representation of transnational interests is constituted. A political unit of all affected interests has typically been defined by territorial boundaries, such as the nation-state. But if nation-states are no longer the sovereign authority in the international legal system, then we need to ask whether and how this principle can be extended to global supply chains. Who legitimately constitutes the transnational demos? Who is included and who is excluded? Whose interests are legitimately represented and through what mechanisms?

## 1.3 Two Approaches to Associational Democracy

In this book, we bring together two distinct approaches to democratic representation: representation as claim and representation as structure as the theoretical underpinning of the approach adopted. While often highly contrasting in their approach, the argument presented is that these two conceptual lenses can be brought together to aid the understanding of the dynamics of an emerging approach to transnational labour governance.

### 1.3.1 A Discursive Model of Transnational Democracy: Representation as Claim

Significant questions exist around the democratic credentials of private labour governance. How can governance through private bodies be democratised when there is a lack of representative structures? Some political theorists have argued that representation can be reconceptualised as 'discursive representation' (Dryzek, 1999; Dryzek and Niemayer, 2008; Mansbridge, 2011). This has focused on the role of discourse, deliberation and communication. Saward (2010), for instance, suggests that representation is about making a 'representative claim'. This means that a wide range of actors can become 'representatives' through claim-making activities. These include NGOs, transnational labour rights and environmental activist groups that work with, within, across and often against states and brands through what is often called global civil society (Kaldor, 2003; Risse, 2004).

For instance, labour rights activists can make claims on behalf of migrant workers in largely unregulated global supply chains who lack a collective voice, or environmental activists can make claims on behalf of future generations who are likely to be most affected by the decisions taken today on climate change. The advantage of these 'self-appointed' claim-makers (Montanaro, 2012; Severs, 2012) is that they are not bound by the fear of upsetting actual and potential allies or rivals. Nor are they bound by 'the realm of necessity occupied by the state' (Dryzek, 1999: 44) – for instance, to attract foreign direct investment (FDI) or appease financial markets. As self-appointed representatives of the interests of workers, labour rights campaigners have produced powerful discourses to activate the sensibilities of consumers and other corporate stakeholders who are in a position to exert pressure on brands to behave in more socially responsible ways.

However, even proponents of the deliberative approach concede that the creation of a transnational public sphere is complicated by a lack of transparency of policy-making, unequal representation of stakeholder concerns in deliberative processes and unequal opportunity to participate in decision-making processes. While attempting to fill global governance gaps, the risk is that over-reliance on discursive and communicative processes creates a 'massive "democratic deficit"' (Nanz and Steffek, 2004) or 'accountability gaps' (Keohane, 2003) as private rule-makers are not elected or otherwise authorised representatives of the people in whose name they claim to act. Rather than being controlled by those who are most affected, NGOs, interest and activist groups act as 'solidaristic proxies' (Koenig-Archibugi and MacDonald, 2013), providing 'surrogate representation' (Mansbridge, 2011). Yet the accountability of self-appointed representatives to their intended beneficiaries in the Global South is increasingly questioned. Often, agendas are driven by the interests and necessities of Western NGOs, companies or the emerging industry of sustainability consultants and accountants (Bendell, 2005; Khan et al., 2007; LeBaron and Lister, 2015; LeBaron et al., 2017). Scholars have therefore argued that the increasing capacity of self-appointed representatives to generate standards and regulations conflicts with democratic legitimacy. The position taken in this book is that private institutions largely fail to enable the democratic representation of those who are most affected.

### 1.3.2 Industrial Democracy and Industrial Citizenship: Representation as Structure

As outlined above, a key feature of democracy is the idea that those affected by rules and regulations have meaningful participation in their development. Industrial democracy as put forward by British social reformers Beatrice and Sidney Webb (1897) applies this principle to the workplace. The Webbs argued that industrial democracy was about developing governance of workplaces by workers for workers. The central feature of the system is the representation of workers by self-governing trade unions. In contrast to representation as claim, we will refer to this position as 'representation as structure'. Trade unions provide a structural mechanism through which workers elect and authorise their representatives, provide mandates and hold them accountable.

Closely related to industrial democracy is the idea of industrial citizenship (Marshall, 1950) where individuals are bestowed with rights to participate in systems to develop their well-being in the sphere of employment. Within continental Europe, industrial citizenship came to be associated with legally mandatory forms of worker representation at the firm and sector level (Müller-Jentsch, 1976). Industrial citizenship therefore saw the development of complementary structures at the national, sectoral and firm levels to include workers in the governance arrangements of their work (Streeck, 1997a). Such structures were not only viewed as a key feature of increasing worker rights but were also attributed with a key role in developing high-quality, sustainable national production systems through the presence of 'beneficial constraints' (Streeck, 1997b). Beneficial constraints placed on employers a duty to encourage innovative practices to improve both productivity and the quality of industrial life.

Within the realm of supply chains, the main manifestation of this approach to date has been the creation of international framework agreements (IFAs). These agreements initially emerged as a mechanism through which brands and GUFs secured rights for workers in directly owned subsidiaries (Wills, 2002; Hammer, 2005). Like corporate codes of conduct, these agreements are not legally binding.

Significantly, though, they are structurally based representation agreements that generally focus on process rights such as representation, freedom of association, the right to collective bargaining and the right to strike. As such, the key strength of IFAs is that they emphasise democratic representation. Yet, while IFAs are generally good at codifying existing democratic rights, their implementation has been poor. Fichter and McCallum (2015) attribute this to the fact that they have been negotiated by GUFs at the transnational peak level, while the local unions at the upstream end of global supply chains, where IFAs are most needed, have mostly not been involved in their negotiation. In this way, their ability to strengthen the representative structures for workers within supply chains has been limited.

Some of these shortcomings stem from the fact that the model of industrial democracy and citizenship is based upon a number of assumptions that are difficult to reconcile with the nature of global supply chains. First, groups such as unions are viewed as being the rightful representatives of workers based on a logic of membership (Webb and Webb, 1897). While there is no doubt that the emergence of unions was highly contested and resisted in many Western economies, their position in developing economies is much more precarious, with state actions designed to suppress the development of well-functioning unions. For example, in the Bangladesh ready-made garment sector, the International Trade Union Confederation (ITUC) (2016) highlighted the establishment of the industrial police force to prevent worker agitation and the creation of 'export processing zones' (EPZs) in which trade unions are prohibited as key impediments to union development. Second, the notion of industrial citizenship is clearly bound to the idea of a defined national space where local, sectoral and even national institutions complement each other. Where production fragments and becomes dispersed across multiple jurisdictions, achieving such complementarity becomes difficult if not impossible. Third, supply chains may have increased social connectedness but building solidarity across globally disparate workers is difficult – particularly when they occupy different positions in the supply chain, such as a retail worker in a UK Tesco store and a seamstress in a Bangladeshi garment factory.

While much has been written about the weaknesses of private governance, finding meaningful alternative mechanisms has proven challenging. As highlighted above, two significantly different approaches to representation have been adopted in the literature to date. While they deal with significantly different domains, they are not necessarily mutually exclusive. In Chapter 3, we return to these approaches and set out a conceptual approach that views the potential for developing a complementary understanding of representation as both claim-making and structure. The following chapters will then empirically investigate this by analysing a series of governance experiments and institutional innovations that have emerged in response to the Rana Plaza tragedy.

## 1.4 In Search of a New Paradigm

These questions render the Rana Plaza disaster and the various governance interventions it catalysed so significant not only from an ethical but also from a theoretical perspective. Without doubt, the sheer scale of the Rana Plaza disaster sent shock waves across the world. Yet over 1,100 people being killed in one site, on one day, was not an isolated event but an implication of Bangladesh being a paradigmatic case of the failure of democratic governance. As Chapter 2 will discuss in greater detail, it typifies many of the challenges of low-cost sourcing destinations that have led to both a governance gap and democratic deficit. Rana Plaza laid bare the tragic consequences of the failure to promote workplace democracy, as Vignette 1 illustrated. Lacking a collective voice, thousands of garment workers were unable to refuse unsafe work conditions as they feared losing their jobs had they not entered the Rana Plaza building. This is despite obvious safety concerns and large cracks appearing the day before the collapse, which led to the evacuation of shops and banks located in the same building. It is clear that the corporate-focused paradigm has failed and a new paradigm to ensure worker safety in low wage supply chains is urgently needed. At the same time, it is clear that this paradigm has to emerge from within the supply chains and involve actors from across those supply chains. Hard regulation is unlikely to be provided by a state in which the garment sector delivers over 80 per cent of total exports and that fears the appetite of neighbouring countries to capture a share of the global garment production market. Hence, a new paradigm has to square the circle. On the one hand, it has to mobilise the market forces that gave rise to the outsourcing model and turn them against its most egregious consequences. On the other hand, it has to make workers and their representatives part of the solution without putting their jobs in danger.

Bangladesh is not only illustrative of the problems that exist but provides important insights into how the principles of industrial democracy can inform labour governance. With unprecedented international attention focused on the ready-made garment (RMG – the term used in Bangladesh to describe the apparel industry) supply chain in the aftermath of Rana Plaza, Bangladesh has become an experimental ground for a range of governance innovations. Brands that had come under immense scrutiny and were confronted with the failure of their social auditing mechanisms were now willing to make considerable investments and trial a range of new approaches. In addition, international actors including the ILO, GUFs and donor countries have focused attention on the importance of strengthening freedom of association, supporting trade unions and worker representation to strengthen worker voices on the ground. Together, this has led to a wide range of both distinct and overlapping private, public or public–private initiatives and programmes aimed at improving factory safety, improving productivity, strengthening industrial relations and trade unions, supporting workplace social dialogue or combinations of all of these. Moreover, Rana Plaza has had significant ramifications for supply chain practices in a range of sectors worldwide. This renders the evolving landscape of governance initiatives that emerged from the Rana Plaza disaster so significant for investigating the possibility and limitations of building institutions for transnational industrial democracy in global supply chains.

In this book, we focus in particular on how actors from across the global supply chain, including brands, GUFs and labour rights NGOs, contribute to private governance interventions on three levels: the sector level, the host country level and in the workplace. It is important to note that these are experiments in transnational governance, which are far from perfect models of transnational industrial democracy. Nevertheless, they provide valuable insights into the process of institution-building.

## 1.5 A Note on the Fieldwork

This book is based on seven years of empirical research that involved six field trips to the RMG cluster around Dhaka, Bangladesh and over

140 interviews with actors involved in the Accord, the Joint Ethical Trading Initiatives (JETI) Social Dialogue Project and/or the Bangladesh RMG supply chain. The research included interviews and meetings with workers, Bangladesh trade unionists, international trade unionists, NGO activists, brand representatives, factory owners, ILO workers and other subjects in Bangladesh, Europe and North America. A summary of our data sources can be found in Appendix 1. Qualitative data sources used in the text are anonymised and cited by respondent category (e.g., GUF), with a capital letter used to distinguish different organisations per category (e.g., GUF A) and numbers used to distinguish whether more than one respondent per organisation is cited (e.g., GUF A.1).

The research journey started in a comfortable restaurant in the small English Midlands village of Kenilworth and brought us to the buzzing and dynamic capital city of Dhaka, home to sixteen million residents and thousands of garment factories in its spreading outskirts. Many of the insights presented in this book would not have been possible without experiencing the Bangladeshi RMG world first hand and, most importantly, without all the generous input we received from all the field actors who live the challenges on a day-to-day basis. Many of the ideas in this book emerged during extended discussions when we were stuck for hours in Dhaka's endless traffic jams on our way to or from visits to factories, trade union offices or brand offices. By the end, we missed the loud honking noises of the traffic, the calls to Islamic prayer and the general hustle and bustle of this vibrant city. We reflect on the challenges of the research in our Appendices.

Qualitative field research is costly and time consuming, yet we believe the insights presented in this book would not have been possible without immersing ourselves in the setting. It made real what we call 'the global supply chain'. It introduced us to the multiplicity of actors, their interests and perspectives that make up the global supply chain. It allowed us to gain a glimpse of their different life-worlds, of the everyday challenges they faced and of the immense work they did to recreate the global supply chain anew every day. While field researchers often aim at 'making the familiar strange rather than the strange familiar' (Van Maanen, 1995: 20), for us much of the challenge was to make sense of a social and cultural setting that was entirely strange to us. This puzzled and surprised and exhausted us, but it mainly enriched our perspective. What seemed contradictory often made perfect sense when seen from each actor's perspective. Yet in this book, we had to put all this complexity back together into some more or less coherent account. On a personal level, seeing where the clothes that we wear were made and meeting some of the workers who made them has also added a human factor to the global supply chain. It provided a sense of global connectivity. Seeing 'Made in Bangladesh' on a garment label catapults us back to the factory floor, to seeing the workers in their colourful dresses bending over the sewing machines, to the cramped spaces of the trade union offices and to the streets of Dhaka.

## 1.6 Summary of the Argument: Why Industrial Democracy Is Needed in an Era of Globalisation

The core argument we develop is that transnational labour regulation is in urgent need of a new paradigm of democratic participation and that such a paradigm needs to find ways to place the most affected – typically the workers – at its centre. This may be achieved when principles of industrial democracy and transnational democracy come together to inform governance institutions within global supply chains. Notwithstanding significant limitations manifest in the institutional arrangements we analysed, we document traces of such a new paradigm of transnational industrial democracy that are evident in some of the emerging strategies and experiments. The argument is not that private governance is preferable to public governance, supported by an effective structure of industrial relations, but that the reality of modern-day capitalism is such that optimal institutional frameworks may not be a reality. Dealing with the institutional landscape in the emerging economies where many global supply chains originate may require what Rodrik (2008) calls a 'second-best mindset'. When cut-throat competition undermines state oversight and suppresses trade unionism, yet the livelihoods of millions of workers depend on global supply chains, investing in first-class legal institutions may fail to produce the intended effects or may even backfire. Alternative avenues and institutional innovations become important strategies to deal with the constraints in highly competitive environments. As such, our aim is to understand better how an approach informed by principles of industrial democracy can enhance emerging forms of private transnational governance.

Another caveat is that our argument does not seek to provide an ultimate assessment of the effectiveness of these initiatives. What we observe is an evolving landscape of governance initiatives that show effects in some but not in other areas and overall is in constant flux. Moreover, effectiveness begs the question of from whose perspective it is assessed and what the baseline is against which effects are compared. In Bangladesh, for instance, the baseline of avoiding death at the workplace is a very low bar but unfortunately one that has to be considered when asking questions about whether recent interventions have, on the whole, been successful. Thus, compared with the baseline of deadly incidents in garment factories, the Accord on Fire and Building Safety in Bangladesh – one of the institutional innovations that will be analysed – has effectively used an approach inspired by industrial democracy in achieving quite dramatic improvements in factories in a remarkably short period of time. Yet, when judged against the yardstick of enabling workers to enforce safety themselves in the workplace, only relatively small steps have been made. Each of the chapters analyses both the potential as well as the limitations of the different programmes and initiatives, with the overall aim of drawing more general lessons for understanding how, why and when certain coalitions of supply chain actors can contribute to building more democratic governance institutions.

Chapter 2 centres on role of democratic participation in supply chain labour governance. First, the supply chain model challenges the established concept of democracy upon which liberal capitalist societies have relied, namely that economic activity is subject to democratic control and oversight. This raises the fundamental question of whether and how existing governance structures can be democratised or whether and how new democratic institutions can be created that extend democratic underpinnings to globally expanding supply chains. We then analyse the types of actors represented in different forms and strategies of voluntary regulation aimed at promoting labour standards. Drawing on this, we highlight that two distinct approaches to supply chain labour governance have emerged: one based on focusing on production relations and collective bargaining and the other based on consumption relations and a CSR approach by brands. These approaches raise important questions, such as what constitutes the relationship between the representation of worker interests and consumer interests, who has the 'right' to raise concerns about labour conditions in global supply chains and whether these contrasting approaches can prove complementary. Answering these questions requires a more fundamental understanding of the concept of democratic representation.

Chapter 3 focuses on the challenges and opportunities of transnational worker representation and their consequences for the development of more democratic governance institutions. We examine these from a number of theoretical perspectives. Starting from the notion of associational democracy, we differentiate between two logics of legitimacy: representation as claim versus representation as structure. The first approach is associated with a discursive or communicative model of transnational democracy, as put forward by political theorists John Dryzek (1999), Jane Mansbridge (2012) and Michael Saward (2010). Rather than thinking of representation in terms of representative structures, representation becomes the dynamic and ongoing process of making 'representative claims' that reflect certain discourses, categories, concepts, judgments, dispositions and capabilities. In contrast, structural ideas of representation are grounded in industrial democracy and the related 'private-interest government' approach (Streeck and Schmitter, 1985). Here, constituents of an organic political unit defined by voluntary membership, such as a trade union, authorise their representatives to deliberate, negotiate or bargain on behalf of members. In practical terms, these logics of legitimacy of associational democracy are exemplified by labour activists making representative claims and trade unions having representative structures. We investigate their theoretical grounding in structuralist and post-structuralist thinking and question the extent to which these approaches may be reconciled with each other to advance prospects for transnational worker representation. Together, these two chapters lay the theoretical foundation for examining democratic representation and participation in global supply chains.

The next five chapters document two novel institutional innovations that have emerged in response to the Rana Plaza disaster, which will be presented as experiments in transnational industrial democracy. These are analysed with a view to understanding how private institutions may enhance the democratic representation of those affected. Chapter 4 is primarily a contextual chapter, which provides an overview of the empirical context of the Bangladeshi RMG supply chain, the labour representation gap and the failure of private codes of conducts to protect workers' rights. It ends by presenting introductions to the Accord on Fire and Building Safety in Bangladesh (the Accord) and the Joint Ethical Training Initiatives' Social Dialogue Project as initiatives aimed at developing more robust forms for the representation of workers' interests in global supply chain governance.

Chapter 5 analyses how and when representation as claim and representation as structure can become complementary in global supply chains: labour rights NGOs can use their power to agitate and mobilise in ways that empower trade unions to negotiate with global brands. As a result, the Accord emerged as a negotiated and legally binding agreement between GUFs and over 200 brands, providing an unprecedented mechanism of transnational co-determination at the supply chain level between representatives of labour and capital.

Chapter 6 explores in greater detail the reasons why transnational industrial democracy yields a different approach to labour governance by presenting a structured comparison between the Accord and the Alliance for Bangladesh Worker Safety (the Alliance). The latter was a parallel initiative set by twenty-nine mainly North American retailers and operated as an alternative to the Accord but is more firmly rooted in a CSR approach. Private governance as a whole has been characterised by competition between overlapping initiatives, which often claim to have the same objectives but differ in their institutional design. The same is true for the Accord and the Alliance. By considering differences and similarities in the design and implementation of these two competing initiatives, we are able to demonstrate how differences in governance design translate into distinct emphases in implementation. In particular, we find that the inclusion of worker representatives in the design of transnational governance structures led to the recognition of divergent interests and hence to a more rigorous model of transnational labour governance.

The next two chapters focus on the relationship of transnational initiatives with national and local level institutions respectively. Chapter 7 examines the relationship between transnational industrial democracy and national institutions in Bangladesh. Empirically, we focus on the contentious relationship between the Bangladesh Accord and local actors from the industry association and government of Bangladesh, for whom the imposition of private labour governance through the Accord undermined local democratic institutions. While collective action from over 200 signatory companies has been vital in driving factory owners to remediate urgent safety issues, it also created quasi-authority to regulate and close sites of production by withdrawing orders from unsafe or non-cooperative factories. Overall, Chapter 7 raises difficult questions about democratic governance at the intersection of transnational and national spheres.

Chapter 8 explores mechanisms of developing transnational industrial democracy at the workplace level. It looks at efforts to promote worker representation, such as the creation of democratically elected occupational safety and health committees under the Accord. We focus in particular on the workplace social dialogue programme by the Joint Ethical Trading Initiatives (JETI). Workplace social dialogue provides a potentially promising mechanism for enabling worker voice in a context of toxic industrial relations. We examine the enabling roles played by brands in developing dialogue at their supplier factories but also unveil the resultant tensions their involvement exposed in their relationship to factories and workers.

We conclude in Chapter 9 by summarising the core argument of the book: that principles of industrial democracy can play a key role in shaping the evolution of transnational labour governance. We consider the extent to which lessons drawn from the garment industry can be instructive for wider supply chains and conclude that, under the right conditions, transnational industrial democracy can help to democratise labour governance in global supply chains. However, rather than being a restraint against market forces, it is dependent on them in order to succeed.

Finally, Appendix 1 offers a reflection on the practical and political questions of doing research on the Bangladesh global supply chain, while Appendix 2 offers a reflection on doing interdisciplinary research. We explore how we – an organisation theory scholar and an industrial relations scholar – brought together our different perspectives and backgrounds.

In summary, this book seeks to stimulate debate about both the need for and potential promise of the incorporation of principles of participatory and industrial democracy regarding debates around transnational private governance. We argue that important lessons can be drawn from the responses to the Rana Plaza tragedy for wider questions of supply chain labour governance.

# 2 | The Democratic Deficit of Global Supply Chains

More than 400 years ago, an unregulated private company, headquartered in the City of London, set out to the Indian subcontinent to source silk fabric, along with spices, tea and other goods, to export them to England. This was the East India Company, a joint-stock company that had secured a royal charter for monopoly trade with the Indian subcontinent. At the height of its power, it was responsible for almost half of Britain's trade. By 1803, this international mega-corporation had transformed into an aggressive colonial power that had an army of 260,000 soldiers. Unlike the East India Company, today's brands are neither militarised nor do they seek to capture territories as the East India Company did. Nevertheless, striking similarities remain. Like many multinational retailers today, the East India Company was a joint-stock company that employed only a small number of permanent staff in its London head office while exploiting the labour of millions of people thousands of kilometres away for the benefit of its shareholders. Similar to how the East India Company (alongside private companies of other colonial powers) wielded enormous economic power through trade, today's multinational textile companies dominate much of Bangladesh's exports with more than 80 per cent of the country's total export earnings now generated by the ready-made garment (RMG) sector alone.

This chapter focuses on how the global supply chain model operated by these brands has become a key, if not *the* key, characteristic of the globalised economy and thus become the dominant form of organising production in the past quarter of a century. Central to the supply chain model is a hard-nosed business approach where resources – physical or human – are sourced at the point where maximum profit can be extracted. In this way, mass-produced goods are often manufactured in low-cost economies, with the bulk of savings being extracted from low direct and indirect labour costs. While Western democracies have developed institutionalised mechanisms to curtail the most exploitative tendencies of capitalism at the national level, the shift to highly flexible transnational sourcing has undermined the economic and social institutions that provided some degree of protection for workers. Not only does the global supply chain model undermine the terms and conditions of workers, it goes further by undermining the institutional configurations of workplace and industrial democracy. Next, the chapter will outline how the supply chain model is a feature of the movement from the Fordist to a post-Fordist economy and the associated ways in which it undermines institutions of workplace democracy. Towards the end of the chapter, the rise of consumption actors and their role in driving global labour governance are highlighted as potentially interesting developments that may increase democratic participation in global supply chains.

## 2.1 Democracy and the Fordist Model

In the period immediately following World War II, the Fordist model came to dominate the social and economic organisation of life in developed economies. While Fordism is often associated with the mass production of goods, it was notable for a number of other key features that link production to consumption and democratic institutions. Wolfgang Streeck (2016) has labelled the post-war period as one of 'democratic capitalism', where markets and democracy reached a relatively stable balance: markets were supervised through multiple layers of democratic control in terms of both representative government and organisational-level democracy. Central to this system of national economic and social governance were the links between production systems and democratic governance under Fordism. A key feature of the models associated with the Fordist period, which typified the 'Golden Age of Capitalism' for Western European and North American economies from around 1950 to 1970 (Boyer, 2001; Vidal, 2015), was that they were based around 'institutional fixes' (Jessop, 2011), focused on a national basis. While the Fordist model is sometimes seen as synonymous with the move to mass production and deskilling through assembly-line organisation (Braverman, 1974; Watson, 2019), the flip side to the approach is equally important (Petit, 1999): a central feature of the Fordist model was to increase consumption of relatively cheap mass-produced goods through real wage increases, thus increasing demand across the economy. Under

Worker = consumer          Creates more demand

Mass employment of workers

Retail organisations

Mass consumption of goods

Real wage increases with increased purchasing power

**Figure 2.1** The virtuous circle of production and consumption under Fordism

the Fordist model, mass production and consumption interacted in a virtuous cycle as illustrated in Figure 2.1: real wage increases led to increases in purchasing power, increased the demand for goods and, in turn, increased employment and real wages (Reinecke and Donaghey, 2021b). As such, the approach that dominated the thirty years post World War II has been labelled as 'wage-led growth' (Baccaro and Pontusson, 2016). In the ideal scenario, wages, determined through collective bargaining, would rise below productivity but above inflation.

The Ford model, however, did more than simply link production and consumption in a given national context. The model sought to achieve full employment by producing domestically most of what was consumed in what was known as 'import substituting industrialisation'. While Fordism did involve cross-border trade, it was built upon a foundation of national economic, social and political institutions that combined to act in complementary and mutually reinforcing ways.

A second feature of the model was thus the growth of a social welfare system governed not through market mechanisms but rather through national-level democratic governance. In this way, peaks and troughs of consumption could be somewhat smoothed through the development of mechanisms of state intervention in the labour market and vice versa (Iversen and Soskice, 2020). In addition, while smoothing issues in the labour market, this welfare system also provided a safety net for individual consumption and helped to manage macroeconomic demand. This type of intervention formed part of the Keynesian consensus, where state policy focused on the achievement of full employment. Crouch (2009) argues that this commitment to a mixed economy became the defining feature of social democracy, where markets and states acted in coordination and a balance was achieved between democratic and market-based activity.

The third feature was that, at the workplace level, workers were integrated into the system through collective bargaining and democratic representation. Many of the representation rights of workers, developed to provide restraints on capital, were achieved through industrial and electoral struggle by unions and their allied social democratic political parties. While there were often attempts by management and owners to resist trade unionism, including at Ford (Beynon, 1974; Starkey and McKinlay, 1989), collective bargaining and representation had become key features of the model by the time of World War II (Clarke, 1992). In this way, workers were democratically represented with management, particularly around issues of pay and conditions through collective bargaining. While, in the English-speaking world, collective bargaining was generally at a company or plant level, in continental and Nordic European economies it was often at a sectoral level. In these systems, workers generally had workplace-level representation through institutions such as works councils, which dealt with issues such as work organisation and staffing levels at individual plants (Rogers and Streeck, 1995; Nienhüser, 2020). To enable this, governments actively – often through statutory means – embedded such representation rights. In addition, as an important counter-balance to the power of capital, workers had the right to take industrial action, such as strikes and work to rule, to achieve a more equitable distribution of economic gains, with those systems that had stronger systems of collective bargaining having lower income inequality (Rueda and Pontusson, 2000). While in some countries, such as the United Kingdom in the 1970s, frequent strikes did cause economic disruption, in many others, such as West Germany, strike action was rarely called upon. In other countries, particularly Sweden under the Social Democratic Party's Rehn–Meidner model, national and sectoral wage bargaining functioned to squeeze out those businesses that could not afford to pay the going rate (Vartiainen, 1998; Erixon, 2008, 2010). This power for both governments and workers to restrain the activities of capitalism was viewed to create 'beneficial constraints' (Streeck, 1997b). These constraints were beneficial because they led to capital seeking more qualitative forms of competitive advantage rather than just acting on a cost basis alone. While there certainly was inequality, and the workforce was predominantly male, national political institutions provided mechanisms through which pay and the quality of life in general were increasing. To use the language of the French Regulation School, during the period, the *mode of accumulation* was Fordism with the *regime of regulation* being social democracy. This model had a very significant effect on the distribution of wealth within society: Thomas Piketty (2014) has demonstrated that, across developed economies under the Fordist system, inequality declined on a fairly continuous basis from the 1940s through to the end of the 1970s.

While this is a stylised account of the Fordist economic model, and generally is confined to the experiences in advanced capitalist societies of Europe, North America and Japan, the key points emerging are that the model was based around achieving a balance between economic growth, equitable distribution, creating a positive cycle between consumption and production and democratic governance. Despite differences between countries, a central feature was an acknowledged role for government in national economic management and the regulation of workplace relations at the enterprise level, with unions as worker representatives at the workplace, sector and national levels (Amable, 2003). In this way, individuals were recognised in terms of their identities as producers, consumers and citizens; the workers were also the consumers and the citizens.

## 2.2 Post-Fordism, Supply Chains and Democracy

With the simultaneous vast changes in technologies and the lowering of trade barriers, alongside the growth in financialisation since the late 1970s, there is a consensus that the Fordist model has been replaced by a post-Fordist model. Consequently, the economic, social and political institutional complementarities of the Fordist approach have been undermined. Central to the erosion of the Fordist model has been the emergence of the supply chain model, which became the key defining feature of late twentieth- and early twenty-first-century production (Reinecke et al., 2018). In their simplest sense, supply chains can be thought of as what links goods from their first stage of production right through to their final consumption. In the modern economy, this essentially means that production is carried out through the partial or entire outsourcing of the production of the product or service. This vast growth in outsourcing has created a situation where retailers in sectors such as apparel have become organisations that often manufacture none of their products in their own factories and essentially become little more than 'brands' that engage with their consumers (Lury, 2004). Here, this means brands effectively minimise their activities into a narrow range of consumer-facing roles and particularly seek not to be directly producing goods sold under their labels. For example, Swedish apparel retail giant H&M states on its website: 'H&M does not own any factories. Instead, our garments are bought from around 800 independent suppliers, mainly in Europe and Asia' (H&M, n.d.). In 2019, the ITUC estimated that H&M employed 132,000 workers in its consumer-facing operations, but had a staggering 1.6 million workers producing its goods through its supply chain.

One of the implications of the supply chain model is that it separates consumption from production and de-democratises the model of production. Most famously, Apple has labelled its products as 'Designed in California; Made in China', but this is an oversimplification of the situation. In reality, the label possibly should read along the lines of 'Designed in California; display made in Japan; accelerometer made in Germany; chips made in the USA; gyroscope made in Italy; touch ID made in Taiwan ... Finally assembled in China most of the time but sometimes in India'. The 2018 UNCTAD report highlighted that the massive expansion in supply chains as a mode of industrial organisation took place between 2000 and 2010 with an annual average year-on-year growth of 11 per cent in developed economies, 19 per cent in transitional economies and 15 per cent in least-developed economies. Between 2010 and 2017, while this figure declined to an average of 1–2 per cent of annual growth by 2017, supply chains still constituted 80 per cent of all international trade and 60 per cent of global production (UNCTAD, 2018). Alongside this was a complicated picture in the area of inequality. First, as demonstrated above, in developed countries since the early 1980s, there has been a significant growth in inequality. Second, there has been a decline in absolute terms in inequality in developing countries, with fewer people in absolute poverty but a growth in inequality in relative terms. Third, there has been a fall in relative inequality between developing countries (Ravallion, 2014).

Global supply chains have thus broken the Fordist model as they are essentially based on increasing consumption not through increasing disposable incomes but by making consumption increasingly cheap for existing consumers. To deliver lower priced goods, consumers often become spatially separated from those who produce the goods (Rainnie et al., 2007) by seeking out producers who operate at significantly lower wage costs than those who are consuming the goods earn. While recent research in the United Kingdom (Hammer and Plugor, 2016, 2019) highlights that the supply chain model can lead to labour abuses in developed countries, the main focus of brands has been to shift to sourcing from developing countries. While this has undoubtedly brought employment and economic growth to these developing countries, it has also meant aggressive price competition, exploitation of workers and thus growing inequality. Brands have little incentive to ensure that the wages of workers are increased to a level where they could also become consumers of the goods they are making. Instead, corporate activity ensures that costs remain low: buyers relocate or threaten to relocate should wage costs rise, particularly in sectors driven by labour cost such as apparel (Feuerstein, 2013; Zhu and He, 2013). The model, as outlined in Figure 2.2, is therefore the opposite of the virtuous cycle: workers do not have a reasonable prospect of being able to consume the type of goods they produce, nor do workers have access to the democratic institutions that regulate the behaviour of brands where they are headquartered.

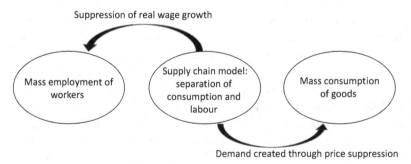

Figure 2.2  The separation of production and consumption under post-Fordism

As discussed above, production is outsourced to legally independent factories, which generally bid through competitive processes for the supply contracts. In doing this, brands have no sunk costs in facilities they own themselves or employment responsibilities towards those who make their goods. Instead, they create markets to supply them (Clark and Wrigley, 1997). The implication of not having sunk costs or direct employees is that brands are free to shop around between potential suppliers for those that will produce at the requisite level for the most competitive price, through what can be thought of as 'regime shopping'. Traxler and colleagues (2008: 217), in the context of EU integration, define 'regime shopping' as 'capital, based on its superior cross-border mobility ... relocating production to what is seen as the most favourable labour market regime'. Where brands pursue an 'efficiency seeking' internationalisation, rather than a resource or market-expansion based strategy, labour regulation and costs become central features of the 'shopping' exercise (Rugman, 2010). For instance, even within wholly owned plants, German car manufacturer Volkswagen played fragmented production sites in Germany, Spain and the Czech Republic off against each other to raise productivity while maintaining low costs (Greer and Hauptmeier, 2012). The factors that are attractive for regime shopping differ according to sector (Haidinger et al., 2014) – for example, in high-end services, the availability of a well-educated workforce may be important, whereas in mass production, such as the apparel sector, the driving factor is generally labour costs.

To attract business from brands, many developing countries have followed a strategy of 'export-led industrialisation' to accelerate economic growth, in contrast to the 'import substitution industrialisation' that was the dominant mode in the Fordist period. To be an attractive site for investment from brands, the emphasis of state action is on increasing national competitiveness. Just as brands compete for customers, the state competes for global buyers of its goods and services and becomes a 'competition state' (Cerny, 1997). As a result, state commitment to maintaining labour rights has weakened. The creation of 'export processing zones', or EPZs, illustrates the strategy of 'export-led industrialisation', with states striving to be hyper-competitive: certain areas are designated specifically to produce at low lost as a method of enticing orders from large brands (Engman et al., 2007). EPZs typically offer a combination of tax incentives, exemptions from labour laws, bans on trade unions and specialised police to ensure that brands enjoy smooth supply (Rahim and Islam, 2020).

Moreover, in many developing nations, states simply lack the capacity to regulate effectively. Many states are rogue and/or failed states, which suffer from corruption and have an inability and lack of resources to enforce labour regulation and impose realistic fines (Brinkerhoff and Brinkerhoff, 2002). In 2020, the Fragile State Index, which measures the vulnerability of states to collapse based on a range of fragility and conflict indicators, issued a 'warning' about state fragility for the majority of states (116 out of 178 assessed). Many outsourcing destinations for the garments sector have an elevated warning (e.g., India, Turkey), a high warning (e.g., Bangladesh, Malawi), an alert (e.g., Ethiopia, Myanmar) or a high or very high alert (e.g., Democratic Republic of the Congo). Due to a lack of state support, important democratic rights at work, such as the right to strike and freedom of association, often face significant curbs.

As outlined to this point, the supply chain model marks a significant move away from the Fordist model in terms of its linkage of production and consumption, but also in terms of its links to wider society in terms of democratic participation. These changes pose significant challenges in terms of how the regulation and governance of labour and employment standards are understood. The implications of this for actors in the capital–labour divide will be taken up in Section 2.3.

## 2.3 The Fragmentation of Employment Relationships

While it is not new to argue that the shifts in the post-Fordist economy have led to the fragmentation and disintegration of workplace representation and democracy (Marchington et al., 2005; Doellgast, 2012), we argue that the supply chain model represents the epitome of such fragmentation and disintegration due to the changed relations and the actors involved. The very nature of the supply chain model brings about a significant reconfiguration of the actors in the employment relationship, which has generally been thought of as the relationship between workers and employers, underpinned by nation-state legislation. In particular, as will be developed next, the role of brands and NGOs focuses particularly on the consumption relationship, which is in addition to employers and unions, who generally focus on the production relationship. While at one level this relationship may seem complementary, the different approaches to mobilisation and power often leave an uneasy relationship.

## 2.3.1 Sourcing Relations in Global Supply Chains

At the heart of the supply chain model, particularly in low wage sectors like apparel, is an extremely efficient form of extraction of surplus labour value. As wealthy consumers clamour to wear goods carrying the label of prominent brands, the price they pay and how it varies compared with other functionally equivalent pieces of clothing often bears little relationship to the labour effort of those making the goods. For example, when visiting apparel factories, it is not uncommon to see production lines within the same facility producing for high-end designer labels cheek by jowl with production for discount retailers, with the workers in these factories receiving the same pay rate whether they are producing for the Tommy Hilfiger brand or a discount retailer such as Aldi. In addition to the straightforward low-wage advantage sought through the model, supply chains also provide brands with a transfer of risk away from them but simultaneously increase their levels of control over their suppliers.

Supply chains in the apparel industry conform closest to what Gereffi and colleagues (2005) label 'market' configurations, where the brands have a large supply base that competes for contracts based on short term price-based competition. While some suppliers do supply brands for many years, this supply is generally based on a series of short-term contracts that are effectively auctioned between suppliers as they arise. By having short-term contracts, brands are able to limit their legal ties to specific factories to these specific orders. Similarly, by procuring from factories that supply to multiple buyers, potential liability around being a 'co-employer' is reduced. To minimise risk in terms of political or natural disaster factors, these contracts are often highly fragmented between many suppliers and often across multiple countries. In these ways, the brands are able to reduce the extent to which they are exposed to risk in individual factories or even countries, while the competitive tendering process gives them considerable leverage and control over their suppliers. Thus, by fragmenting their procurement into supply chains, they are able to achieve increased economic efficiency and a high degree of control with limited legal liability.

Traditionally, employers generally form a key, if not *the* key, constituent of the employment relationship (Kaufman, 2004), as it is with the employer that workers have their contract of work. That said, within the CSR (Welford and Frost, 2006; Sobczak, 2007; Scherer and Palazzo, 2011; Scherer et al., 2016), supply chain and global value chain literature (Gereffi et al., 2005; Barrientos and Smith, 2007; Taylor et al., 2013), employers have often been viewed as rather passive recipients and powerless enactors of the policies of brands, with little ability to influence or resist downward pressures. This is true to some extent: employers are often heavily dependent on brands in terms of the provision of work and are also bound by the constraints of items like employers' codes of conduct. Moreover, brands' purchasing practices and their business models shape the pressures faced by employers (Reinecke et al., 2019). That said, employers do have agency. In reality, the costs involved with switching suppliers in highly fragmented, fast-moving supply chains mean that brands are far less flexible when it comes to withdrawing purchases from suppliers (Locke, 2013). In addition, suppliers typically produce for multiple brands at the same time, so the loss of a contract with one supplier can be compensated for by orders from other buyers. Factory managers can therefore exercise some autonomy in terms of responding to the demands of buyers in the extent to which they substantively adopt, ceremonially adopt or minimally adopt brand codes of conduct (Zhu and Morgan, 2017). This agency of employers is generally dependent on their ability to meet brand pressures and thus, in theory at least, workers could have power to disrupt. In this way, the employment relationship becomes more opaque, with the interaction and power relations between brands and their suppliers playing a key role in shaping the regulation and governance of the relationship.

## 2.3.2 Labour Representation in Global Supply Chains

The nature of global supply chains, where brands spread their purchasing from across a wide range of suppliers, combined with immature systems of employment relations, often with few unions present and low labour power (Bartley and Egels-Zanden, 2016; Jenkins and Blyton, 2017) and aggressive states (Anner, 2015), provides for difficult environments for workers in terms of leveraging employers and brands. The logic of unions is based on workers being organised collectively and having the ability to disrupt, or at least to threaten credibly, the production process (Donaghey et al., 2014; Reinecke and Donaghey, 2015). In this context, the main transnational vehicles for organising workers are the nine global union federations (GUFs), which bring together unions from across much of the world. Yet the nature of GUFs makes coordinating activity difficult (Croucher and Cotton, 2008). Two interrelated issues raise challenges for GUFs in the supply chain context. First, GUFs are organised on a sectoral basis. Thus, even in the unlikely event that workers at both ends of the supply chain are unionised, unions at one end of the supply chain – for example, manufacturing unions – are more likely to be in a different global union than those at the consumer end, which can create impediments to worker solidarity across the supply chain. Second, GUFs are organised on a broadly sectoral model without regard for the political, institutional and economic differences that Anner and colleagues (2006) highlight as being potential hurdles for international union cooperation. In addition, leverage over actors is most often felt by targeting the buyer firms rather than the actual employers. Wright (2016) argues that reputational risk among consumers is a lever that unions can utilise to improve labour standards in production networks. However, he goes on to argue that such leverage is not automatic but rather contingent on the different types of organisations and the markets within which they are embedded.

While unions are at best weak in these global supply chains, NGOs, movements and other civil society actors have emerged as central to transnational supply chain governance. Even if these organisations advance workers' rights, they typically direct their campaigns to Western consumers and the media, often with the aim of putting pressure on brands, rather than on the employers who are directly responsible for working conditions. For instance, in 2019, Oxfam Australia produced a 'Naughty or Nice' list of brands in the lead-up to Christmas in an effort to get consumers to buy from those brands that Oxfam viewed as having a more positive approach to labour issues. In response to such pressures, many brands have engaged directly with these NGOs as part of their CSR programmes. NGOs have also been constituents and sometimes initiators of 'multi-stakeholder initiatives', where they engage with business interests in the formation and implementation of labour standards. In this space, NGOs become an important actor for labour rights (Bartley, 2007,

2018; Egels-Zandén and Hyllman, 2006, 2011). While sharing many
substantive objectives around issues of labour standards and rights,
unions and NGOs do not always operate in a symbiotic relationship
(Egels-Zandén, 2009). This is generally due to the differing underlying
logics of representation on which their political legitimacy rests, which
will be discussed in Chapters 5 and 6. A key claim of unions regarding
their legitimacy is that their membership is a voluntarily coalition of
workers who pursue an agenda to advance their own material interests
at work through a logic of industrial democracy (Donaghey and
Reinecke, 2018). In contrast, many NGOs are composed of people
who wish to express solidarity with workers with poor conditions but
who are not necessarily subject to such conditions themselves.

The supply chain context has therefore significantly altered the
constellation of actors and their roles in governing the employment
relationship of production. It is particularly noteworthy that brands,
even though generally the most powerful actor, are by design and
choice directly employing fewer and fewer production workers. For
those seeking improvements in labour standards, this raises issues
about how these powerful actors and the relationships they have with
other actors, such as global unions, local unions, employers and states,
can be used to improve labour standards. With the marginalisation of
organised labour, NGOs have emerged as key actors in terms of labour
activism in the supply chain model. However, the nature of their
activity is significantly different from that of unions in terms of who,
how and where they represent labour issues. Section 2.4 addresses this
issue in terms of the governance tools and power resources of the
labour actors.

## 2.4 From Production to Consumption-Based Labour Governance?

While the role of the state in terms of the regulation of the employment
relationship varied greatly under the Fordist model, states were generally viewed both as prescribing a minimum floor in terms of employment rights and standards and enforcement of both publicly legislated
standards and private contracts. This has changed significantly under
globalisation. As Cerny (1995, 1997) argues, the pressures of globalisation and the significant shift in power towards global capital have
led to states becoming highly competitive in terms of their attempts to

attract brands. The implications of this shift have meant that states are incentivised to liberalise labour market regulation, which drives down labour standards.

With this denudation of the capacity and willingness of states to regulate, it has been argued by some that the development of forms of meaningful global governance (Scholte, 2008) is necessary – in other words, that private actors should take on the capacity to direct actors across national boundaries. While at the national level the term 'governance' has been viewed as the replacement of public regulation by private forms (Jessop, 2002), at the global level it can be argued that governance has emerged from the absence of a global government rather than as the replacement for it. This perspective on global governance is generally based around the argument that there is no meaningful prospect of the development of democratic global government and that what is instead emerging is a complex web of global governance institutions (Scholte, 2008). Private, transnational governance in the form of CSR is thus viewed as filling gaps in global regulation and/or substituting for the lack of regulatory capability or willingness of nation-states (Djelic and Sahlin-Andersson, 2006; Bartley, 2018). In this way, brands are viewed as taking on 'state-like characteristics' in terms of being the bodies that devise and implement rules across national boundaries (Scherer and Palazzo, 2007). This is part of a more general trend where brands have become the dominant actors for most forms of global labour governance, with some arguing that the defining feature of the neoliberal era has been the rise and consolidation of corporate power and, rather than neoliberalism being about deregulation, it is in fact re-regulation in favour of the interests of oligopolistic corporations (Hathaway, 2020).

With this power shift, the idea that brands are the dominant actor within their supply chain and thus are able to dictate actions to others within their network, is central to the CSR approach. Gereffi (1994) and Gereffi et al. (2005) famously argued that, within supply chains, not all firms are equal and those that exert more power are labelled 'lead firms'. In global apparel supply chains, global brands are the 'lead firms' because their purchasing power and ability to switch producers endow them with significant leverage over other supply chain actors. For this reason, lead firms are central to private governance and also become key targets for leverage in terms of how changes to working conditions can be achieved in the supply chains.

The core asset possessed by MNCs – their 'brand' – is the recognisable name that attracts consumers to purchase their products; however, it also becomes their core vulnerability. While MNCs' divorce from production and 'relative autonomy' from other actors (Ruggie, 2018) give MNCs significant flexibility, power and control over production, they open their reputation up to vulnerability. MNC brands have also essentially become political actors themselves because they have assumed public governance roles that were once the domain of the nation-state (Scherer and Palazzo, 2011). This is because the supply chain model undermines the division of labour between governments that regulate corporate power and corporations, which operate within the confines of regulatory frameworks. Brands therefore engage in political forms of CSR that take the role of regulatory functions, such as imposing labour standards on their suppliers in their private contracts (Scherer and Palazzo, 2007, 2011). Yet the very nature of this brand governance, aside from the obvious conflicts of interest, is that a multiplicity of rule-making regimes emerges with no uniform method of enforcement. However, despite lacking central enforcement authority, private governance standards can have law-like effects (Terlaak, 2007), becoming binding and enforceable rules through independent, third-party, certification systems and diffusing globally as a result of institutional pressure (Bansal and Roth, 2000; Lim and Tsutsui, 2012).

What does this mean for the employment relationship? So far in this chapter, it has been argued that the very nature of the supply chain model brings about a significant reconfiguration of the actors in the employment relationship and the extent to which workers' interests are represented democratically. The remainder of the chapter argues that the shifting nature between industrial relations and CSR is based around a recasting of power relations away from production and towards consumption. This shift necessitates a reconsideration of how we understand democratic participation in global labour governance. While the idea of governance relationships being based on production relations is well established, we argue that in the supply chain context, greater attention needs to be placed on the interaction of industrial relations and CSR. The CSR approach sees NGOs and the rise of 'ethical consumerism' as an important factor in driving market-based forms of global labour governance with the key relationship in CSR being the relationship between the brand and their consumers.

To understand better the interface between industrial relations and CSR, we conceptualise power within production and/or consumption relations as drivers of particular labour governance regimes. It is argued that greater labour power drives labour-based collective agreements regimes and greater consumer power drives market-based forms of labour governance. While the power bases of industrial relations and CSR governance regimes differ considerably, they may be complementary in the context of establishing labour standards. In particular, we focus on Wright's (2000) use of structural and associational power to conceptualise the power of labour. We use Hirschman's (1970) 'exit, voice and loyalty' framework, originally developed to explain declining consumer loyalty in nationalised industries in Africa, to conceptualise the power of consumers in terms of their ability to pressurise 'lead firms'.

### 2.4.1 Production-Based Governance of Global Labour through Collective Agreements

The production-oriented view of the employment relationship generally views employment governance as being provided by 'producer groups' – that is, employers and trade unions. To complement this, states set minimum procedures such as union recognition laws, dismissal procedures and legal enforcement of contractual obligations, as well as substantive minimum standards such as levels of minimum wages and worker compensation levels, which employers within their jurisdiction are expected to meet (Traxler, 1999). Collective bargaining has long been viewed as the means by which workers can democratically exert influence over their terms and conditions of employment, providing a counter-balance to the economic power of employers (Webb and Webb, 1897; Commons, 1919). However, globalisation and the associated supply chain model pose many issues for the future of collective bargaining (Standing, 1997; Thelen, 2003). Widescale collective bargaining and joint regulation are primarily Western European phenomena and the industrialisation of many developing countries is occurring under systems where state and/or managerial determinism dominate, leading to weak collective bargaining regimes. The ILO (2022) estimates that in about half of the 98 countries for which they have data, less than 25 per cent of wage earners were covered by collective bargaining agreements, with the Asia and

Pacific region having coverage of 12.8 per cent. In addition, the expectation is that those countries not covered by the ILO data have even lower coverage levels. The ILO (2022) also highlights that of its eight fundamental international labour conventions, the two covering collective bargaining and organising (Nos. 168 and 157) have the lowest ratification level. Alongside this, the nature of the supply chain relationship, where multinational brands set labour standards for workers in their supply chain, obfuscates the clarity of who actually is the employer in the relationship. This issue has been challenged in various courts – most famously in Germany, where KiK was sued as a co-employer by the widow of a victim of the Ali Enterprises disaster in Pakistan but settled before the court rendered its judgment, thus preventing a precedent being set. The case was viewed as potentially path-breaking as it was felt that it could potentially lead to recognition of the concept of 'co-employers', where brands were viewed as such due to their control over both their suppliers and the workers.

Within this constrained public space, IFAs have emerged as the main mechanisms in global supply chains for regulating labour through negotiated, collective agreements. Hammer (2005: 512) describes IFAs as 'agreements [negotiated by GUFs] on fundamental labour rights with MNCs', which democratise the labour standards–setting process. The first agreement was signed in 1988 by the French food multinational Danone, followed by the Accor hotel chain in 1995 (Wills, 2002). Agreements can take the form of either 'bargaining', where substantive agreements are made, or 'rights', where procedural agreements such as freedom of association and the right to collective bargaining are set. Generally, these agreements are built around the brand headquarters committing to enable the exercise of freedom of association and collective bargaining with the details of the individual sites to be negotiated locally. IFAs generally cover MNCs' subsidiaries and often place requirements on independent suppliers. As a result, they can differ significantly in terms of who they cover. They may cover those directly employed by the brand, the workers in the supply chain or both (Niforou, 2012). Take the apparel giants Inditex (most famously associated with the chain Zara) and H&M. Both have two IFAs, one with UniGlobal, generally covering direct employees, and another with IndustriALL, covering those workers within the supply chain. Spanish brand Inditex's IFA with IndustriALL emerged directly out of the Spectrum fire in Bangladesh in 2005 and was signed in 2007

(Miller, 2011). Interestingly, Inditex's IFA with IndustriALL, which covers 1.5 million non-directly employed workers worldwide across 50 countries and 7,000 factories in their supply chain, pre-dates the 2009 one with UniGlobal, which covers its own direct employees.

### 2.4.1.1 The Structural and Associational Power of Labour

The strength of labour is drawn primarily from the structural and associational power held by labour vis-à-vis employers (Wright, 2000). Structural power can be defined as 'power that results simply from the location of workers within the economic system' (Wright, 2000: 962). Thus, structural power effectively refers to how labour is positioned vis-à-vis other actors and interests within the economic system, including institutions such as legal frameworks, employer structures and the physical location of work. Within supply chains, three factors shape labour's structural power: the structural power of workers is high when workers are not easily substitutable, when they have effects on other parts of the economic system and when know-ledge of the structure of a supply chain enables workers to upset the flow of the chain to claim better wages and employment conditions. In sum, the greater the potential of labour to affect the production pro-cess, the more power it exerts. For example, workers in logistics tend to have higher structural power compared with assembly line workers. Logistics workers possess valuable information about the flow of production, including transportation, supply chain consultants and financiers, as well as labour-friendly investors and shareholders (Quan, 2008). Second, labour gains leverage points in the supply chain when it is 'highly driven' – that is, when a strong lead firm governs supply chains in a hands-on manner, irrespective of whether the lead firm is situated at the consumption or production end of the chain (Riisgaard and Hammer, 2011).

The associational power of labour can be defined as 'the various forms of power that result from the formation of collective organiza-tions of workers' (Wright, 2000: 962), such as trade unions and, at the supranational level, the GUFs (Croucher and Cotton, 2008). GUFs are distinguished by industrial sector and have a formal internal govern-ance system comprising a worldwide network of national affiliates (industry union federations) spanning more than 120 countries. High associative power depends on the coexistence of three factors: the relationships between supplier-firm unions and lead firm unions, the degree of unity among unions and the ability of unions across a supply chain to coordinate solidarity actions. While GUFs play an important mediating role, affiliation of a local trade union with a GUF does not necessarily translate into local compliance with core labour rights (Ford and Gillan, 2015). Differences in perceptions regarding local strategies and international campaigns, as well as differences in political orientations, can result in inter-union conflicts and therefore the absence of a shared collective identity among global and the local labour representatives. Associative power is not independent of structural power. Awareness of production details allows workers to identify potential allies to organise international campaigns. Workers may leverage the lead firm's unionised operations/suppliers to gain solidarity and support (Quan, 2008).

### 2.4.1.2 Analysis of the Power of Labour

It is accepted that globalisation has seen the power of labour decline. While many have written about the potential for labour revitalisation and renewal, the supply chain context presents an exemplar case as to the difficulties of achieving this. The very nature of the model, where production is separated from those who capture the largest value and is dispersed across multiple countries, is one where the ability of exercising the power of labour is greatly diminished. But it is not just the power relations that are diminished: in addition, the nature of democratic participation and representation of worker interests are also diminished. In this context, other forms of power and representation have emerged, and it is in this context that we discuss the emerging role of consumption-based representation of labour issues.

## 2.4.3 CSR-Based Governance of Global Labour through Consumption-Driven Standards

While consumption is typically considered a post-production issue, rising consumer awareness of ethical issues has resulted in actors outside the employment contract having an influence on industrial relations. Traditionally, consumers and workers have been uneasy bedfellows (Compa, 2004), and consumers have been associated with greater market pressure, flexibility and service quality (Heery, 1993; Kessler and Bach, 2011). Nevertheless, the consumer is increasingly being seen as a fundamental post-production actor and driver of labour governance, rather than an enemy of labour as a result of labour standards. This is particularly in the context that MNCs, as outlined above, have essentially become consumer-facing entities ('brands') and now devote significant resources to shaping their public perception in the form of CSR. The implications of this for the workers who produce their goods is significant. Most importantly, due to the highly flexible nature of the supply chain approach, brands become the actors who have the most constant presence in the market as they have significant capacity to switch suppliers and exclude employers from participating. In this way, the core vulnerability of the brand is not the potential disruption of goods to their consumers but that for some reason consumers would no longer wish to purchase goods from their brand. Second, due to the fragmented nature of production under the supply chain model, brands spread their risk across multiple suppliers. Thus, should workers disrupt production through strike action or the like, brands can acquire produce from other suppliers. While in theory this could give workers leverage over their individual employers, it also carries with it the risk of ending all orders to their factories and thus also ending employment.

In this context, NGOs such as faith groups, student organisations and human and labour rights activists have shifted their attention from seeking states to take action and instead have focused on the private sector in the form of brands (Soule, 1997; den Hond and de Bakker, 2007; King and Pearce, 2010). In the face of globalised industries, where no single national body can ensure the enforcement of workers' rights, activists have mobilised consumers to use their power at the end-point in the global supply chain to put pressure on brands. Campaigns such as the student-led anti-sweatshop protests against Nike exposed the complicity of brands in human rights abuses in industries ranging from rug-weaving in South-East Asia to cocoa farming in Africa (Bartley, 2007; Vogel, 2008). While the extent to which these concerns actually do affect consumption is unclear, the threat to brand image has increased the possibility of consumer power as a counter-force to globalisation's race to the bottom (Barnett et al., 2005; Conroy, 2007).

In response to such activism, firms have invested significantly in CSR in attempts to demonstrate that they contribute to society beyond narrow profit maximisation. CSR is broadly understood in terms of socially beneficial activities that go beyond a corporation's legal obligations to stakeholders (Carroll, 1999). While the term is broad, in this context it is taken to mean that brands create governance systems to which their suppliers are expected to conform to supply that buyer. In global supply chains, CSR activities typically take the form of voluntary, private social auditing initiatives, such as codes of conduct and other forms of industry self-regulation (Fransen and Burgoon, 2015). Corporate-driven CSR codes have the advantage that brands can impose them upon their suppliers using contractual relationships. Corporations, subject to activist campaigns and media exposés, often make CSR commitments to reduce reputational risk emanating from poor labour conditions (Khan et al., 2007; Wells, 2009; Wright, 2016). Thus, the CSR approach generally is framed as one of responding to customer concerns over issues such as the treatment of workers and environmental concerns through the notion of 'ethical consumerism'. Without doubt, there have been numerous debates about whether CSR is leading to genuine efforts by firms to fill the governance gaps that are arising from the globalised production model (Matten & Crane, 2005; Scherer et al., 2006; Scherer & Palazzo, 2011) or whether CSR is just a form of 'organized hypocrisy' (Krasner, 1999; see also Banerjee, 2008), where multinational corporations adopt a few isolated social projects doing good to distract from a continuing self-interested, socially harmful approach to profit generation (Banerjee, 2018). Nevertheless, the exercise or even threat of consumer power and its potential to harm brands' reputation can often drive firms' voluntary engagement in private labour governance.

### 2.4.3.1 Bases of Consumer Power: Consumers' Purchasing and Voice Power

The consumer is the raison d'être for the existence of, and theoretically the most powerful actor in, a global supply chain. Ethical consumerism taps into the consumer's purchasing power by encouraging them to evaluate goods and products in terms of price and quality but also in terms of labour practices and environmental criteria. Consumer power can be conceptualised using Hirschman's (1970) exit, voice and loyalty framework within the domain of the consumption relation (Donaghey et al., 2014; Reinecke and Donaghey, 2015). Consumers can articulate dissatisfaction with goods and services through 'exiting' the consumption relationship by boycotting goods (or threat thereof), consistent with Hirschman's (1970) notion of 'exit'. Consumer boy-cotts as a form of negative purchasing behaviour express protest against ethical issues ranging from animal testing, genetically modified food and unethical corporate behaviour to goods from objectionable political regimes such as apartheid in South Africa (Soule, 1997). But instead of actual exit, the mere threat of exit may suffice to alert brands to avoid inflicting damage on the ethical reputation of their brands.

The realisation of consumer power requires the existence of substi-tute products with the desired ethical attributes, along with access to information and the transparency provided by ethical labels (Hirschman, 1970). Fairtrade-labelled goods, for instance, enable consumers in rich industrialised countries to use their buying power to improve the incomes and working conditions of producers in less-developed countries (Nicholls and Opal, 2005). In sum, when consumers' purchasing decisions are shaped by consideration of companies' ethical reputations and 'credence factors' (Dolan and Humphrey, 2004), conception of consumers' ethical expectations may become an important driver shaping firm practices. The second form of consumer power can be described in terms of the strength of the consumers' 'voice', defined as 'any attempt at all to change rather than to escape from an objectionable state of affairs' (Hirschman, 1970: 30). The notion of 'consumer voice' resonates with Bendell's (2005) argument that ethical consumerism contains a consumerist, as well as a 'citizen', element, allowing consumers to gain political voice and hold brands responsible for their corporate conduct (Conroy, 2007; Schmelzer, 2010). But such consumption power is not simply the outcome of 'changes in consumer demand met by more or less elastic market supply'; rather, it is 'the result of organised and strategic conduct by collective actors who are highly attuned to the potentials of consumer-activism' (Barnett et al., 2005: 46).

Similar to the importance of collective action by workers, consumer power is created through the mobilisation of collective consumer voice – for instance, few individual workers or consumers in retailers that sell No Sweat or Fairtrade products know the actual details of what workers actually receive. This is why labour rights NGOs run-ning campaigns naming and shaming companies play a central role in bringing issues to public attention and in mobilising consumer pres-sure. Hence, it is often the laborious work of numerous social advo-cacy organisations that has pressured corporations into the adoption of private standards and/or participation in multi-stakeholder initiatives. The mobilisation of consumer voice, rather than consumers' actual changes in purchasing preferences, is often the main driver for corporate engagement. For this reason, the mere threat of consumer exit may suffice to alert companies to avoid inflicting damage on their actual sales or reputation of their brand, a significant intangible asset in the global economy. Bartley's (2007) study of voluntary standards initiatives in forestry and apparel demonstrates that their rise was driven by political struggles led by NGOs and activists, rather than actual changes in ethical purchasing behaviour or commercial strategies to adopt a profitable market niche (see also Bartley, 2018). The growing anti-sweatshop movement publicly exposed firms' behaviour in a variety of 'naming and shaming' campaigns targeting high-profile American companies (Bartley, 2007). Similarly, the 2000 decision by Starbucks – the world's largest speciality coffee retailer – to offer Fairtrade coffee in all of its 2,700 US chains, was preceded by a country-wide campaign by human rights activists against the coffee house chain, enhanced by media reports of child labour practices in a coffee plantation in Guatemala that supplied Starbucks (Conroy, 2007). Voice can be highly effective in the absence even of actual consumer demand for ethical products or the reality of consumer exit.

In sum, NGOs, media and consumer movements are effective mechanisms enabling and amplifying consumer voice. The result is a civil society coalition consisting of NGOs, activist groups and consumers that acts as societal watchdogs, scrutinising corporate behaviour and creating awareness of corporate abuses to exert pressure on brands to take action and enhance the livelihoods and working conditions of branded products. However, companies targeted by social movements, NGOs and the media are not necessarily those engaged in the most offensive and least responsible behaviour but may be those most vulnerable to societal exposure – for example, well-known firms enjoying high brand value selling to final consumers in Western markets that may have shifted their production offshore to benefit from lower labour costs (Bansal and Roth, 2000; Terlaak, 2007; Lange and Washburn, 2012).

### 2.4.3.2 Analysis of Consumer Power

Without doubt, a key Achilles heel for capitalism in the supply chain model is the vulnerability of brand reputation in terms of human and labour rights. However, the nature of this relationship is fundamentally different from that of employment: while the employment relationship is ongoing over a significant period of time and indeterminate in terms of the actual amount of labour exchanged, the consumption relationship is generally one-off or maybe periodic at best. In addition, while workers are generally a relatively well-defined and small number of actors who give significant amounts of their time to their employer, when people act as consumers, the extent to which it is a significant and ongoing commitment is much less. This has implications for democratic participation and the nature of the relationships between who, how and where individuals are represented in terms of their working and consumption lives. These issues will be developed in Chapter 3.

## 2.5 Conclusion

The supply chain model has become the dominant mode of organising production in the modern economy and it is accompanied by significant challenges in terms of the development of democratic governance of labour rights. Central to the argument is that the supply chain model inherently undermines the Fordist model, which linked production, consumption and democracy. In addition, the development of democratic forms of transnational modes of labour governance has been challenged by a lack of institutional support at the transnational level. A patchwork of initiatives has emerged, but often these are examined in terms of their efficiency and effectiveness rather than the power relations and democratic principles that underpin them. This book puts these issues of the changed nature of power relations and democratic participation to the centre of these debates. In Chapter 3, we examine the implications of the separation of production and consumption for the representation of worker interests in labour rights.

# 3 | *Democratic Representation*
## *Structures and Claims*

In 2018, the Clean Clothes Campaign launched a social media campaign under the hashtag '#WeDemandTk16000' to support the National Garment Workers' Federation (NGWF), which had lodged a demand in Bangladesh to double the national minimum wage for garment workers. Rather than joining the NGWF in focusing on the Bangladeshi Minimum Wage Board, which is the democratic body to make such decisions, the sector's employer associations or individual employers, the labour rights NGO sought to mobilise Western consumers and targeted brands such as H&M. No Bangladeshi worker is formally represented in the Clean Clothes Campaign, yet consumer-oriented campaigns such as these may prove equally (and sometimes more) effective in changing workplace conditions than modes of formal representation that are available to workers. The example raises important questions with regard to democratic governance: Who has the right and the capacity to represent workers in transnational spheres and on what grounds?

Many global supply chain contexts are characterised by what we call 'representation gaps' – spaces where constituents affected by business activity in global supply chains are not part of transnational rule-making processes. Modern democracies have been built on the idea that laws and rules are legitimate and binding because those who are governed by them have an input into choosing who makes these rules. Achieving this democratic ideal requires some form of democratic representation in rule-making processes. For this reason, democratic representation – being authorised to speak or act on behalf of someone – has generally been thought of as the cornerstone for democratic legitimacy (Pitkin, 1967; Rehfeld, 2006; Urbinati and Warren, 2008). At the national level, elections are the most recognisable form of democratic representation, while at the workplace and sectoral levels, established structures of representation in the form of trade unions and workplace social dialogue are mechanisms for workers to have an input in the governance of their workplaces. However, the Bangladeshi worker, who earns less than 2 per cent of the production price of a t-shirt (Hasan et al., 2020), has had no say in the codes of conduct that Western buyers impose on their workplace, even if these codes of conduct might be their best hope of ensuring minimal labour standards. Moreover, their employer is much more likely to ensure formal compliance with their buyers' codes than to listen to the concerns of employees. This is because worker representation mechanisms are largely absent in global supply chains that span multiple countries. Even if participation rights for workers are enshrined in law, they remain largely unenforced in production contexts. This chapter seeks to provide the theoretical foundation to grapple with the question of democratic representation in the context of global labour governance.

As outlined in Chapter 2, an increased number of private actors in consumer countries, including campaigning groups, NGOs and brands, have become involved in new forms of labour governance beyond the nation-state, purporting to fill global governance gaps. These private actors participate in transnational rule-making on behalf of citizens, consumers, local communities, workers and others in largely unregulated global supply chains. They derive their legitimacy from the claim that they act in the name of marginalised and otherwise unrepresented stakeholders, including workers – albeit often without the representative structures needed to convey democratic legitimacy to the generated rules. Indeed, private rule-makers at the global level are rarely elected or otherwise authorised representatives of the people in whose name they claim to act. As a result, global governance – rule-making and power-exercising on a global scale – is increasingly shaped by entities that are not necessarily authorised by general agreement to act but that instead derive rule-making power from market and consumer demand. While some see these private politics as a viable route to fill global governance gaps (Scherer and Palazzo, 2007), others fear that the lack of representation perpetuates the 'massive "democratic deficit"' (Nanz and Steffek, 2004), and accentuates 'accountability gaps' (Keohane, 2003). There have thus been questions about the democratic legitimacy of such new forms of governance beyond nation-states and the role of 'self-appointed' representatives such as NGOs and consumer campaigning organisations (Montanaro, 2012; Severs, 2012; Hahn and Weidtmann, 2016).

To provide a conceptual foundation for understanding the role of democratic representation in private labour governance, this chapter begins with a short excursion into political theory to introduce the notion of representation and its legitimising role in democratic governance. It then presents and discusses two different approaches to interest representation outside electoral politics: industrial democracy, through the notion of 'representation as structure', and deliberative democracy, through the notion of 'representation as claim'. Building on this, the chapter develops a sensitising framework that will guide our analysis of transnational industrial democracy in the chapters to come.

## 3.1 Representation in Political Theory

In nearly all Western-style liberal democracies, democratic representation through popular election is typically seen as the cornerstone of political legitimacy (e.g., Cohen, 1989; Benhabib, 1996). Representation is the 'process in which one individual or groups (the representative) act on behalf of other individuals or groups (the represented) in making or influencing authoritative decisions, politics, or laws of a polity' (Thompson, 2001: 11696). The concept of representation in modern political theory is rooted in Thomas Hobbes' (1651) *Leviathan*. Hobbes was particularly concerned with the question of authorisation and whether the political agent has the authority to act in the name of the represented: political authority itself is legitimate only because it was consented to by individuals who, explicitly or implicitly, surrender some degree of their individual freedom in exchange for the protection of some rights or social order. Representation is seen as important to convey legitimacy to the rules generated by representatives and their enforcement, typically by a governing authority. As formulated in the political slogan that inspired the American Revolution, 'no taxation without representation', a basic democratic claim is that a populace should not be subject to binding rules and regulations unless that populace is represented in the political process of creating regulation. In the so-called standard account of political representation (Pitkin, 1967; Rehfeld 2006; Urbinati and Warren 2008), authorisation of a representative (i.e., through elections) by a constituency and accountability to that constituency are the defining institutional features of democratic representation.

The concept of democracy has generally been based on democratic representation as developed through electoral democracy that ensures authorisation and accountability. Elections authorise a representative and enable the constituency to hold their representative accountable for their performance in subsequent elections. In such a system, political claims can be submitted to democratic decision-making procedures, in which the interests of affected parties are advanced and/or defended by their elected representatives. Apart from electoral democracy, representation is also the legitimising principle in other democratic institutions, such as associations and other voluntary organisations where workers participate in electing union officers and office-holders in professional associations.

However, representative politics is currently undergoing a crisis in many societies where representation itself has come under threat from several sides. There are two main lines of critique: one territorial and one radical. First, democratic politics has largely been conceptualised at the level of the nation-state in territorial terms through what has been labelled the Westphalian model. At the transnational level, 'long-held assumptions about democracy and representation can no longer be taken for granted' (Bohman, 2012: 74), thus the practice of representation is changing. While the standard account of representation is based on a pre-existing constituency – members of a political community – who are to be represented, some political scientists question the assumption that democratic representation needs to 'have its origins in a [territorially defined] constituency' (Disch, 2011: 130). From a normative perspective, representation should be proportional to the extent that people are affected by collective decisions, which Goodin (2007) calls the 'all affected interests principle'. However, large sections of people and future generations are currently not represented under the traditional model of representative democracy. A territorially based electoral democracy seems poorly suited to deal with global social and environmental challenges that are territorially unconstrained (Scherer and Palazzo, 2011). For instance, global production has become increasingly fragmented across complex supply chains spanning borders. Production has shifted to locations often because of their lack of regulation and effective representation, while national home country legislation does not reach beyond national borders. The commercial practices of Western brands as well as their CSR standards have a significant effect on the working conditions of workers in South and

South-East Asia. Yet these workers often have no democratic say over whether and how Western brands are regulated (Reinecke and Donaghey, 2021a). Hence one of the central challenges concerns 'the lack of congruence between those who are being governed and those to whom the governing bodies are accountable' (Risse, 2006: 180). In sum, the lack of global representative institutions has created a 'representation gap' (Towers, 1997) where those adversely impacted by global challenges, including workers, future generations or non-human aspects, are often under-represented or unrepresented.

Second, a more radical critique of representative politics has emerged, which argues that, for the majority of citizens, democratic participation is reduced to voting in regional or national elections. One proponent of this critique is political theorist Hanna Pitkin (2004: 339), who argues in her later work that 'the arrangements we call "representative democracy" have become a substitute for popular self-government, not its enactment'. Pitkin is dismissive of representation in arguing that 'representation has supplanted democracy instead of serving it . . . .. The representatives act not as agents of the people but simply instead of them' (Pitkin, 2004: 340). In this view, the real-world limitations of politics, dominated by structural inequalities and biased towards more powerful agents, justify engagement in critical oppositional activity beyond formal institutional (and representative) structures (Young, 2001). This is a position echoed by some New Left, feminist and anarchist movements, which have rejected representative politics in favour of direct or participatory democracy (Maeckelbergh, 2011; Razsa and Kurnik, 2012; Reinecke, 2018). In their search for an alternative to centralised forms of representative power, they focus on the 'how' of decision-making (= processes) while declaring the 'who' (= representation) obsolete (Maeckelbergh, 2011). Whether or not one agrees with this radical critique, this position has given rise to an alternative view of representation to which we will return in order to help us understand different logics of representation.

## 3.2 Logics of Representation in Global Labour Governance

How can we conceptualise representation in transnational governance when the option of representation through electoral democracy is not available? To be sure, there are legitimate forms of political representation beyond the state's system of electoral democracy. The modern territorial state and the capitalist market economy have developed ways to incorporate organised social and professional groups and interest-based associations (Streeck and Kenworthy, 2003). These elements of a collective-associative order are typically seen as part of democracy and present important forms of self-government. Political theorists have argued that organised representation through membership of interest-based associations ensures the incorporation of a greater plurality of interests and complements public regulatory efforts.

It is important to note that this is not seen as hollowing out the state's democratic structures but complementing them (Cohen and Rogers, 1992). The incorporation of interest groups in public policy-making can be explained in terms of both power politics and functional expediency (Streeck and Kenworthy, 2003). On the one hand, institutions of self-government are a concession of the state to the mobilising power of social groups. On the other hand, the state devolves power to interest groups because they also increase problem-solving capacity since they create an interface between the state, market and private citizens. For instance, in the system known as 'neo-corporatism' that emerged in European post-war democracies, parliamentary representation shares the public space with organised social groups that are entitled to various forms of collective participation and self-government (Schmitter, 1974). The state devolves regulatory and public policy functions to organised social groups, which can complement public regulatory efforts. The emphasis in the corporatist literature is on centralised associations and other formal organisational structures, particularly those representing labour and capital, which self-organise to perform functions of rule-making and collective goods production. One example is occupational health and safety. Relying on an inspectorate to monitor commercial establishments is likely to leave significant gaps in law enforcement. Here, the public enforcement mechanism can be supplemented through enlisting institutions of self-government such as workplace committees on occupational health and safety to reduce workplace hazards. Similarly, 'private multipliers of enforcement' (Cohen and Rogers, 1992: 464) can enhance the state's capacity to regulate environmental and social issues.

In Chapter 2, we presented and contrasted the production-based from the consumption-based approach to global labour governance. Below, we argue that both can give rise to different forms of political representation, based on organised social groups that are under-pinned by different logics of representation: The first is based on representation as structure, as exemplified by industrial democracy. It relates to a production-based approach to governance through 'producer groups' – that is, trade unions and employer associations. The second approach is based on representation as claim-making, which emerges from the deliberative tradition in democratic theory. In the context of supply chain governance, it typically is based on an approach where 'consumption actors' – civil society organisations and brands in consumer countries – play an important role in governance. While often perceived as competing approaches, the argument will be developed that in the area of transnational governance, these two approaches can be complementary in providing worker representation and that utilising principles of industrial democracy can augment transnational labour governance. Table 3.1 outlines the key features of these two logics of representation, which will be explored in the sections below.

Table 3.1. *Comparing logics of representation*

|  | Industrial democracy | Deliberative democracy |
|---|---|---|
| Logic of representation | Representation as structure | Representation as claim |
| Who represents? | Trade unions as elected representatives | Civil society organisations as self-appointed representatives |
| Capacity to represent | Labour power: structural, associational and institutional power | Consumption power: exit, voice and loyalty |
| Where does representation take place? | Employment relation/workplace and tripartite sphere | Consumption relation/public sphere |
| What is the content of labour governance? | Process rights: freedom of association and other participation rights | Greater focus on outcome rights: health and safety, working hours, etc. |
| Challenges in Global Supply Chains | Low coverage/low union membership in actual workplaces | Surrogate, skewed to simply failed representation |

## 3.3 Production-based Labour Governance: Representation as Structure

The first approach to representation in private labour governance systems originates from industrial relations scholarship and the idea of industrial democracy. Industrial democracy, as put forward by Sidney Webb and Beatrice Webb (1897), applies this principle to the role of unions in democratising the nature of workplace relations. This production-based approach focuses on the employment relationship and the traditional employment relations actors – workers and employers – in places of production (workplaces, factories, etc.). Central to industrial democracy is the idea of participation in rule-making and implementation by those affected by these rules and regulations. Here, representation provides a mechanism through which constituencies voluntarily delegate their authority for the aggregation and pooling of individual interests through collective bodies, including trade unions, employers' associations and industry bodies. Coming from the reformist tradition,[1] Webb and Webb (1897) argued that these representative structures were about establishing democratic governance for engaging with management, rather than replacing it. As industrial relations scholar Hugh Clegg (1951) put it, unions were the opposition who could never become the government. Industrial democracy conceptualises representation as 'structure' in the sense that it emphasises the role of representative structures. Trade unions, independent of employers and electing their own leaders, are thus democracies in their own right, as in the words of Webb and Webb (1897: 38): 'that is to say their internal constitutions are all based on the principle "government of the people by the people for the people"'.

Industrial democracy bestows industrial citizenship upon workers in systems where producer groups, such as unions and employer associations, were devolved the authority to take public action (Marshall, 1950; Streeck, 1992). The idea of industrial citizenship was viewed as central to the 'associative order' and the related 'private-interest

---

[1] 'Reformism is a political doctrine advocating the reform of an existing system or institution instead of its abolition and replacement.' The idea is that gradual changes through existing institutions can eventually lead to lasting change. It stands in opposition to revolutionary socialism, which seeks revolutionary upheaval as a means for transforming political and economic systems.

government' approach outlined by Streeck and Schmitter (1985). Here, interest associations present a 'fourth' logic of social order alongside the logics of community, markets and state. Interest associations are 'organizations defined by their common purpose of defending and promoting functionally defined interests, i.e. class, sectoral and professional associations' (Streeck and Schmitter, 1985: 10). These privately organised interests can be put to public purpose and act as 'private-interest governments', where they take on devolved public responsibilities and voluntarily regulate their members in the public interest. In such an approach, governments devolve rule-making authority to private interest associations, generally in the form of unions and employer organisations, allowing the representatives of labour and capital to negotiate to reach agreement (Streeck, 1992). Rather than substituting public with private governance, this model is viewed as being facilitated and authorised by the state, as well as complementing state regulation based on electoral democracy (Streeck and Schmitter, 1985).

While private-interest government did occur in pluralist contexts such as the United Kingdom (Atkinson and Coleman, 1985), it is most associated with the neo-corporatist system of interest group–government intermediation in Northern and Central Europe. For instance, the German system of sector-based vocational training sees industry associations provide occupational licensing in the apprenticeship model (Lynch, 1994; Thelen, 2007). For private-interest government, the organisations that represent producer interests should be encompassing, member-based organisations with a democratic mandate that reflects the agendas of those they represent (Olson, 1965; Schmitter, 1974, 1983). As representative organisations, these thus have both democratic accountability in making agreements but also the legitimacy to expect the agreements to be respected by those they represent.

### 3.3.1 Principles of Industrial Democracy

While not synonymous, the concepts of industrial democracy and private-interest government are highly complementary. In particular, industrial democracy is a key concept in terms of how worker interests are represented to employers at various levels when interacting with employers and their representatives. Industrial democracy carries with it important assumptions about who should represent workers and participate in governance systems, where representation takes place and what is the content of labour governance.

First, industrial democracy stresses the importance of who represents workers and participates in labour governance, with emphasis placed on workers having a democratic input into decision-making in the industrial process and hence their workplace (Wilkinson et al., 2014). This is in line with Scharpf's (1997: 19) democratic ideal of input legitimacy, where 'political choices should be derived, directly or indirectly, from the authentic preferences of citizens' – here, the worker-citizens of the firm. This emphasises the ultimate right of the represented in determining and defining what is in their interest and in judging the claims made on their behalf. Without doubt, union representation is viewed as the optimum vehicle (Webb and Webb, 1897; Dawkins, 2019), but other forms of workplace dialogue can be complementary. The Germanic system of works councils generally functions alongside union representation. It is often viewed as an exemplar of workplace dialogue (Freeman and Lazear, 1995), as it requires management to consult with workers over contentious issues such as redundancies or restructuring.

The second area of concern is the where of representation – that is, the level at which democratic representation takes place. The employment relationship defines a union's sphere of operation and where political presence is being created: a union's representative approach and capacity are inherently linked to an exchange of labour between workers and employers. The relationship is not based around particular issues but is an ongoing relationship that covers the entirety of this exchange, including pay levels, hours of work and even the continuing nature of the relationship. As the origin of 'where' is the employment relationship, the ultimate legitimacy to represent workers is derived from the workplace: worker representatives gain their legitimacy to represent due to their mandate received from the shop floor level in a bottom-up manner and this can be used to establish dialogue at higher levels within the organisation and the economy. This ensures dialogue focuses on the underlying pressures in the workplace.

While the main focus is the workplace, where trade unions create the political presence of workers through negotiating with employers or employer groups, unions engage at multiple levels, including the sector, national and transnational levels – for example, the ILO – to influence the regulation of employment. Within continental Europe, industrial citizenship came to be associated with legally mandatory forms of worker representation at the shop-floor level (participation, works councils), firm level (codetermination, workers' directors) and sectoral level (sectoral collective bargaining) (Müller-Jentsch, 1976). As such, industrial citizenship saw the development of complementary institutional structures at the national, sectoral and firm levels to include workers in the governance arrangements of their work (Streeck, 1997a).

Third, in terms of what, industrial democracy focuses on process rights such as collective bargaining and the right to join a union. Process rights are enabling rights because they seek to enable workers to defend and improve their rights and conditions at work through participation in negotiation processes. At their minimum, all IFAs therefore reference the ILO's eight core labour conventions, which are summarised in the four core labour standards as defined by the ILO Declaration of Fundamental Principles and Rights at Work in 1998: freedom of association and the right to collective bargaining, freedom from forced labour, freedom from child labour and freedom from discrimination at work. Together, they form the basis for allowing workers to participate in the regulation of their workplaces and working conditions. Worker participation not only means periodic involvement in negotiating universally applicable codes of conduct or standards but requires ongoing worker involvement in local, workplace-level decision making and problem-solving. Therefore, process rights are important as they reflect that divergent interests cannot be solved in a once off manner but are subject to ongoing negotiation and renegotiation of issues at the workplace (Edwards, 1986, 2003).

## 3.3.2 Challenges of Establishing Industrial Democracy in Global Supply Chains

Industrial democracy is based upon a number of assumptions that are difficult to reconcile with the nature of global supply chains. First, and as developed in Chapter 2, the very nature of supply chains is based on a representation gap due to the suppression of unions. The assumption that unions are the most appropriate representatives of workers is based on workers having the freedom to choose to join or not join a union. While there is no doubt that the emergence of unions was highly contested and resisted in many Western economies, their position in developing economies is much more precarious, with state actions designed to suppress the development of well-functioning unions, even if host country states have ratified ILO core conventions. The International Trade Union Confederation (ITUC) (2020) highlighted that in 2019, 85 per cent of countries violate the right to strike, 80 per cent of countries restrict the right to collective bargaining and in 80 per cent of countries workers face restrictions on the right to join unions. Methods used to suppress workplace democracy vary as well. Mark Anner (2015), for instance, highlights that suppression of worker representation in the apparel sector can take a number of forms, but is also often done alongside the state either directly or indirectly being involved in the suppression. Efforts to redress the 'representation gap' have also been contested. While some see the strengthening of union organising as the only route to effective worker representation (Thomas, 2011; McCallum, 2017), others have criticised the efforts to support and fund union organising in the Global South as just another way of imposing imperialist and neo-colonial agendas. For instance, Rahman and Langford (2014) describe the AFL–CIO solidarity work in Bangladesh as 'hegemonic trade union imperialism' that aims at controlling and shaping unionism in line with the foreign policy goals of the US imperialist nation-state.

Second, the complementarity of private interest associations and the state, which endows private-interest governments with their beneficial public-interest orientation, is often lacking. This is because the notion of industrial democracy is clearly bound to the idea of there being a defined national space where local, sectoral and even national institutions complement each other. Where production fragments and becomes dispersed across multiple jurisdictions, achieving such complementarity becomes difficult if not impossible. Powerful interest associations, such as the Bangladeshi employer association Bangladesh Garments Manufacturers and Exporters Association (BGMEA), may 'capture' the state for their instrumental interests rather than the wider public good. In combination with union suppression, collective interest representation will be heavily skewed towards capital and the regulation of work skewed towards capital interests.

Finally, the global governance instruments that have emerged based on industrial democracy are insufficient. Supply chains may have increased social connectedness but building representation across globally disparate workers is difficult, particularly when they occupy different positions in the supply chain, such as a retail worker in a UK Tesco store and a seamstress in a Bangladeshi garment factory. In this context, IFAs can provide powerful representative structures because they can create a constituency based not on territorial lines but rather on global production relations within a brand's supply chain. They are based upon gaining recognition at the corporate level and then aiming to ensure effective implementation down to workers in every site, which can be difficult to establish (Niforou, 2014), as discussed in Chapter 2. However, their spread and coverage have been limited to date, and legal enforcement mechanisms are lacking. Of the 115 IFAs in place in 2018, the ILO (2018) highlighted that 94, or 82 per cent, of the MNCs are headquartered in social market economies in Europe, where the institutions of collective interest representation are already in place. In addition, in sectors where employment standards are worst, according to the ILO (2018), the global union federation, IndustriALL, which organises workers in the manufacturing sector, has IFAs with only five retailers in the garment retail sector, including Inditex (Spain), H&M (Sweden), Mizuno (Japan), Tchibo (Germany) and ASOS (UK). IFAs can strengthen union organising within an MNCs' supply chain and have provided existing worker representatives with important leverage (Riisgaard and Hammer, 2011), but they are much less effective in establishing unions in new sites (Niforou, 2012). This has prompted criticisms that the rights guaranteed through IFAs often exist on paper alone. GUFs also carry the danger of unions in developing countries becoming 'clients' of donors from wealthier societies (Spooner, 2004). The Bangladesh apparel sector illustrates this challenge. Even based on the most generous calculation, union density is no higher than 3–4 per cent of the workforce with coverage of 6 per cent or less. As a result, IFAs remain top-down approaches that often are detached from local union organising (Thomas, 2011; Fichter and McCallum, 2015). Thus, they are far from being a panacea for workers' rights.

In sum, the industrial democracy approach relies on the existence of trade unions and supportive institutional frameworks to provide effective forms of political representation in the realm of employment relations. This points to the limited ability of global unions to claim legitimately to represent the workers in a sector where union membership is so low.

## 3.4 Consumption-based Labour Governance: Representation as Claim

The second approach to democratic representation in private labour governance brings the voice and purchasing power of consumption actors at the downstream end of the supply chain into the regulation of the employment relation at the upstream end. Here, we will more closely examine the democratic legitimacy of such as approach in terms of representative claim-making. Since there is no enduring, structural relationship with consumption actors, their democratic legitimacy relies on the force of discourse, deliberation and communication in transnational governance.

The representation as claim perspective has its normative basis in deliberative democracy, which emerged as a critique of the aggregative view of democracy that dominated post-war democratic theory (Dryzek, 1999, 2010; Dryzek and Niemayer 2008; Mansbridge, 2011). Rather than aggregation through elections, the deliberative approach suggests that democratic legitimation can be generated by means of deliberation between a variety of social actors (government, scientific experts, civil society, NGOs, consumers, etc.). The role of civil society is seen as central to a well-functioning democracy with civil society actors bringing new issues to public attention through extra-institutional politics to advance societal demands that are not processed effectively through established channels.

Central to deliberative democracy is the notion of the public sphere – a domain of social life where public opinion can be formed through deliberation (Habermas, 1989). The public sphere generates debate about political decisions and subjects them through a deliberative process where participants discuss, justify and scrutinise decisions in view of the common good of a given constituency. On this account, global civil society (Kaldor, 2003; Risse, 2004) plays a vital role in establishing a transnational public sphere. Thus, Western consumers (and citizens) can legitimately participate in the discourse about labour standards in the Global South. This has the potential to enable demo-cratic and legitimate decision-making at the global level. Hence, the focus shifts from representative structures onto the quality of the representative process through public reasoning and argumentation.

In line with the shift towards discourse and communication, pro-ponents of deliberative democracy argue that we need to rethink the concept of representation to understand contemporary democratic practices in the emerging system of global governance (Mansbridge, 2003). The argument goes like this: If what counts is deliberation, not aggregation of votes, then this allows for different modes of representation, namely those that best advance the deliberative qualities of deliberation. Dryzek and Niemayer (2008) propose the notion of 'discursive representation' to reflect the fact that transnational actors do not represent real people but rather certain discourses that convey legitimacy to the generated rules.

So how is representation discursively generated? Saward (2010) proposes that representation is accomplished through the making of a 'representative claim'. Representation is here reconceptualised as a dynamic and ongoing process of making and receiving claims (Saward, 2008, 2010; Severs, 2012). According to Saward (2008, 2010), the 'representative claim' consists of five key elements. Someone makes the claim (a maker), and they make the claim about someone or something (a subject) standing for something (an object) to a group (an audience). Representative claims can 'operate across borders and even across species; they denote shifting power relationships rather than fixed institutions' (Saward, 2010: 1). Representation becomes the representation of the concerns of stakeholders and affected parties in deliberative processes. Civil society actors are vital in this process, as they engage in representation of certain interests, themes and demands.

Proponents see this 'renewal' of representation as an opportunity to reconstruct democratic politics. It clearly breaks with the traditional idea of 'representation' as an aggregation of their interests through a 'delegate' or a 'trustee' acting in the name of the person represented. The capacity to be a 'delegate' or a 'trustee' would assume the knowability of the interests of the represented, as if they were fixed and knowable in advance. Instead, in this approach, the interests entering the political process are constantly being renegotiated (Whittle and Mueller, 2011). Thus, rather than transmitting the will of the represented, representation is thought of as 'the constitution of that will through the very process of representation' (Laclau, 2005: 159).

Proponents argue that representative claim-making may play an important role in a global context where electoral constituencies fail to coincide with those affected by collective decisions (Montanaro, 2012). The 'representation gap' that leaves workers, marginalised communities, future generations or non-human nature without representation in global supply chains, requires alternative forms of representation beyond formal institutional structures. Thus, 'self-appointed representatives bring constituencies into being' (Montanaro, 2012: 1100) that would not otherwise have political presence in traditional political spaces. Claim-making can thus contribute to the democratic process, since 'without this intervention there would be no incorporation of those marginal sectors into the public sphere' (Laclau, 2005: 116). With global civil society, the creation of deliberative participatory publics can enable democratic and legitimate representation at the global level. Where participation in structural democracy is not available, the involvement of (non-elected) activists, campaigners and spokespersons plays an important role in creating a discursive interface between international organisations and global citizens (Nanz and Steffek, 2004).

### 3.4.1 Principles of Representative Claim-Making

When applying discursive ideas about representative claim-making to global labour governance, we can discern a different set of assumptions about who should represent workers and participate in governance systems, where representation takes place and what is the content of labour governance. First, in terms of who, claim-making at the transnational level raises the question of who represents workers' interests and participates in deliberation. Representative claims typically are made by self-appointed representatives, who Koenig-Archibugi and MacDonald (2013: 517) call 'solidaristic proxies', such as NGOs, interest and activist groups. They often mobilise consumer power, rather than being controlled by the workers in whose name they mobilise claims. In the absence of a direct relationship between producers and consumers – as in global supply chains – NGOs create 'a chain of social connectedness' between downstream consumption acts and upstream production actors (Schrempf-Stirling and Palazzo, 2016). But even if NGOs do often claim to act on behalf of the common good, claiming 'moral' legitimacy (Baur and Palazzo, 2011), they are often seen as unrepresentative or unaccountable. Indeed, the accountability of self-appointed representatives to their intended beneficiaries in the Global South is increasingly being questioned. There is also the risk that NGOs are more accountable to their donors and engage in symbolic politics that satisfy their internal constituencies while remaining 'unresponsive to the real needs of the people whom they claim to serve' (Keohane, 2003).

Second, in terms of the where, representative claims are made in the context of the consumption relationship. Since there is no formal membership, the consumption relationship is negotiated in and through the public sphere – a domain of social life where public opinion can be formed through deliberation (Habermas, 1989). In the context of private labour governance, NGOs often address citizens in their role as consumers or citizen-consumers. Since consumers have no power through electoral democracy, NGOs mobilise the purchasing power of citizens as consumers to pressure brands. Thus, it is typically through public campaigning that NGOs disseminate their claims in the public sphere and bring workers as affected constituencies into being in transnational governance processes. Claim-making can thus contribute to the democratic process, since 'without this intervention there would be no incorporation of those marginal sectors into the public sphere' (Laclau, 2005: 116).

On the downside, claim-making within the context of the consumption relationship can also mean that deliberation in the transnational public sphere is skewed towards consumer markets and brand head-quarters in Europe or North America, rather than where outsourced workplaces are located (Ehrnström-Fuentes, 2016; Alamgir and Banerjee, 2019). In their examination of the Social Accountability 8000 standard, Gilbert and Rasche (2007: 202) acknowledge this shortcoming by concluding that 'no clues are given how these dialogical processes are supposed to be organized' with stakeholders at the local level. For these reasons, Banerjee (2018: 802) warns against conflating deliberation with democracy because 'processes might be deliberative without being democratic'. Instead of promoting dialogue on contentious workplace issues, CSR standards are typically imposed on supplier sites and monitored by third parties (Locke, 2013), allowing companies to deflect blame if things go wrong.

Finally, in terms of what, representative claims are more likely to focus on the ideological agendas of consumption-based actors. For instance, it has been widely documented that CSR standards – typically adopted as a result of consumer-pressure – tend to focus on outcome rights, such as health and safety, rather than promote process rights such as freedom of association (Dawkins, 2012; Egels-Zandén and Merk, 2014). Process rights focus on incorporating workers and their representatives in the 'negotiation of workers' rights facilitating progressive change in labor relations' (Barrientos and Smith, 2007: 717). The focus on outcome rights aligns with the view of Gilbert and Rasche (2007), who conclude that there is a need to enable forms of practical reason whose purpose is not to establish universal principles but rather to confront the micro-political complexities at the local level.

### 3.4.2 Challenges of Making Representative Claims in Global Labour Governance

The multi-stakeholder model of governance illustrates how the logic of 'representation as claim' underpinned by deliberative democracy may be operationalised in global supply chains. Multi-stakeholder initiatives are exemplified by the Forest Stewardship Council (Scherer and Palazzo, 2007), Social Accountability 8000 (Gilbert and Rasche, 2007) and Fairtrade (Reinecke and Ansari, 2015), where rules and norms governing labour and environmental standards across global supply chains are developed through deliberation between business firms and civil society actors. The deliberative democracy model and its operationalisation through multi-stakeholder initiatives are at times interpreted as an attempt at re-embedding corporations and their economic decision-making in democratic processes with civil society and recruiting them into regulatory roles intended to solve social problems and fill the regulatory vacuum in global governance, maybe even assuming a state-like role to fulfil governance roles where state systems fail (Matten and Crane, 2005; Scherer et al., 2006, 2016; Scherer and Palazzo, 2007, 2011). This model of governance shares an important similarity with the industrial democracy model and the associated projects of neo-corporatism and private-interest government. Like neo-corporatism, the deliberative democracy project assumes that 'private actors such as corporations and civil society organizations play an active role in the democratic regulation and control of market transactions' (Scherer and Palazzo, 2011: 901). In this sense, both approaches emphasise that private actors can play important roles in fulfilling regulatory functions. But the similarities end here.

Whereas in the industrial democracy tradition, the state explicitly devolves regulatory functions to certain interest groups in a complementary relationship, here the relations between civil society, corporations and the state are much more spontaneous and rarely formalised – even if some hybrid forms have emerged (see Baccaro, 2006). Due to the challenges associated with global production, the state's role in global governance has changed significantly. In countries such as Bangladesh, we see how private regulation becomes an enforcer of public regulation, such as the labour law or national building code. And rather than the employer groups and trade unions in production sites acting as the representatives of capital and labour, multi-stakeholder initiatives typically see brands and NGOs in consumer countries emerge as central governance actors. Rather than industrial democracy, where citizenship rights are accorded to trade unions, the role of brands has been conceptualised as 'corporate citizenship', where brands become the actors that pledge to protect, enable and implement citizenship rights (Crane et al., 2008).

In industrial democracy, political bargaining based on divergent interests is the engine of collective interest representation, which restrains the power of capital. In contrast, multi-stakeholder initiatives are aimed at consensus-based decision-making through deliberation between voluntary participants with the political legitimacy of rule-making resting on the discursive quality of the deliberative process rather than on representative structures that involve intended beneficiaries in the rule-making process.

The multi-stakeholder governance model exemplifies many of the problems of how the logic of 'representation as claim' is operationalised in global supply chains. In fact, critics argue that multi-stakeholder initiatives 'represent a new form of privatized, elite regulation, and that these systems are mainly designed to protect multi-national brands, rather than to actually solve labor or environmental problems' (O'Rourke, 2006: 899). Even proponents of deliberative democracy concede that the creation of a transnational public sphere is complicated by the lack of transparency, unequal representation of stakeholder concerns and unequal opportunity of marginalised actors to participate in and contribute to deliberative processes (Nanz and Steffek, 2004). While attempting to fill global governance gaps, private rule-makers are often not elected or otherwise authorised representatives of the people in whose name they claim to act.

To understand whether representative claims work democratically or undemocratically (Saward, 2010; Disch, 2015), we need to consider whether representative claims provide 'political presence to those whose interests are affected, or potentially affected, by collective decisions, and empowers them to exercise authorization and demand accountability' (Montanaro, 2012: 1098). If they don't, then, representative claims can be labelled surrogate, skewed or simply failed representation (Montanaro, 2012). In multi-stakeholder governance, representation of labour is often surrogate, as workers have no means of authorising representatives and are largely excluded from participation in governance activities, despite being their alleged beneficiaries (Donaghey and Reinecke, 2018). An asymmetry therefore emerges: deliberation takes place at the so-called global level of brands and/or international NGO headquarters in consumer countries, while production actors at the upstream end of the supply chain are often passive recipients of regulation, with little deliberation taking place at the level of production. Excluding worker voice from view may cast labour governance as an overly benign, consensus-oriented process that conceals the inherently conflicting interests between capital and labour. The lack of worker participation may also result in skewed representation, whereby representatives provide disproportionate political presence for a constituency. A political presence is thus disproportionately skewed towards certain constituencies, such as business interests or the agendas of Western activists (Siddiqi, 2015).

Skewed representation would then be a situation where self-appointed representatives drive governance on behalf of their intended beneficiaries, such as workers, while the agenda remains driven 'driven by what Western NGOs push for, what large companies consider feasible, and what consultants and accountants seek to provide' (Bendell, 2005: 362). As a result, issues that matter to Western activists and consumers find stronger representation and can even overshadow and displace local matters of concern. As members of the Bangladeshi activist group Activist Anthropologist (Sumon et al., 2017) argue, Western activist campaigns for compensation of the victims of industrial disasters have undermined local efforts to hold the Bangladeshi state and factory owners accountable. At worst, many examples of transnational governance regimes illustrate failed representation. For critics, transnational governance initiatives 'represent a new form of privatized, elite regulation, and ... these systems are mainly designed to protect multi-national brands, rather than to actually solve labor or environmental problems' (O'Rourke, 2006: 899).

In sum, multi-stakeholder governance exemplifies how 'representation as claim' may be operationalised in global supply chains with the participation of brands. Claims typically address consumption actors – retail brands and consumers in consumer countries. Representative claims provide a powerful source of transnational representation, but they are inscribed into the logic and power asymmetries of supply chain capitalism and therefore risk being skewed towards Western agendas. The 'representation as claim' perspective hence leaves us with some important questions about the democratic legitimacy of self-appointed representatives and their participation in governance: Who is able to act as a legitimate representative for workers in the transnational space? Can self-appointed representatives fulfil global governance functions in ways that are democratically legitimate? If representative claims are discursive achievements, what and who determines which claims are democratically legitimate? In many cases, there is no objective yardstick to decide whether representation is democratically legitimate, surrogate, skewed or even failed. Instead, legitimate representation is highly contested.

The claim-making perspective does not provide a definitive toolkit to evaluate the legitimacy of representative claims. Instead, it invites us to focus on studying the political dynamics through which some claims become seen as legitimate. In contemporary political practice, those claims that 'stick' and garner broad support are likely to be the ones that are acted upon. Those claim-makers who tell convincing 'causal stories' (Stone, 1989), even if thereby crudely simplifying complex causal relationships, are more likely to be successful. For instance, when seeking to allocate responsibility for addressing armed violence in the Democratic Republic of the Congo, Western human rights NGOs purposefully framed the 'victims' in need of representation and constructed a causal narrative of responsibility that simplified the complex situation, focusing on female victims of sexual violence because this would attract the most attention among target audiences: Western consumers (Reinecke and Ansari, 2015). Thus, which are the relevant constituents, who can claim to represent them and what that means in terms of governance decisions constitute an ongoing political struggle.

## 3.5  A Framework for Democratic Representation in Global Labour Governance

Based on our discussion in this chapter, we can consider the interface between different forms of representation. Figure 3.1 proposes two

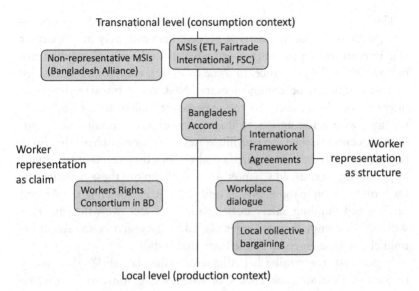

**Figure 3.1** Conceptualising worker-driven supply chain governance

dimensions to consider: whether workers are represented by structure (membership in unions) or by claim (discursive representation by proxies) and the level at which representation takes place (transnational level of or workplace level).

As a first distinction (Figure 3.1, X-axis), workers can be represented either by elected worker representatives (typically representation as structure) and they can be represented by proxy (typically representation as claim). An example of elected worker representatives at the transnational level (Northeast quadrant) are GUFs, such as UNIGlobal or IndustriALL. International Framework Agreements, which we discussed above, are collective agreements negotiated by elected worker representatives at the transnational level with brands but also aim to apply at the local level. An example of elected worker representatives at the local level (Southeast quadrant) is factory level unions in Bangladesh, who engage in collective bargaining with employers to improve conditions in the workplace. Unfortunately, there are very few collective agreements in the Bangladesh RMG sector. As formal representation through unions is suppressed in many production contexts such as Bangladesh, it also becomes important to understand how non-unionised workers, such as informal labour and marginalised communities, can represent themselves.

Thus, representation as claim through self-appointed representatives, such as NGOs and activist groups, may also play an important role in representing the interests of workers and other affected parties in transnational governance. In some cases, representation as structure and as claim can be complementary. NGOs can translate workers' interests and bring them to the agendas of global actors and work together with trade unions to improve workplace conditions in production contexts. The Accord illustrates such a case where the direct representatives of affected parties and proxies became complementary in pressuring brands. In Chapter 5, we will explore these complementary roles of labour rights NGOs and GUFs in establishing the Accord on Fire and Building Safety in Bangladesh. In fact, we will argue that without the complementary roles played by these actors, the Accord is unlikely to have emerged in the form that it did.

In contrast, the retailer-led Alliance for Bangladesh Worker Safety (Alliance) illustrates the effects of excluding unions, and therefore structural representation, from participating in global labour governance. As we will show in Chapter 6, the creation of the Alliance, a parallel initiative that lacked the democratic pluralism in its governance structure provided a sort of 'natural experiment' in terms of how more democratic governance structures can create fundamentally different outcomes.

As a second distinction (Figure 3.1, Y-axis), representation can take place at the transnational level or at the workplace level. While in reality there will be blurred boundaries between these levels, the workplace level denotes the sphere of employment relations and the transnational level is more likely to involve the sphere of consumption relations. Here, the focus is on the different institutional mechanisms that promote democratic forms of participation at different levels of the global supply chain. As we will show in Chapter 8, brands can play an important role in establishing the institutions and processes through which workers get involved in dialogue; in this case, brands played an important role in engaging their suppliers to initiate factory-level workplace dialogue with elected workers' representatives or, where present, factory-level unions.

So far, we have discussed modes of worker representation. Yet any system of labour regulation through collective interest representation necessarily also involves representative of capital. Thus, in Chapter 7 we will consider shifts in the representation of capital in transnational industrial democracy with regard to the role of employers. Brands, rather than employers, typically become enrolled as governance actors by both GUFs and NGOs. So what is the role of employers in transnational labour governance?

## 3.6 Conclusion

We began this chapter by demonstrating how transnational governance arrangements challenge conceived ideas about democratic legitimacy. While the standard account of representation is based on a pre-existing constituency – members of a political community – who are to be represented, a core challenge in transnational governance is that constituencies must be brought into being through representative processes beyond territorial boundaries. However, who can or should represent whom across global supply chains has become a contested question in transnational labour governance, with no single actor being able to claim monopoly over representation. This conundrum motivates the analysis in this book of the modes of representation and their interplay in contested arenas of transnational labour governance. The case studies that follow show what can be learnt from the interface of the different logics of representation and across different levels of the supply chain. As alluded to above, each case will explore a specific puzzle and constellation of consumption and production-based actors and provide specific insights. Taken together, these cases inform our theory of transnational industrial democracy, which we will return to and outline more fully in the book's conclusion (Chapter 9).

# 4 | *After Rana Plaza*
## *Mending a Toxic Supply Chain*

Almost one-fifth of the value of garments imported into the European Union are produced in Bangladesh (Eurostat, 2020). Most people in developed economies have garments 'Made in Bangladesh' in their wardrobes. However, and because of this, the conditions in which they are produced involve labour abuses and, for a long time, they have also involved significant safety hazards. In this context, the Rana Plaza disaster did not occur as an isolated event: the Bangladesh garment sector was bedevilled by deadly industrial incidents for many years. Since 2013, the number of fatal accidents in the RMG industry has radically reduced, while total export volumes have increased by over 40 per cent since Rana Plaza. The number of lives saved might seem like a low bar for improving working conditions, but sadly it could not be taken for granted. Since first embracing the apparel sector in the late 1970s, Bangladesh has been at the forefront in trying to compete with its rivals for orders from multinational buyers. This imperative of keeping prices low has seen worker rights severely constrained and ultimately ended in a series of deadly incidents from the beginning of the millennium, culminating with the Rana Plaza disaster. In this context, after Rana Plaza, a number of initiatives that differed from the established systems in the apparel sector were adopted in an attempt to build institutions to ensure greater worker safety in the sector. This chapter will outline the contextual features of the Bangladesh garment supply chain and the two main innovations upon which this book focuses in response to Rana Plaza: the Bangladesh Accord for Fire and Building Safety (Accord) and the Joint Ethical Trading Initiatives' Social Dialogue programme.

## 4.1 The Bangladesh Ready-Made Garment Supply Chain

The apparel sector has become one of the most globalised in the world. Between 1975 and 2005, the Multi-Fibre Agreement and its successor, the Agreement on Textiles and Clothing, played a key role in insulating developed economies from the most extreme competition from developing countries (Morelli, 2021). Because of the labour-intensive nature of the industry, lower labour costs in developing nations gave them a significant competitive advantage over developed economies. While they were far from being universally implemented – for example, the EU famously never imposed Multi-Fibre Agreement quotas on Bangladesh – the existence of the system certainly slowed down the competitive nature of the sector. However, with the expiration of the MultiFiber Arrangement in 2005 and the sector falling back on bilateral trade agreements and WTO rules, a further intensification of the competitive nature of the sector took place (Yang and Mlachila, 2007). A vast web of suppliers, retailers and sourcing agents has emerged in the apparel sector, with retailers – often from the most developed economies – sourcing products from thousands of suppliers in developing economies.

The national economy of Bangladesh is possibly as dependent on any one form of export – apparel (generally referred to as ready-made garments, or RMG in Bangladesh), as any economy could be. Because of the importance of this sector, economic and political life in Bangladesh is dominated by it. Economically, in Bangladesh, RMG exports constituted about 80 percent of Bangladeshi exports at the time the Rana Plaza disaster occurred, rising to 84 per cent and 11 per cent of GDP in 2018. Since the 1980s, Bangladesh had become the second largest exporter of garments after China (though in 2020 it was overtaken by Vietnam), growing from US$12,000 in exports in 1978 to annual exports exceeding US$34 billion by 2018 (BGMEA, 2020). The sector has created employment for around 4.1 million people directly, about 65 per cent of whom are women, and five million workers indirectly (BGMEA, 2020). However, given the nature of the sector, the work is based on low wages and poor working conditions: the minimum wage (which for many workers acts both as a floor and a ceiling), at the time the Rana Plaza disaster occurred in 2013, was US$38 per month, which increased to US$68 per month late in 2013 and US$95 per month in 2019 (BGMEA, 2020). Alongside these low wages, employment has contributed to the country's rapid economic development and poverty reduction, having halved the percentage of people living under the US$1.90 per day poverty line since 1991. The political importance of the sector became clear on our first visit in 2014 when we attended the Dhaka Apparel Summit, organised by the powerful industry association, the BGMEA. The economic and political objective of reaching US$50 billion worth of exports by 2021 to coincide with the celebration of the 50th anniversary of the birth of the nation was declared as the theme of the event. This would mean a doubling of garment exports since the Rana Plaza disaster. The inaugural event was attended by the country's political and economic elite, reflecting the significance of the summit, including the Prime Minister Sheikh Hasina, the Minister of Finance, the Minister of Commerce, the Minister of Labour and other government and industry officials.

It is not hard to see how a country of over 170 million people, which is reliant on a single industry driven by some of the world's cheapest labour, feeding orders from Western retailers who have no legal liability over labour abuses, can spell disaster for the protection of labour rights. In fact, the Bangladesh RMG sector epitomises the global supply chain model, both in terms of the economic development and job opportunities it brings to the country, as well as in terms of the lack of regulation and exploitation of labour. It is a prime example of how the hyper-competitive market dynamic of globalised industrial capitalism has overwhelmed worker protection, such as protective labour market institutions of the state and trade unions, and shifted the human cost of cheap fashion to the most vulnerable element of the chain – garment workers in developing countries. As part of this regime, Bangladesh also epitomises the 'competition state' (Cerny, 1995), where states compete for inward investment through cheap labour and a lack of public regulation to keep prices low: in effect, the interests of the sector have captured state institutions (Alam and Teicher, 2012). As a result, public regulation has largely failed to protect workers' rights in the Bangladeshi RMG industry, as the Bangladesh Labour Law and the country's Building Code have remained largely unenforced. At the time Rana Plaza occurred, the government's labour inspectorate had fewer than 100 inspectors for more than 24,000 factories across all industrial sectors, three million shops and two major ports, including more than 4,300 export-oriented garment factories.

Uncontrolled growth and unregulated buildings led to a pattern of recurrent industrial disasters in apparel factories: residential and commercial buildings in densely populated urban areas were repurposed for industrial use, often by adding additional storeys without permission, as in the case of Rana Plaza – a commercial complex housing garment factories. On our various field trips to Bangladesh, we visited a number of newly built, state-of-the-art, flagship factory complexes with their own fire water ponds and fire engines. We also visited small, crowded sweatshop factories tucked away on the fifth and sixth floors of residential buildings. These 'factories' could only be reached by climbing up narrow staircases of busy buildings. The floors would often be loaded with heavy machinery and large volumes of highly flammable materials next to poorly maintained electrical systems.

As the industry grew, so did the number of industrial disasters: before Rana Plaza, more than 600 Bangladeshi garment workers had died due to unsafe buildings between 2006 and 2012 (IndustriALL, 2012). There were 64 deaths in the Spectrum Sweater factory disaster in 2005, 21 people killed in the Garib & Garib Sweater fire in 2010, 117 killed by the Tazreen factory fire in 2012, before more than 1,100 ultimately died and a further 2,000 were severely injured in the Rana Plaza collapse in 2013. While the Rana Plaza disaster has become a by-word for labour standards reaching their lowest levels, the recurring events in Bangladesh showed it was more than just a one-off event in a poorly run factory: this was an industry where the loss of human lives to produce cheap goods for Western consumers had become normalised. As such, the focus of initiatives after Rana Plaza was placed on raising the levels of occupational safety and health (OSH) across Bangladeshi factories supplying Western brands, rather than just on the direct outcome of the Rana Plaza disaster itself.

Despite the significant labour abuses in Bangladesh, it is important to recognise that Bangladesh is not the only country in which labour rights violations occur in low-paid factory work. We need to look no further than the United Kingdom's garment-manufacturing hub of Leicester. The majority of the city's estimated 10,000 textile workers in 700 factories producing for online super-fast fashion retailers are paid below the national minimum wage, do not have employment contracts and are subject to intense and arbitrary work practices (Hammer et al., 2015) with even anonymous reports of locked fire doors in Leicester factories (UK Environmental Audit Committee, 2019). Our focus on Bangladesh is not about pointing fingers at one country. Instead, Bangladesh is illustrative of some of the challenges that bedevil low-paid factory work globally, including in developed economies such as the United Kingdom. Focusing on Bangladesh allows us to study positive change in terms of improvements to factory safety as well as creating mechanisms for worker representation.

## 4.2 The Representation Gap

A major focus of initiatives responding to the Rana Plaza disaster has been attempts to enable the representation of workers' interests in the supply chain. The Bangladeshi garment supply chain provides a prime example of a 'representation gap' (Towers, 1997), where workers lacked effective representation at both the workplace and sectoral levels, as well as the supply chain level. The Bangladeshi government and garment industry have been complicit in suppressing any type of worker representation that could threaten the low-cost production model that generates over 80 per cent of the country's total exports. It exemplifies the model that Anner (2015) calls 'despotic market labor control': workers lack both market power and the power to demand effective state protection as citizens through electoral democracy. The position of unions is fragile due to union fragmentation (involving over thirty union federations in the garment sector alone based on the enterprise unionism model, where legally unions can only operate in any one place of employment), low membership density (generally estimated as about 4 per cent), an immature system of industrial relations and political suppression. We often found it hard to keep track of the many union federations organising in the RMG sector, many of whom had very few affiliated unions in factories. In 2017, the Dhaka branch of the American Federation of Labor and Congress of Industrial Organizations (AFL-CIO) Solidarity Center counted eighteen different trade union federations in the RMG sector, with affiliated factory-level unions ranging from three to forty-eight, and another nine federations with fewer than three registered factory level unions each. As a result of the challenges we describe below, the Solidarity Center in Dhaka (2017)[1] also estimated that as few as 20 out of 425 registered

---

[1] Even though freedom of association – workers being able to join independent trade unions – constitutes one of the ILO Core Labour Standards and typically forms a key provision in buyers' codes of conduct, efforts to achieve unionisation faced stiff opposition from employers. Bangladesh consistently features in the list of the ten worst countries to be a trade unionist due to physical threats to the lives, freedom and physical health of trade unionists (ITUC, 2018, 2020).

unions across 4,296 garment factories had fully functional, independent unions with collective agreements.

Despite various international programmes designed to strengthen union organising (Zajak, 2017) and the efforts and courage of local organisers to strengthen unions, the challenges to unionisation have remained considerable. Pressure by the ILO and Bangladesh's most important trading partners in the EU to encourage union formation led to a short-lived period of union growth post–Rana Plaza, before facing renewed government-led suppression. This is illustrated by the difficulties of union registration – which has remained a challenge even if the revisions to the Bangladesh Labour (Amendment) Act in 2013, to which Bangladesh committed in line with the Sustainability Compact with its international trading partners – improved conditions for union registration. As outlined in Figure 4.1, in the RMG sector the number of registered unions in factories increased from 132 in December 2012 to 659 in April 2018. However, up to 63 per cent of applications were still denied, according to data provided by MoLE (European Commission, 2018).

After a steep rise in union registrations in 2014, union leaders found that their efforts to organise in factories and meet the demanding threshold of convincing 30 per cent (later 20 per cent) of the factory workforce to join the union were increasingly defeated. Union leaders

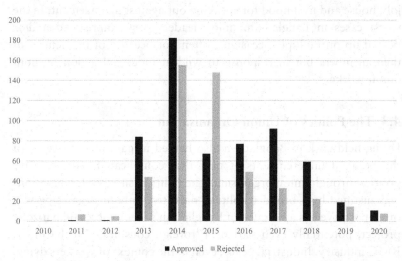

Figure 4.1 RMG union application approvals and rejections, 2010–2020

complained to us about the bureaucratic hurdles to registering independent unions. The Bangladeshi government rejected a high number of union applications on dubious formalistic grounds or minor mistakes, such as misspelt names or without any explanation at all – rejections that felt arbitrary to union leaders. Moreover, employer retaliation against workers who filed union registration papers or who organise workers once registered is common. We came across numerous cases of workers being physically attacked, losing their jobs or being placed on unofficial 'blacklists' to prevent the workers from finding employment in other RMG factories.

There is no doubt that union organising in Bangladesh faces fierce resistance from employers and government. We were confronted first-hand with the challenges faced by politically suppressed, poorly financed and poorly organised unions whose members had to fear retribution from hostile factory management as well as constant surveillance and even physical violence from the industrial police. As we visited the small, cramped and poorly equipped offices of union federations, the contrast between unions working out of tiny offices with hardly any equipment, resources or paid staff members compared with the shiny offices of factory management, let alone the big BGMEA headquarters with its hundreds of staff to represent employers' interests, was stark. While people talk of fearless trade unionists in developed countries, it is often in the context that they could lose their job, house and livelihood for speaking out against management. In the worst cases in Bangladesh, union leaders were imprisoned and/or beaten up on multiple occasions, often not because of the actions of their members but in response to wildcat industrial action by non-union workers.

## 4.3 The Politics of Union Organisation

Doing fieldwork in Bangladesh also helped us gain a better sense of the political undercurrents at play that complicated representative politics through union organising. The political suppression of unions was justified by a broader political narrative: labour organising was often portrayed as a betrayal of Bangladesh's ideological and patriotic project, potentially even part of a 'foreign conspiracy' to harm the RMG industry. Industrial peace, even in the context of workers dying, was cast as necessary to sustain the country's competitive advantage (of cheap labour) in the garment sector. Accordingly, a trope that prominently fed nationalist narratives about the need to discipline labour was that of the 'militant worker as anti-national' or as 'the embodiment of national betrayal' (Siddiqi, 2020: 387). There was a widespread narrative that the decline of the once thriving jute industry was due to unionisation in the 1970s and it had to be resisted to stop the garment sector going down the same route. In the name of national interest and industrial progress, workers were expected to submit to managerial control and exploitation and to make sacrifices to support the economic goal to double the size of garment industry exports to US$50 billion by 2021. In fact, union organising, as well as the Bangladesh Accord, were repeatedly identified as the product of 'outsider conspiracies' to destroy the RMG industry and weaken the nation. In informal conversations, we encountered widespread fear amongst factory managers that 'outside leaders' could come in and mobilise workers to strike for political reasons, become violent and destroy factory equipment. We noted that union leaders themselves were sometimes caught in between these contradictory interests – class interest versus national interest, to use Hyman's (2001) terms. Class interest justified them to align with international allies to defend workers' rights, while national interest also explained an ambivalent relationship to their international allies and a certain overlap of interest with the BGMEA to further the interest of the RMG industry at large.

While the 'foreign conspiracy' was often used as an excuse to discipline labour, scholars have indeed noted that many conflicting interests and ideological agendas were inscribed into the representation of Bangladeshi garment workers through Bangladeshi unions, such as Northern labour interests – for example, unions receiving finance for rent, training programmes, salaries for union leaders from their Northern labour allies (see Rahman and Langford, 2014; Tanjeem, 2017). Rahman and Langford (2014: 169) critiqued the AFL-CIO's solidarity work in Bangladesh as 'hegemonic trade union imperialism' – foreign-sponsored unionism aligned with foreign policy goals. International solidarity efforts thus had to navigate between supporting politically suppressed and under-resourced unions without feeding suspicion against trade union organisers for having 'foreign links'. For instance, we witnessed the AFL-CIO Solidarity Centre in Dhaka as a vibrant meeting space for local labour organisers but also heard complaints about them for creating relations of dependence by financing unions rather than encouraging them to become independent by collecting dues from their membership. Yet it is too easy to dismiss unions for receiving this support. While undoubtedly being a trade union member is not something that should come for free, when facing highly hostile environments, having such international solidarity can be a lifeline.

Among the thirty or so trade union federations operating in the RMG sector, many had no active factory unions but were in receipt of foreign aid, leading to the realisation that the legitimacy of these Bangladeshi union federations varied greatly. We met many hard-working, courageous trade union federation leaders who literally showed us the scars of their activism but also others who seemed to benefit from international donations without doing too much organising. Other obstacles included so-called yellow unions, which were set up by factory owners with the goal of preventing the registration of genuine independent trade unions, or 'dalal'/double agents cooperating with employer organisations (Siddiqi, 2020). Due to these complexities, who was seen a 'legitimate' union leader could differ greatly depending on the audience.

In sum, the enormous challenge that union leaders faced amidst adverse circumstances meant that the representation of worker interests by Bangladeshi unions was not straightforward. Overall, garment workers were in a very disadvantageous position to represent their own interests vis-à-vis local employers and governments through collective organising, let alone confronting global buyers whose prime motive to source from Bangladesh were its low production and labour costs. It is in this context, as will be discussed particularly in Chapter 5, that labour rights NGOs, such as the Worker Rights Consortium (WRC) and the Clean Clothes Campaign (CCC), have emerged as important, albeit self-appointed, representatives of Bangladeshi workers.

## 4.4 The Failure of Corporate Codes of Conduct and Social Auditing

While Bangladesh provides Western brands with cheap produce without the burden of legal liability over factory conditions, years of campaigning and 'naming and shaming' by Western NGOs, labour activists and global unions have exposed these brands to negative publicity over poor working conditions. In response, brands invested heavily in social auditing of factory compliance, with estimates that it could account for up to 80 per cent of their ethical sourcing budget (ETI, 2014). Yet while social auditing helped companies manage their supply chains, safeguard individual reputation and claim social responsibility, it has largely failed to improve working conditions. Shortcomings have been tragically demonstrated by the failure to prevent a series of fatal industrial disasters: Rana Plaza infamously housed two factories, Phantom Apparels and New Wave Style, which were audited against the Business Social Compliance Initiative's (BSCI) standard shortly before the building's collapse.

Critics have long argued that social auditing is designed primarily to limit buyers' legal liability and to manage reputational risk, rather than improving working conditions (Egels-Zandén and Lindholm, 2015; LeBaron et al., 2017). In theory, the threat of sanctions – withdrawal of orders – encourages suppliers to address non-compliance. In practice, the necessary incentives to promote improvements in labour standards are often missing (Reinecke et al., 2019). Commercial contracts are rarely terminated by buyers even if suppliers are found non-compliant with a company's code of conduct (Locke et al., 2009; Amengual et al., 2020), not least because this would create disruption to the supply chain. Studies have even found that factories whose standards worsened tended to see their orders from Western buyers increase (Amengual et al., 2020). This renders the threat of an individual buyer withdrawing orders ineffective. Companies and their suppliers thus both have an interest in hiding labour violations rather than reporting them. The result is corporate complicity in a system where multiple buyers re-monitor the non-compliance of their supplying factories, leading to duplication of audits and 'audit fatigue', yet without significant remediation taking place.

Another problem with social auditing is the almost complete lack of worker involvement, a theme we will pick up on in more detail in Chapter 8. Even though tools such as worker hotlines have emerged and factory walls are plastered with different buyers' posters about corporate codes, meant to ensure minimum worker rights, there is very little active participation from workers in their monitoring, let alone enforcement. Workers and their representatives have no access to audit reports. They are at best interviewed by auditors, typically on factory premises, yet have to fear reprisal for revealing potentially compromising information about their working conditions.

While the many other industrial deaths in the RMG sector had barely made a ripple in much of the media in consumer countries, the sheer scale of the number of deaths and the horrific pictures of the collapsed Rana Plaza building did send shockwaves across developed economies. For a brief period, the spotlight turned onto the consequences of cost-driven supply chains, and in this context, a range of initiatives were implemented to try to improve the situation. The responses to Rana Plaza – especially the creation of the Bangladesh Accord (Chapters 5–7) and workplace social dialogue programmes (Chapter 8) – represent an important departure from social auditing in two dimensions: accountability regarding enforcement and worker involvement. In many ways, both of these initiatives, which provide the empirical context for this book, were attempts to move beyond the previous position, which clearly had failed. That said, as in all innovations, the extent to which they could be successful was unclear. It is within that context that these programmes will now be outlined.

## 4.5  Post–Rana Plaza as Ground for Institutional Innovation

### 4.5.1  *The Bangladesh Accord for Fire and Building Safety*

In the aftermath of the 2013 Rana Plaza tragedy, GUFs and labour rights NGOs leveraged global public pressure to force apparel brands and retailers sourcing from Bangladesh into an unprecedented collective and legally binding agreement to reform worker safety: the Bangladesh Accord for Fire and Building Safety, which is the empirical focus of Chapters 5–7. Coming into existence in May 2013 and being extended from its original expiry date in May 2018 until May 2021, it grew to over 200 corporate signatories covering over 1,600 supplier factories. As will be discussed in Chapter 5, the Accord emerged from a highly politicised approach to worker safety and health adopted through an alliance of unions and international NGOs. The ILO acted as neutral chair, lending significant institutional legitimacy to the Accord.

The Accord (2018) sought, in its own words, 'to enable a working environment in which no worker needs to fear fires, building collapses, or other accidents'. Programme activities included:

- independent fire, electrical and structural safety inspections carried out by trained Accord engineers
- monitoring remediation progress and facilitating brand support for remediation
- transparent online publication of all Accord-covered supplier factories, inspection reports and corrective action plans (CAPs)
- mobilising collective brand leverage through escalation and termination of business relationships with non-participating supplier factories
- a training programme for joint labour–management safety committees
- an Accord Safety and Health Complaints Mechanism to resolve safety complaints.

Brands also committed to ensuring that factories had the financial capacity to maintain safe workplaces and comply with remediation requirements through providing loans, accessing donor or government support or through offering other business incentives. To ensure a solid commitment to the Accord, companies agreed to a long-term sourcing relationship with Bangladesh, maintaining purchasing volumes for two years, thus providing an incentive for suppliers to invest in safety improvement.

The success of the Accord is most clearly demonstrated by improvements to safety, reducing workplace accidents. The average remediation rate had reached over 84 per cent by the time the first Accord expired in April 2018, rising to 93 per cent by May 2021 (see Figure 4.2).

The Bangladesh Accord was unique, and it marked a departure in transnational labour governance for several reasons:

### 4.5.1.1 Transnational Co-determination

Central to the Accord was a recognition that worker representatives, not just representatives of capital, must be included in the design and oversight of transnational labour governance regimes. The Accord Steering Committee was established to consist of equal representation by trade union and company representatives. Rather than promoting common business interests in protecting reputation, inclusion of recognised labour representatives was developed with a view to ensuring the representation of the interests of the agreement's intended beneficiaries: garment workers. Two obvious actors missing from the Accord as an employment relations agreement were, however, the Bangladeshi

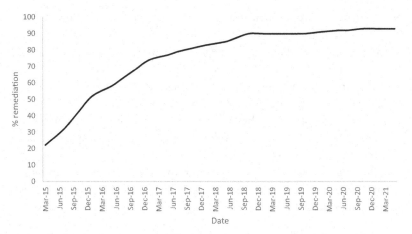

**Figure 4.2** Accord percentage remediation progress, 2015–2021

employers and the Government of Bangladesh. For this reason, the BGMEA and Government of Bangladeshi fiercely contested the quasi-regulatory authority of the Accord, which will be the focus of Chapter 7.

### 4.5.1.2 Legally Enforceable Commitment

By signing the Accord, company signatories made legally binding commitments that were enforceable in the national courts in the country within which they were registered. Due to its legally binding nature, the Accord departed from voluntary CSR standards in creating an enforceable contractual relationship in the home country of the buyer brands. The point about the establishment of a legally enforceable contract was a very significant new departure in global supply chain labour governance. Through the Accord, brands transferred oversight of their supply chain to a body that had a right to initiate legal action against the brands where they did not meet their commitments. While heavily resisted in the past, a legally binding agreement was achieved due to the pressure placed on brands by the harnessing of the complementary capacities of labour rights NGOs and trade unions, as will be discussed in Chapter 5. This legally binding nature was tested when two cases were filed in October 2016 at the Permanent Court of Arbitration in The Hague by IndustriALL and UNI Global to hold two unnamed signatory companies to account for failing to meet Accord terms (Permanent Court of Arbitration, 2018) – in particular, to require their suppliers to complete their remediations and to agree on commercial terms that were financially feasible for their suppliers to cover the remediation costs. The first case settled in December 2018. The second case settled in January 2019 and involved agreed payments of US$2.3 million to cover remediation in more than 150 garment factories in Bangladesh (US$2 million) and pay into IndustriALL and UNI's joint Supply Chain Worker Support Fund (US$0.3 million).

### 4.5.1.3 Leverage through Collective Action

The Accord created collective leverage through the combined power of its corporate signatories. Unlike IFAs, which are generally agreed between one brand and a GUF, the Accord covered multiple brands (in excess of 200 in the first Accord). Collective action by a large proportion of buyers provided far greater leverage for effective sanctioning than any buyer would have individually. Signatory firms agreed to terminate contracts with factories that failed to make safety improvements. As expressed by a buying brand, 'If you don't remediate you lose your orders from 215 brands. That's leverage, that's how you get things done in Bangladesh' (Interviewee Brand A.1). Under Accord rules, when a factory was found unsafe, no signatory brand could source from this factory. Facing the loss of orders from not just one but a large group of buyers commits the factory to invest in remediation. Effective sanctioning led to the most unsafe factories being temporarily or permanently shut. In 17 factories, safety concerns were so severe that the Accord recommended immediate evacuation. Immediate remedial actions were necessary in another 110 factories. While not all factories were covered by the Accord, approximately half of all workers in the sector and most of those in directly exporting firms were covered by the Accord.

### 4.5.1.4 Pooling of Resources

The Accord brought brands together to pool resources and share costs, information, responsibility and risk. The brands assumed responsibility for funding the activities of the steering committee, safety inspectors and training coordinators based on their annual volumes of garment purchases from Bangladesh on a sliding, pro-rata scale up to US$500,000 per annum. To illustrate the scale of the task, by the time the first Accord expired in April 2018, Accord engineers had carried out a total of 25,656 follow-up inspections in a total of 2,055 factories.

This yielded 134,489 findings, with safety hazards present in every factory, such as a lack of fire escapes. Respondents repeatedly stated that another large-scale disaster would have been imminent without immediate intervention. Pooling of resources helped to overcome the deficiencies of single brand approaches such as lack of expertise, under-funding of specialised inspections and protocols for follow-up action and remediation.

### 4.5.1.5 Developing Worker Voice
A core pillar of the Accord was the aim to strengthen the representation of workers in factories on the ground in Bangladesh by giving them an explicit role in the monitoring of factory health and safety. As such, the Accord oversaw the development of a more comprehensive structure of worker voice in the area of OSH, including the creation of joint worker–management OSH committees in all factories, workers' right to refuse unsafe work and the inclusion of worker representatives in inspection visits (Donaghey and Reinecke, 2018; Reinecke and Donaghey, 2021b). It also created an independent complaints mechanism, a key difference from the corporate-led Alliance, the implications of which we will discuss in Chapter 6. By December 2020, the Accord Safety and Health Complaints Mechanism had resolved over 693 complaints raised by workers and ensured the creation and training of over 1,260 joint labour–management safety committees.

### 4.5.1.6 Highly Focused Approach
One of the criticisms of the Accord was also one of its strengths. The Accord had a narrow focus on building, electrical and fire safety. Critics pointed out that the Accord drew attention away from the preferences and interests of Bangladeshi workers beyond narrow definitions of factory safety (Siddiqi, 2017; Tanjeem, 2017; Kabeer et al., 2020). Indeed, while preventing fatalities within the industry, the Accord's focus was not to increase poverty wages or extend worker rights beyond safety or even to contest the systemic asymmetries generated by neoliberal capitalist relations. This narrow focus, however, enabled the Accord to concentrate attention on protecting lives by significantly reducing deadly factory accidents. In contrast, IFAs and private labour standards often cover a wider variety of industrial relations issues but may be less able to deliver in terms of the expertise required and monitoring involved.

In summary, the Bangladesh Accord certainly marked a new departure on a number of fronts in terms of transnational labour governance that went beyond both NGO standards/certification and GUF IFA approaches. Central to this was the extent to which a system of transnational labour governance could be devised that incorporated the representation of the interests of workers and how this played out vis-à-vis the interests of the actors of capital. In the next three chapters, we chart the politics of its creation (Chapter 5), its operation when compared with the CSR-approach of the Alliance (Chapter 6) and its legacy and decline (Chapter 7).

## 4.5.2 The JETI Workplace Dialogue Project

Since the Rana Plaza disaster, the Bangladesh RMG sector has become a site for experimentation on various fronts, including new approaches to developing worker participation. Despite various international programmes designed to strengthen union organising, considered the first-best route to worker participation, many policy actors have become resigned to the idea that developing some level of non-union worker participation may be better than none in a context as hostile to union organisation as Bangladesh. It was in this context that the Joint Ethical Trading Initiatives (JETI) embarked on its workplace social dialogue programme, with which we engaged, and its development.

The JETIs are multi-stakeholder platforms, composed of high street retail brands, trade unions and NGOs that operate in the United Kingdom, Denmark and Norway. In 2015, the JETIs launched a pilot programme to develop a scalable and replicable model of workplace dialogue. The aim was to develop a mechanism through which workers could participate in resolving workplace conflicts peacefully. While the project was smaller than the likes of the H&M project, which sought to introduce social dialogue in over 200 factories, and the various ILO projects, the programme contained many similarities. In particular, the training developed for workers and managers in the factories was the same and was delivered by the same people as the H&M project. In this context, size (or lack thereof) was also helpful to the research team, as it enabled the possibility of tracking the project closely and helped us to engage meaningfully in qualitative research.

While the ETI base code emphasised the need for independent worker representation, two exogenous pressures also emerged to focus minds on the need to develop workplace-level representation. First, under pressure from the international community and the ILO, amendments to the labour law (Bangladesh Labour Act 2006, sections 205–208, and 2013 amendments) were made to strengthen industrial relations, including provisions for mandatory elections to participation committees (PCs). Section 205 of the Labour Act, 2006 requires all employers with more than fifty employees to have a participation committee composed of both worker and management representatives, although management representatives should not exceed the number of worker representatives. The law outlines the areas to be covered by the PCs as (1) promoting mutual trust, understanding and co-operation; (2) ensuring the application of labour laws; (3) fostering a sense of discipline and to improve and maintaining safe and healthy working conditions; (4) encouraging vocational training, workers' education and family welfare training; (5) adopting measures to improve welfare services for the workers and their families and (6) meeting production targets, improving productivity. Explicitly, the law excludes PCs from engaging in collective bargaining, which is to be the sole preserve of registered unions. Thus, in theory, with its provision for elected PCs, the Bangladeshi law supports the principle of workplace dialogue and provides a legal framework for it, which, at least on paper, is broadly similar to German Works Councils. Notwithstanding such de jure legal support, most observers of the Bangladesh RMG sector agreed that the law on participation committees had been widely disregarded. This was generally done in a number of ways, including factories failing to establish participation committees and, where they were set up, management selecting the representatives rather than workers electing them.

Second, as will be outlined in Chapters 5 and 6, under the Accord each factory was under an obligation to establish an OSH committee, which was to be composed of both worker and management representatives. While it was initially viewed that the worker representatives on these committees would be elected directly by the workers, when the regulations emanating from the amendments to the Bangladesh Labour Act emerged, these worker representatives were to be a sub-committee of the participation committee. Thus, for factories to be eligible to supply Accord brands, they required both an OSH committee and a participation committee and the Accord recognised the workplace dialogue committees developed under the JETI project as fulfilling its requirements.

In the project, JETI member companies in the United Kingdom, Denmark and Norway were invited to nominate suppliers willing to participate. This led to the workplace dialogue programme being piloted in nine factories of varying sizes, including two unionised factories, and expanded to twenty-one further factories. The programme built on the Bangladesh labour law mandating elected PCs by ensuring, and in some cases facilitating, democratic elections together with brands. Training included a designated training schedule for elected worker representatives or union office holders (four days plus one day for women), factory management (one day), production staff (one day) and combined worker–management (half a day). Training content included the concept of workplace dialogue, the labour law, ILO core conventions/buyer codes, meeting procedures, handling problems at work, representing workers, gender equality and the route to collective bargaining.

Close engagement with the JETIs and participating member companies resulted in a wide range of data sources being available, including observations, interviews, documents and workshops. The JETIs provided us with regular updates on their workplace dialogue projects in face-to-face project meetings and invited us to participate in biannual stakeholder meetings in London as well as stakeholder meetings held in Dhaka with participating brands, factories and union leaders. We visited four of the nine participating factories in Bangladesh, interviewed factory management and worker representatives and observed training sessions and PC meetings, with the help of translation where required. Observations yielded important insights into the dynamics of dialogue at the workplace. In turn, we presented our findings at regular intervals at stakeholder meetings in London, Oslo and Dhaka and organised a joint workshop with the ETI and ILO Better Work in London, which was attended by about fifty participants involving ETI members companies, unions, NGOs and representatives from Bangladeshi industry. The key features of our findings on the JETI project are presented in Chapter 8.

## 4.6 Conclusion

After Rana Plaza, a number of initiatives emerged to try to remedy the toxic supply chain in the sector. In this book, we focus primarily on two initiatives, the Accord and the JETI social dialogue programme, although there is some focus on the Alliance as a comparison with the Accord in Chapter 6. The key unifying features of both focus initiatives are the role and prominence of the representation of worker interests. Also significant is that in both initiatives there were a number of overlaps in terms of the actors involved. First, nearly all brands that are members of the JETI had signed up to the Accord (the one major exception being Gap, which had signed up to the Alliance). Second, the GUF IndustriALL and its Bangladeshi affiliates were involved in both the Accord and the unionised part of the workplace social dialogue programme. Third, and very significantly, when the Accord set about training worker representatives for their OSH committees, the training of workers who had participated in the JETI programme was recognised. It is in this context that we now move on to focus specifically on the Accord.

# 5 | Representative Alliances in the Creation of the Bangladesh Accord

Over 100 [later: 200] brands and retailers, covering over 2 million workers in 1,600 factories, are now working together with IndustriALL Global Union and UNI Global Union [in the Bangladesh Accord for Fire and Building Safety] .... Trade unions as partners are the only actors able to ensure accountability and reliable monitoring of conditions and the inspection process. (IndustriALL 2013a)

The work that the campaigning groups such as Clean Clothes Campaign have done over the last decade or decades particularly on the conditions of garment workers in Bangladesh, Cambodia and other places, has greatly helped us to get the Accord because they are the, they were the ones that continued to publicly raise awareness about these issues. The unions have, you know, because the unions are so weak in these countries for all kinds of reasons, legislative reasons, political reasons, and so on, the unions have not been able to really make a lot of progress there. And it was the campaigning organisations that brought hope to the workers in those countries .... So I think we have to give them a lot of credit for, you know, paving the way for the Bangladesh Accord. (Interviewee GUF B.1)

What were the conditions that made the creation of the Bangladesh Accord possible, a move away from years of failed social auditing to a legally binding collective labour agreement? How were over 200 companies convinced to sign up to the Accord? Our research suggests that the fatal events of the 2013 Rana Plaza disaster alone provided the context within which such an agreement became possible. To understand the conditions that enabled the creation and implementation of the Accord, we need to examine the dynamics of labour representation. A core challenge is that transnational governance no longer depends on a pre-existing, territorially bound constituency or electoral forms of representation. This is because electoral constituencies typically fail to coincide with those affected by the social consequences of global economic activity (Bohmann, 2012; Disch,

89

2012). Instead, representation must be created in global supply chains across nation-state boundaries. In other words, a transnational constituency of those affected by a global supply chain must be created and a political presence must be given to this constituency. This raises the question of the basis on which a particular constituency be represented, by whom and how.

The chapter's opening quotes capture the challenges and contradictions of worker representation in the Bangladesh RMG supply chain. As seen in the first quote, trade unions claim to be the legitimate representatives of workers' interests to ensure the proper functioning of global governance initiatives – here the Bangladesh Accord. At the same time, GUFs are aware of the limitations of union organising in contexts such as Bangladesh and the limited progress achieved by unions. They acknowledge the role of labour NGOs and campaign groups such as Clean Clothes Campaign and Worker Rights Consortium in enabling the creation of the Bangladesh Accord. While neither is perfect on its own, both approaches to representation – NGOs' claim-making and trade unions' representative structures – are needed to fill representation gaps. In this chapter, we explore the interplay of the logics of representation as a way of identifying constructive approaches 'for improving democratic practice without looking for some optimal design or blueprint' (Bohman, 2012: 73). Taking as our case study the creation of the Bangladesh Accord, we explore the questions: How do representation as structure and representative claims interact in transnational labour governance processes? How might they become complementary (or clash) in strengthening the democratic representation of workers' interests?

## 5.1 Representative Alliances in the Creation of the Accord

Central to the emergence of the Accord was the coalition between unions and NGOs forming the Labour Caucus that united behind a shared objective: making workplaces safe and protecting workers' lives. The Labour Caucus created a representative alliance, in which unions' and NGOs' respective logics of representation became highly complementary. The Labour Caucus consisted of the GUFs IndustriALL (representing manufacturing workers globally) and UNI Global (representing retail workers globally) and six local Bangladeshi unions, all affiliated to IndustriALL (see Table 5.1), which became full

Table 5.1. *The Accord's labour caucus*

| Name | Founded/HQ | Constituency | Representative approach |
|---|---|---|---|
| Accord full signatories – worker representation as structure | | | |
| IndustriALL Global Union | 201/ Geneva, CH | Affiliate unions in over 140 countries with about 50 million mining, energy and manufacturing workers | Global-level structural representation of supply chain workers: Bangladeshi garment workers covered through IndustriALL Bangladesh Council International Framework Agreements with Inditex / H&M Institutional recognition in tripartite structures (e.g., ILO) But: low union coverage in Bangladesh |
| UNI Global | 2000/ Geneva, CH | 900 affiliate unions in 150 countries of about 20 million service sector workers | Global-level structural representation of retail workers employed by MNCs through affiliates, e.g., Handels in Sweden International Framework Agreements with H&M Institutional recognition in tripartite structures (e.g., ILO) But not formally representing garment workers |

Table 5.1. (*cont.*)

| Name | Founded/HQ | Constituency | Representative approach |
| --- | --- | --- | --- |
| Bangladeshi union federations affiliated with IndustriALL Bangladesh Council[a] | Various/Dhaka, Bangladesh | 1–20 factory-level union members per federation in Bangladesh, or about 6% of Bangladeshi garment workers covered by unions at time of Rana Plaza | Structural representation of Bangladeshi garment workers Some federations enjoy a level of national recognition through party affiliation However, credibility challenges due to fragmentation, low union membership, suspected 'yellow' unions |
| Witness signatories – Worker representation as claim | | | |
| Worker Rights Consortium (WRC) (2001) | 2000/Washington DC, USA | >150 college and university affiliates in USA and Canada | Representation of student/ university voice Labor rights monitoring organisation, conducting investigations of working conditions in factories around the globe with focus is the labor practices of factories that manufacture university-licenced apparel. |

| Clean Clothes Campaign (CCC) | 1989/ Amsterdam/ NL | Global network of 16 campaigning organisations in Europe and partner network of 200 organisations and unions | Representation of consumer voice Educate and mobilise consumers, lobby companies and governments, and offer direct solidarity support to workers as they fight for their rights and demand better working conditions. |

[a] Bangladesh Textile and Garments Workers League, Bangladesh Independent Garments Workers Union Federation, Bangladesh Garments, Textile and Leather Workers Federation, Bangladesh Garment and Industrial Workers Federation, IndustriALL Bangladesh Council, Bangladesh Revolutionary Garments Workers Federation, National Garments Workers Federation, United Federation of Garment Workers.

signatories with 50 per cent voting rights on the Accord Steering Committee. In addition, four labour rights NGOs (Clean Clothes Campaign [CCC], Worker Rights Consortium [WRC], International Labor Rights Forum, Maquila Solidarity Network) were involved in the creation of the Accord and became the Accord's 'witness signatories'. The Labour Caucus was supported by online campaigning groups and a range of other labour rights NGOs.

Yet neither the GUFs nor the NGOs could claim a monopoly on worker representation. GUFs had representative membership structures but lacked actual members in workplaces, which undermined their legitimacy to represent members. In contrast, labour rights NGOs were self-appointed representatives who staked representative claims, but they were neither electorally authorised by, nor directly accountable to, workers or consumers themselves. Whereas each on their own would have lacked representative legitimacy, unions and NGOs formed a 'coalition of the weak' (Baccaro and Lim, 2007), which enabled them to create the momentum and synergies to establish the Accord. The remainder of this chapter explores the symbiotic relationship between representative claims and structures in the set-up of the Accord but also emergent divisions due to differing underlying logics.

## 5.2 Negotiating the Accord

Relationships between the parties within the Labour Caucus had built up over time following the Spectrum factory collapse in 2005 and intensified after the Tazreen factory fire in 2012. Frustrated with existing voluntary CSR activities by brands that had focused mainly on social auditing of suppliers, the WRC and the CCC attempted to establish a memorandum of understanding (MoU) for brands to invest in building safety in Bangladesh, yet it failed to gather the necessary support of at least four brands to sign the commitment with only two brands, US brand PVH and German brand Tchibo, being willing to sign the MoU. An NGO campaigner recalled companies' unwillingness to commit to collective action: 'there wasn't the commitment and buy-in for that at that time' (NGOA.1).

When the Rana Plaza disaster occurred despite the factories inside having undergone social audits on behalf of individual brands, the Labour Caucus regarded the disaster as confirmation that the prevailing corporate social auditing paradigm was 'a model that has failed' (GUF A.1) to address the entrenched structural problems within the Bangladeshi industry. Moreover, the sheer scale of the disaster made the actors realise that 'the industry as a whole has a problem it needs to deal with' (Brand B.1). Worker safety could not be tackled through individual corporate social responsibility but was an industry-wide, endemic problem, the scale and complexity of which required a more substantive and collective response. The emphasis became creating a proper, legally binding collective agreement with IndustriALL and UNI Global being the GUFs involved.

The power of the Labour Caucus was illustrated by its ability to trump an industry-driven solution in favour of a legally binding, collective agreement. The German Agency for International Cooperation (Gesellschaft für Internationale Zusammenarbeit, or GIZ) was simultaneously attempting to develop an alternative initiative with the Global Social Compliance Initiative that was in line with the industry-driven social auditing regime. Shortly after the Rana Plaza disaster, both the MoU and the Global Social Compliance Initiative proposals were being discussed at a meeting of unions, NGOs and brands in Eschborn, Germany, where the headquarters of the GIZ is based. The Labour Caucus united and aligned its position to insist on a broad line: a binding agreement, financial responsibility of brands, a governance role for unions and independent and transparent inspections. Using the momentum created by the disaster, the representative alliance of unions and NGOs created a 'pressure cooker' effect on companies. In contrast, companies lacked a unified position. The meeting ended without a clear outcome but with the Labour Caucus demanding that companies sign the MoU by a deadline of 15 May 2013.

Both GUFs and NGOs went beyond their normal 'roles', which had earlier divided them. Previously, IndustriALL had invited brands and NGOs to a meeting in Geneva to negotiate a compromise, as unions do. But following Rana Plaza, widely described as a 'game changer', and frustration with the response of brands, IndustriALL was now ready to insist on a binding agreement. In turn, the CCC and WRC were ready to leave the negotiations to IndustriALL rather than campaign against companies. The Accord became a very high priority for the GUFs, to the extent that the General Secretaries of IndustriALL and later UNI Global became involved and negotiated directly with brands over the Accord. Between 29 April and 15 May 2013, numerous bilateral and multilateral conversations were led by IndustriALL to negotiate the content of what became the Accord.

While some corporate actors were pushing for watering down of the MoU to a more principle-based agreement, IndustriALL, supported by the other actors in the Labour Caucus, insisted on a substantive agreement. The Labour Caucus recognised the unique opportunity that they had to reach an unprecedented binding agreement. If such a demand could not be formulated in a situation in which the bargaining power of the Labour Caucus was backed by the enormous consumer pressure faced by Western companies, then they would never be able to do it. 'I think that's why, that's what made us so determined to stand by it, to fight it out with the companies', as a global unionist (GUF B.1) explained. Through this coordinated approach within the labour caucus, the MoU evolved behind the scenes into the Accord. It retained the key feature of being binding while integrating two key changes: linking to the Bangladeshi National Action Plan and bringing in the ILO as the chair of the Accord Steering Committee.

## 5.3 Mobilising Companies to Sign Up to the Accord

Even though Rana Plaza was a 'shock for many companies' that 'upped the ante enormously' (ETI.1), many brands were reluctant to engage with trade unions in negotiations for a legally binding agreement. The Labour Caucus took a collective approach and united behind a single demand of Western retail companies: sign the Accord. Compressing the complexity of factory safety in Bangladesh into one single demand helped to focus attention and coordination of actions. Pressure was created by the combination of unions leveraging their representative membership structures and NGOs making representative claims by leveraging the public outcry following the Rana Plaza disaster to put pressure on global brands. In this way, unions' and NGOs' different representative approaches became highly complementary in expanding coverage of affected constituents. Both unions and NGOs admitted that the Accord would not have been possible without leveraging each other's representative capacity.

Due to low levels of union coverage, unions' ability to negotiate with employers in Bangladesh or to threaten industrial action was negligible. As outlined in Chapter 4, the vast majority of garment workers were not covered by representative structures and existing unions were highly fragmented in multiple associations. As a result, the Bangladeshi unions' ability and legitimacy to negotiate collectively with employers in Bangladesh on behalf of all garment workers was limited. Representative structures were stronger in consumer countries and with brands sourcing from Bangladesh. Here, global, national and Bangladeshi union relations could reinforce each other. A trade union-ist from the United Kingdom's TUC describes how unions were able to mobilise solidarity across the supply chain to add legitimacy to the demand to sign the Accord:

We got Amirul [prominent trade union leader from the National Garment Workers Federation in Bangladesh] to speak at the TUC Congress in September [2013] ... that was a very important moment because it marked the kind of solidarity that got lots of the UK brands to sign up. And USDAW, the [UK's] shop workers union, was putting forward a motion on Bangladesh solidarity and saying we want all UK high streets to sign up. That was an important interplay between the retail workers here and the ones who were making the clothes being sold in the shops. And obviously that was being supported by Uni Global .... So you've got that interplay between the global unions, the national unions and the backing of the Bangladeshi unions there, so all kind of tied up quite well.' (TUC.1 12.2013)

In the aftermath of Rana Plaza, NGOs were able to draw media attention and public anger to the role of the brands through intensive campaigning and outreach:

The campaigning role that they have that they're able to go out and put public pressure on companies to sign the Accord has been invaluable. Because we simply wouldn't have had the capacity to do that and we wouldn't have anything like the number of companies that we have that have signed the Accord. (GUF A.1)

By creating political presence for Bangladeshi workers in the media, NGOs mobilised consumer power to make a credible threat to damage brand reputation and to disrupt the consumption relationship. Aggressive online campaigns by SumOfUS and Avaaz demanding brands to sign the Accord created additional 'surge capacity' (Online Campaign B). Their online petitions encouraged their large subscriber base to use their voice as citizens and consumers to demand brands to 'protect your workers. Sign the Bangladesh Safety Accord now, and offer fair compensation to all the victims of factory disasters there'

(SumofUs, 2013). Mobilising the 'massive, public outcry … on tipping-point moments of crisis and opportunity' (Online Campaign A), such as Rana Plaza, validated the claim and diffused its reach.

The campaign to get H&M, the largest buyer from Bangladesh, to become the first signatory to the Accord illustrates the unions' ability to leverage pre-existing relationships. Due to the existence of IFAs, respondents emphasised that IndustriALL and UNI Global had very constructive relationships with Inditex and H&M respectively, both on the manufacturing side and the retail side. Union representatives reported that they 'used a lot of credit that we had from developing those relationships to exert pressure on them. It was not always pleasant but I think it paid off to have an Accord' (GUF A.2). But due to their union affiliates in Bangladesh, they also had the legitimacy to present the Accord as a demand from workers themselves, rather than Western actors. To convince these brands to sign the Accord, UNI negotiated with H&M and IndustriALL with Inditex. To exert pressure on the Swedish fashion retailer, UNI leveraged both its existing IFA with the company with 63 per cent of its employees worldwide then covered by collective bargaining agreements (H&M, 2014), as well as the particularly high union density of its Swedish affiliate, Handels. In coordination with UNI Global, Handels used its relationship with H&M to have a dialogue at the company's Swedish headquarters. Union negotiation was strengthened by the threat of renewed negative publicity. Simultaneously, the Swedish chapter of the Clean Clothes Campaign was planning a massive campaign against the retailer in Stockholm in its various stores, which was called off when H&M signed on the day of planned action. After having previously been exposed over living wages in Cambodia and pulling out 'of its Swedish comfort zone' as an NGO interviewee (NGOA.1) described it, H&M was vulnerable to consumer activism and the retailer was aware that the CCC had been preparing a large-scale campaign against it. On 15 May 2013, H&M became the first signatory to the new Accord, followed by Inditex. Once these industry behemoths had signed, other brands quickly followed suit. By the deadline of 16 May 2013, a total of 41 companies had signed up, covering more than 1,000 Bangladeshi garment factories (IndustriALL, 2013b).

Moreover, the close link between the WRC and university students – an important consumer group for many collegiate super brands such as Adidas – created consumer pressure in key markets. In particular, the

WRC, founded by the US-student activist group United Students Against Sweatshops, engaged students in its over 180 affiliate colleges and universities in the United States and Canada to advocate for university administrators to add the Accord to licensing requirements. Student-led campaigns at five prestigious US campuses led Fruit of the Loom to sign the Accord in November 2013, despite already having been a member of the industry-led Alliance, as the company could not afford to lose consumers in the important collegiate market.

Both unions and NGOs celebrated their representative alliance as 'a really good demonstration of the division of labour between the different types of organisations and the roles that they play in this' (GUF A.1). Both realised that by 'working collaboratively together we bring different things', which 'together actually it's a really strong force for change' (NGO A.1). As respondents explained, their representative alliance pressured brands into signing the Accord:

It really created a kind of boiling pot moment where it was like you're either in or you're out [of the Accord]. And I think that was most powerfully really, that labour rights and unions as a group had ever been before ... the two sides really joined together in a common purpose and I think that really scared the shit out of companies. (NGO A.1)

In sum, the representative alliance between NGOs and unions brought together representative structures and claims in ways that each logic's respective strength compensated for the other's weakness: NGOs' ability to create a political presence of workers in consumer countries through the mobilisation of public pressure compensated for unions' low coverage in Bangladesh. In turn, the unions' relationship with Western brands as well as their affiliate membership links with Bangladeshi workers endowed them with the legitimacy to present the Accord as a demand from Bangladeshi unions. While far from perfect, this significantly expanded the presence of the affected constituency.

## 5.4 Representation of Labour in the Accord

As a union–company agreement, the Accord provided equal representation of corporate and labour interests. However, while the Labour Caucus had insisted on equal representation of corporate and labour interests, clashes started to resurface in terms of deciding who represented labour on the Accord steering committee. Despite low membership in Bangladesh, union interviewees insisted that the Accord – a collective agreement between unions and companies – existed within their sphere of operation. They claimed the right to be full signatories with 50 per cent voting rights on the Accord steering committee, with one vote each for the Bangladesh IndustriALL Council, IndustriALL and UniGlobal: 'we play a representative role because we've representative structures' (GUF A.1).

The four NGOs were to be 'witness signatories' with observer status but without voting rights. NGOs somewhat reluctantly 'agreed to play that role' (NGO A.1) in recognition of their role vis-à-vis that of a union:

We don't technically represent workers ... ultimately, we had to respect certainly what the unions wanted. You know, we have long term working relationships with the local unions in Bangladesh ... and we respect their role as the body that represents workers. Although we certainly would have liked to be signatories, we respect their decision. (NGO A.1)

The Worker Rights Consortium and the Clean Clothes Campaign agreed that their 'role is more sort of an advisory role and being able to support the unions where we can' (NGO B.1).

The reluctance of unions to cede a seat on the table finds roots in unions' 'long held suspicion' that NGOs sought 'to occupy the space that trade unions should be in', as a campaigner herself noted (NGO B.1). 'We have a very big problem with that. We certainly fight with that' (GUF A), as a trade unionist explained. The difference in status in the Accord governance structure, with unions being full signatories and NGOs being witness signatories, was seen as an important acknowledgement of the difference in the approaches to representation:

This to me is an acknowledgement by the NGOs of what the role of an NGO is vis-à-vis the role of a trade union. And it's when those roles get confused that we run into difficulties .... But in the context of the Accord it is a lot easier to deal with because those roles have been made very clear from the start. They're the campaigning organisations, and we are the representative membership based organisations that have the power to enforce the Accord on behalf of our members. (GUF A.1)

In sum, we saw how the latent conflict between unions and NGOs surfaced and was averted only because NGOs yielded to union demands to be recognised as the institutionally legitimate representatives of labour.

## 5.4.1  Tensions within the Labour Caucus

The combination of unions' ability to leverage pre-existing relationships through IFAs and NGOs' public campaigning against companies had been highly complementary in getting the Accord off the ground. But these differences also became a source of conflict. They led to some tensions and divergence on tactical issues. There was a fine line when it came to deciding when a public campaign should start or end and when negotiation with a company through the inside should begin. NGOs mostly coordinated with unions but also insisted that there might be a situation 'where we'd have to break ranks and do a campaign' (NGO A.2). As a result, campaigning NGOs were both useful and distracting in the process of negotiating the Accord:

The campaigning NGOs were a double-edged sword in the sense that yes, the campaigning got the media involved and yes, the campaigning helped create the noise, but in my opinion they didn't know when to switch off and move into negotiation. So there is a time when you've got them [brands] round the table, so stop shouting at them and listen and engage. (ETI.1)

Conflict over where this fine line was situated was illustrated in the joint campaign between the UK's Trades Union Congress (TUC) and Labour Behind the Label, the UK chapter of the Clean Clothes Campaign, against Edinburgh Woollen Mills. The UK knitwear company was targeted on two fronts: first, for its refusal to sign the Accord and second, for its failure to pay adequate compensation for victims of the Tazreen factory fire in 2012, when 117 workers died. The joint action planned to take place outside a number of Edinburgh Woollen Mills stores across the United Kingdom on the Tazreen anniversary was celebrated as a coming together as the alliance of the British trade union movement and civil society:

Not only do you have the whole union movement, 6 million workers in the UK, but there's a broader based alliance ... with all those different NGOs coming together. (TUC.1)

However, just a few days before the planned action, Edinburgh Woollen Mills signed the Accord. This led to a divide between the unions and NGOs. The Accord, being their mandate, meant the TUC called off the 'wonderfully planned' (TUC.1) day of action and commended the company for signing the Accord. One union interviewee

(TUC.2) admitted that signing the Accord 'obviously doesn't solve the compensation issue'. Yet the mandate was to strengthen the Accord as an institution that could prevent future disasters.

In contrast, NGOs saw only marginal benefit in getting another signatory to the Accord, which at the time had already secured over fifty signatories including large retailers. NGOs established themselves as representatives of the dead and injured victims and their families. Labour Behind the Label had invested considerably in the campaign for victim compensation and was unwilling to let the company get away with what it saw as an 'attempt to undermine any kind of calls for compensation'. As one campaigner stated:

> The frustration from our side is that in the rush to celebrate the victory of the Accord there's been a tendency to sweep under the carpet the reality that those families affected by the [Tazreen] disaster still don't get anything. (NGO A.2)

Eventually, an agreement driven by IndustriALL, the fashion retailer C&A, the C&A Foundation and the Clean Clothes Campaign led to total compensation of US$2.17 million for the Tazreen victims. However, the conflict damaged the representative alliance between the TUC and Labour Behind the Label, leading to reluctance to work together in the future.

Similarly, online campaigning groups such as SumOfUs or Avaaz were also seen as 'uncontrollable' and their interventions could sometimes be non-constructive. At best, their aggressive online campaigns created additional 'surge capacity' (Online Campaign B) that diffused the reach of the claim. Online petitions against companies to sign the Accord, such as Gap and Walmart in the United States, Coles and Rivers in Australia, Loblaw in Canada or River Island and Edinburgh Woollen Mill in the United Kingdom, helped to raise consumer awareness and exert consumer pressure. These online campaign groups did coordinate some of their actions with organised labour. For instance, in the United Kingdom, the TUC and SumOfUs coordinated a successful campaign against River Island with about 17,000 signatures from UK consumers, which played an important part in persuading the UK-based fashion retailer to sign the Accord.

Generally, though, surge capacity was a short-term oriented campaigning strategy that attempted to build on outrage about news in the media rather than longer-term coordinated action with other parties.

The delicate complementarity between union-led negotiations and activist agitation is illustrated by online campaigning against Topshop. Online campaigners, who neither had direct relationships with the company nor pursued negotiations, were building a public petition against Topshop, a UK high-street fashion retailer, to pressurise it into signing the Accord. Yet the brand was simultaneously in negotiations with unions and threatened to walk away from the Accord if it were publicly campaigned against. The petition was withdrawn after the negative reaction in the test phase and shortly afterwards Topshop signed the Accord. While this success was attributed to the skills of union negotiators, trade unionists acknowledged the contribution of 'having that implicit threat helped focus minds' (GUF A.1). But they also accused online campaigners of using the plight of the affected workers to 'feed their campaigns' (GUF A.1) to sustain a business model that relied on external visibility in the public sphere, rather than seeking pragmatic solutions that helped workers. Unions thus found it difficult to work with online groups strategically due to their unwillingness to cooperate in the same way as the CCC and the WRC.

In sum, these cases illustrate how unions' membership structures meant that they focused more narrowly on their mandate to represent current workers and build the Accord. In contrast, NGOs' freedom from structural ties allowed them to focus on seeking justice for a neglected group of victims, who were bereft of a voice. While the different logics of representation – structure versus claim – can expand coverage of relevant constituents, here it also weakened the representative alliance.

## 5.5 The Logics of Representation: Structure versus Claim

The creation of the Accord clearly illustrates the interplay of the different logics of representation. In this section, the Accord is used to explore this interplay in further depth to determine what distinguishes them, what allows them to become complementary and where sources of tensions originate, using the criteria of political representation (Pitkin, 1967; Rehfeld, 2006; Urbinati and Warren, 2008; Montanaro, 2012) outlined in Chapter 4. These are summarised in Table 5.2. First, we focus on where representation is created. Then we examine (1) whether the representatives of affected interests – the

Table 5.2. *The logics of representation*

|  | Representation as claim | Representation as structure |
|---|---|---|
| **Representatives** | Self-appointed claim makers NGOs: Workers Rights Consortium, Clean Clothes Campaign Online campaign groups | Membership-based organisations Unions: Global Unions Federations IndustriAll and UNI Global; IndustriAll Bangladesh Council and affliated Bangladeshi union federations |
| **Creation of presence of affected constituency** | | |
| Mode of creating presence | Create political presence through representative claims | Create political presence through representative structures |
| **Sphere of operation** | Public sphere | Employment relationship |
| **Authorisation by affected constituency** | | |
| Mode of authorisation | Attention-based, discursive authorisation validated by attention to, and agreement with, claim. | Authorisation by members and affiliated to represent their interests. |
| Plasticity of authorisation | High. Transient claims are flexible and allow NGOs to claim authorisation to pursue issues more flexibly. | Low. Pre-existing structures prescribe the mandate that unions are authorised to pursue. |
| **Accountability to affected constituency** | | |
| Mode of accountability | Attention-based, discursive accountability. | Membership-based accountability to the explicit mandate given by constituents. |
| **Logic of securing accountability** | Logic of attention | Logic of membership |

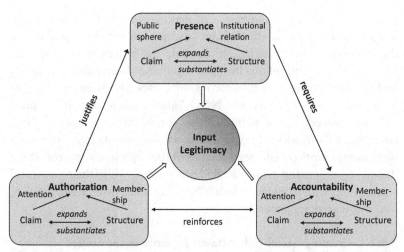

**Figure 5.1** A framework of transnational representation based on complementarities between representative claims and representative structures

Bangladeshi workers – give political presence to those whose interests are affected ('affected interests standard'), (2) whether the affected are empowered to authorise and (3) whether they can hold a representative accountable. We argue that the interaction of representative claims and structures can strengthen input legitimacy if it (1) makes affected interests politically more present, (2) enables authorisation by a greater number of affected interests and (3) creates stronger forms of accountability to affected interests than without the interplay.

Our case suggests that this happens when approaches are able to compensate at least partially for each other's limitations. As depicted in Figure 5.1, the strength of representative claims is that they can expand presence, authorisation and accountability and at least partially fill representative gaps by including those who would otherwise be excluded from structural forms of representation in transnational governance. In turn, the strength of representative structures is that they can substantiate claims.

## 5.5.1 Creating Political Presence of an Affected Constituency

Democratic representation depends on the ability to bring affected constituents – here workers – and their interests into the political process. Thus, the first dimension of making representation legitimate is whether it makes the affected constituency present. As seen above in the context of the Bangladesh Accord, the representative alliance between NGOs and unions brought together representative structures and claims in such a way that each actor's respective strength compensated for the other's weakness: NGOs' ability to create political presence of workers in the public sphere compensated for unions' low coverage in Bangladesh. In turn, GUFs' affiliate membership links with Bangladeshi workers endowed them with the legitimacy to present the Accord as a demand from Bangladeshi unions, while their structural relationship with Western brands allowed them to turn public pressure into negotiated agreements.

### 5.5.1.1 Creating Membership-Based Presence in the Sphere of Employment Relations

We play a representative role and it's because we have representative structures. (GUF A.1)

Unions follow a logic of membership, where their ability to represent workers is both enabled and constrained by the nature of union membership – the voluntary association of workers with a collective body that is authorised to act as their representative. As expressed in the quote above, trade unions therefore ground their democratic legitimacy to represent members through representative structures. They provide a mechanism through which members voluntarily delegate their authority for the aggregation and pool their individual interests through collective bodies. This creates a structural relationship with the workers who are union members and provides unions with a strong, formal role as the official bargaining agent for workers. Ideally, high levels of membership or coverage in any given sector allow all or most affected constituents to participate in the representative process. The logic of membership establishes unions as the official representatives of labour within the sphere of the employment relationship.

However, in the Bangladeshi case, the unions' traditional sources of labour power were low, lacking the associability to disrupt production processes through collective industrial action or the threat of it (Wright, 2000). Nevertheless, the unions' representative membership structures gave them a high capacity to represent workers at the transnational level across the supply chain. We describe these representative capacities in terms of relational power and institutional embeddedness.

GUFs could mobilise their relational power to negotiate directly with Western brands. IndustriALL and UNI Global's representational capacities were highly complementary. While IndustriALL's official mandate was to represent factory workers in the Bangladesh RMG sector, UNI Global had significant membership in some areas of retailing and could leverage industrial relationships with many brands. This enabled the global union federations to both mobilise bottom-up voices through their network of affiliate members as well as negotiate directly with Western brands. For companies with union recognition, the relevant unions, such as GMB, USDAW and UNITE in the United Kingdom or Handels in Sweden, could both negotiate with brand management to make internal demands or use the threat of mobilising their members to exert pressure. What was important was that unions were viewed by many of the brands as being legitimate 'insiders' to the employment relationship and regarded as more appropriate negotiation partners because they shared a mutual interest in the well-being of the company and responsibility for the success of collective agreements. Being embedded in the well-established structure of collective bargaining with companies on a local, national and international level also gave unions direct access to and influence at those company headquarters where unions were recognised. Having such ongoing relationships enabled more cooperative bargaining and a willingness on both sides to compromise to retain existing relations. This enabled union federations to leverage existing national collective bargaining institutions – for instance, by contacting staff at corporate headquarters.

Finally, the global union federations' institutional embeddedness contributed access within the global governance arena – access that NGOs mostly lacked. The unions leveraged their formal role in the institutionalised governance landscape, particularly as constituents of the tripartite structure of the ILO. This institutional embeddedness helped gain the official endorsement of the ILO for the Accord through its agreement to chair the Accord Steering Committee. It also enabled the unions to link to a broad network of global-level institutions as well as local-level agencies.

### 5.5.1.2 Creating Presence in the Sphere of Consumption Relations

In cases in Bangladesh, as you will know, where you haven't got mature systems of industrial relations that exist for whatever reasons, whether it be resource, whether it be politics, whether it be corruption. They [NGOs] provide another avenue towards worker representation, how it can be affected. (Accord.1)

Self-appointed representatives can contribute to democratic representation by providing 'political presence to those whose interests are affected' (Montanaro, 2012: 1098). Broadly speaking, and in line with a constructivist interpretation of Hanna Pitkin's (1967; see Disch, 2011, 2012) foundational definition, to 'represent' means, literally, to 'make present again' – making people's voices, opinions and perspectives 'present' in governance processes. But rather than making 'present' through 'mirroring' or 'reflecting' an already existing constituency, proponents of discursive representation go one step further in suggesting that constituencies are themselves constituted in the process of representation. This approach conceptualises representation as performative: 'acts of representation do not simply reflect constituencies and their interests but help to bring them into being' (Disch, 2012: 600). In other words, NGOs bring constituencies into being that would not otherwise have political presence in traditional political spaces, including marginalised people or future generations.

In the case of the Clean Clothes Campaign's '#WeDemandTk16000' campaign mentioned in Chapter 3, no Bangladeshi worker is formally represented in the Clean Clothes Campaign, yet their claim makes 'present' the worker and her claim to fair wages in the eyes of consumers who might not otherwise reflect on the conditions of workers making brand-name clothes. As seen in this example, representative claims can be ambiguous about their 'object' of representation: The '#We' can either or both refer to the Bangladeshi workers or the Western consumer as constituents of the claim. Representative claims form constituencies around issues rather than fixed structures. Moreover, rather than focusing on Bangladeshi institutions or employers, this representative claim is directed where the greatest attention can be generated: at brands such as H&M, Tesco, Inditex and their consumers.

The example also illustrates that NGOs follow a logic of attention, where their ability to represent workers is grounded in their ability to focus public attention – that of media, consumers and policy-makers – onto a particular issue and claim to represent the concerns of a particular constituent. This establishes NGOs as self-appointed representatives of labour within the sphere of the consumption relationship. Thus, whereas unions' representative capacities were relational/ negotiating power and institutional embeddedness, NGOs representative capacities were based on mobilising power and freedom to agitate based on institutional disembeddedness. In terms of mobilising power, NGOs seek to mobilise what Hirschman (1970) terms exit and voice – the power of consumers to boycott or 'buy-cott' products based on their perceived ethical qualities or mobilise consumers' voice. Placed at the end-point of the global supply chain and within a highly competitive consumer market, NGOs had considerable power to mobilise voice and exit power. Similar to GUFs, whose representational capacities were directed at Western brands rather than employers, the power of NGOs was to mobilise Western consumers in the name of Bangladeshi workers. The key leverage point of campaign groups was creating a reputational risk to companies by damaging or threatening to damage their brand image through repeated negative press or 'naming and shaming' campaigns.

This freedom to agitate is based on institutional dis-embeddedness. Standing outside the tripartite system of industrial relations afforded NGOs far more freedom to agitate and engage in contentious politics to raise awareness and pressurise companies. Rather than negotiating behind 'closed doors', hard-hitting NGOs found it more productive to engage in public campaigns, using print media, social media, and 'off-line' street protests to disseminate their claims and make workers present. An extreme example of institutional disembeddedness is the online activist and campaigning networks, which 'act like a megaphone to call attention to new issues' (Avaaz.org). They are also transient and momentary, needing to be recreated on an ongoing basis to maintain the political presence of the represented. However, as seen in the mobilisation against Topshop, their freedom to agitate can also interfere with unions' ongoing attempts at negotiation.

## 5.5.2 Authorisation by an Affected Constituency

The second condition is whether affected constituents exercise authorisation. Authorisation by the represented to speak and act on their behalf is a defining institutional feature of democratic representation (Pitkin, 1967; Rehfeld, 2006; Urbinati and Warren, 2008).

### 5.5.2.1 Membership-Based Authorisation

Representation through trade unions is based around the idea of workers voluntarily delegating their authority for the aggregation and pooling of their individual interests through collective bodies with elected representatives. In forming or joining a union, workers are formally authorising the union to represent them in negotiations and collective bargaining with employers. Membership seeks to ensure explicit consent from members through democratic processes as workers collectively form a union, aggregate their representative capacity through affiliation and delegate interest representation to a collective body. This is a key feature that differentiates unions from NGOs, as a respondent explains:

> The NGOs are not democratically authorised ... they claim themselves representatives of workers and civil society but ... there is no democratic process here to enable NGOs to claim that they are representatives of civil society. This is different from the unions. The unions they are set up by workers, workers decide on their unions, workers on the unions, there is a democratic process and it's even carried on from the local unions to the international unions where they are joining in federations: there is a democratic basis!' (Brand A.1)

The logic of membership creates a clearly defined constituency that authorises. Thus, a union's authorising constituency is defined by the boundaries of union membership and affiliation. Authorisation also happens through participation: regular union meetings or locally elected committees provide their members with local democracy (Martin, 1968). Union members are expected to feed into and vote on policies that mandate the local leadership over issues such as industrial action and thus should bring strong features of participatory democracy to union representation (Benhabib, 1996). Wider structures emerge where branches form federations, and federations become part of national and transnational structures, thus creating links of democratic authorisation. In the case of the Bangladesh Accord, GUFs were formally authorised to represent Bangladeshi workers through the Bangladesh IndustriALL Council and its union affiliates. International unions deliberately mobilised these chains of affiliation across the supply chain to legitimise their demands. A trade unionist from the United Kingdom's TUC describes how the presence of and support from a prominent trade union leader from the IndustriALL-affiliated National Garment Workers Federation in Bangladesh added urgency and legitimacy to its demand for brands to sign the Accord:

It [Accord] didn't have that feeling of like 'Oh, the West telling the Global South what to do.' Because we were having Bangladeshi union leaders coming here and saying what we want you to do is sign the Accord because this Accord, unlike any other kind of CSR process, has within it that you must work with the trade unions and the factories. Or where there are no trade unions you must work with worker representatives. So it actually has the engagement with workers within its very core. So it's something that trade unions actually want. (TUC.1)

As alluded to in this quote about the role of Bangladeshi unions in authorising the Accord, unions ensured that representatives were 'acting in the interest of the represented, in a manner responsive to them', which is core to Pitkin's (1967: 209) widely applied definition of substantive representation.

Still, it is also worth highlighting that at no point have Bangladeshi workers ever voted on and thus authorised the Accord as a collective agreement covering their working conditions. Bangladeshi union federations have signed the Accord on behalf of workers, even though they cover less than 4 per cent of the workforce. Such low levels of union density meant that authorisation came from a relatively small percentage of Bangladeshi workers: those who were members of unions affiliated with the Bangladesh IndustriALL Council. This highlights the limitations of traditional union approaches to claim a monopoly on democratic representation in transnational governance.

### 5.5.2.2 Attention-Based Authorisation
In contrast to unions, where the boundaries of membership and affiliation clearly defined a union's authorising constituency, the question of authorisation poses not just a practical but also a conceptual difficulty for NGOs (Montanaro, 2012). Since there is no pre-existing authorising constituency, such as a territorially bound political community (Disch, 2012), self-appointed representatives such as NGOs lack formal authorisation. Claim-makers instead need to gain attention-based or 'discursive authorization' (e.g., Dryzek and

Niemeyer, 2008) in the form of attention drawn to an issue and public agreement with the claims being made. If no attention whatsoever is generated for a claim, then claim-makers have simply failed to mobilise a constituency around it that could authorise the claim. Public agreement can be expressed through support of protests, boycotts, letter-writing and petitions, which contributes to a self-appointed representative's public reputation.

Representatives may employ different mechanisms of discursive justification (Schormair and Gilbert, 2021). For instance, campaign groups often invite signatures to public petitions to validate their representative claims retrospectively, or NGOs may seek to gain authorisation by creating close connections with affected constituents and seek their input into campaigns. This allows NGOs to present themselves as transmitters of workers' own demands into global discourses to build legitimacy around their claim. For instance, NGOs invited Bangladeshi labour leaders, such as Nazma Akter, executive director of the labour NGO Awaj Foundation, Kalpona Akter, executive director of the Bangladesh Centre for Workers Solidarity, and Amirul Haque Amin, general secretary of the NGWF union, to speak at events in consumer countries.

One characteristic tenet of representative claims is that they can form flexibly around particular issues or problems. For this reason, discursive sources of authorisation endowed NGOs with significantly higher levels of plasticity: not being limited to fixed authorising structures makes NGOs highly flexible. Representative claims can 'operate across borders and even across species; they denote shifting power relationships rather than fixed institutions' (Saward, 2010: 1). Being so spontaneous and highly flexible, representative claims can contribute to democratic representation because they can generate attention around particular issues quickly when needed. This can be incredibly helpful for mobilising public outcry on tipping-point moments of crisis, such as Rana Plaza or other disasters where there might be short windows of opportunity to prompt responses through fast and aggressive mobilisation of public anger. In the creation and implementation of the Accord, this allowed NGOs to make representative claims and fill representative gaps where unions lacked an organisational mandate to represent, when the affected – such as those killed by the Rana Plaza tragedy – could not speak. Here, attention-based, discursive authorisation might be the only authorisation available.

For instance, NGOs made representative claims on behalf of those killed by the Rana Plaza tragedy. Immediately after the disaster occurred, Dhaka-based investigators from the Worker Rights Consortium photographed and collected documents, tags and labels amidst the rubble with the aim of 'putting together testimony about the brands that were sourcing from the factory' (NGO B.2). Even if some brands claimed they did not source from Rana Plaza, labels found in the ruins of Rana Plaza provided the evidence needed to draw attention to these workers as victims who were working and dying for these brands. Justifying the representative claim through evidence on the ground allowed activists to demand compensation from brands on behalf of the dead and injured. This illustrates how an NGO's plasticity – that is, its ability to offer representation more flexibly without formal authorisation – can fill representative gaps by including those who would otherwise be excluded from representation in transnational governance by the structural boundaries of union membership and affiliation. In turn, we saw that a union's ability to mobilise substantive sources of authorisation through enduring structural links of membership and affiliation across the supply chain could substantiate representative claims.

## 5.5.3 Accountability to an Affected Constituency

The final dimension for establishing democratically legitimate representation concerns sources of accountability: how do representatives demonstrate accountability to their constituency? To claim legitimacy under the logic of membership, unions must be accountable to their union members and affiliates. This creates clear boundaries in terms of to whom they are accountable and for what. In contrast to claim legitimacy under the logic of attention, self-appointed NGO representatives must demonstrate public reputational accountability by drawing attention to their claim.

### 5.5.3.1 Membership-based accountability

We would always rather try and negotiate things than go out after companies publicly or resolving issues publicly. (GUF B.1)

We often are in a situation that we have relationships with these companies, or our affiliated unions in the countries have relationships and often good relationships with these companies. And they have to make a judgement call in terms of how far they can go without really putting lasting damage to the relationships that they have developed .... So we always have to kind of weigh up our means and tools and methods that we're using. (GUF B.2)

Being insiders to the employment relationship has important implications for accountability towards the represented. For unions, internal membership structures clearly define the boundaries of representation and relations of accountability: the boundaries are set by membership, the interests of their members and the preservation of the employment relationship. As several of our respondents emphasised, membership creates 'that great responsibility of accountability to our members' (GUF B.1). Not only can union members hold their union officers accountable for their performance (accountability through election), but unions have an important stake in the employment relationship and therefore the economic sustainability of the business: if the employment relationship ceases to exist then the representative loses her raison d'être. This reality has important implications for how unions negotiate with employers on behalf of their members. As insiders, they need to balance interests and demands with economic sustainability. This is seen to make them legitimate participants in negotiations with employers because their members will suffer the consequences of 'unreasonable' demands or solutions that threaten the viability of the enterprise (Budd, 2004). 'Beating people around the head and saying you're evil and you must sign this or else you'll burn in hell is never a great negotiating stance for a partnership', a respondent from the ETI explained, adding that unions therefore regarded the Accord 'not as a chance to bash companies but as a chance to engage them' (ETI.1).

The unions also viewed the Accord as a joint programme that both corporate and labour signatories had to deliver – they were jointly accountable for its success or failure. In contrast to NGOs, the unions were insiders and viewed as having 'as much skin in the game on this as the companies have', as an interviewee from the United Kingdom's Ethical Trading Initiative observed. 'So they're not sitting on the outside and watching: they're in the centre!' Hence, whereas NGOs were seen as enjoying 'freedom to agitate' because they lacked direct accountability for the effects of their campaigns, unions had to weigh up the interests of other parts of their membership. This came to a head when, in 2015, the NGO witness signatories published a report highly critical of the level of remediation carried out in H&M's supplier factories. This infuriated the GUFs but particularly IndustriALL, which believed they were accountable to H&M workers not just in Bangladesh, but across the world, and that in many spheres H&M was a high performer compared with nearly all other brands. They were reluctant to do 'lasting damage' to their relationship with H&M, with whom they have an IFA, because this could harm their ability to represent workers in other supply chains. As insiders to the employment relationship, they adopted the 'general position that we are a reasonable organisation and we will make demands on the basis of what we think is a kind of a reasonable thing to do' (TUC.1).

### 5.5.3.2 Attention-Based Accountability

We're always getting frustrated that they don't move quickly enough and they're always getting frustrated that we don't act without thinking it through. (NGO B.1)

So ... the typical labour rights campaigning NGOs ... they argue with very good reason that you'll get more from the campaigning end if you aren't talking behind closed doors. The position of ... labour right NGOs, is that you will achieve far more through public campaigning than you will through talking to companies. Or, you know, exclusively trying to negotiate with companies. And that's a very persuasive argument ... [they] are continually calling out the companies and they're in the media naming and shaming, Email actions, all that sort of stuff. (TUC.2)

Without a clearly defined authorising constituency, it is even less clear how workers can hold self-appointed NGO representatives accountable. Lacking such substantive authorisation, NGOs sought reputational accountability by basing their claims on those made by Bangladeshi workers themselves while placing them where greatest attention could be generated. By operating in the public sphere of consumption relations, accountability was hence generated from the public sphere – where claims could be accepted or rejected. Public reputational accountability, then, serves as an important discourse-based mechanism of accountability for self-appointed representatives, who are unlikely to be subject to more formal forms of accountability (Montanaro, 2012). Self-appointed representatives subject themselves to what Mansbridge (2009) calls 'deliberative accountability', where representatives seek accountability through public reasoning and discursive justification (Schormair and Gilbert, 2021). Ideally, they engage 'in two-way communication with constituents, particularly when deviating from the constituents' preferences' (Mansbridge, 2009: 370). Self-appointed representatives establish a reputation for certain positions and may be held accountable for their claims through the court of public opinion.

The NGOs' role as 'international watchdog' was particularly important in the context of the Bangladeshi textile sector. Not having to worry about doing damage to pre-existing relationships means that representative claim makers can both 'move quickly' – they can mobilise on the spot without having to worry about how this will affect relationships going forward. Thus, 'NGOs work differently and they can move faster' (NGO B.1). In interviews, union officials themselves recognised 'procedurally the TUC and unions act slower than NGOs which can probably make NGOs feel a bit like we don't do enough, we are not doing things ....  Whereas NGOs they're part of their currency ... they can kind of go to 100 immediately to get a quick media hit and a quick response' (TUC.1). The NGOs were thus regarded as 'vital in creating the energy and the noise and the push' (ETI.1) for companies to sign the Accord.

Legitimate claims thus differ from those that are merely successful in that they are perceived as legitimate 'by appropriate constituencies under reasonable conditions of judgment' (Saward, 2010: 144–145). For instance, authorising constituencies can hold NGOs accountable by removing themselves from mailing lists, cancelling donations or ceasing participation in programmes. This may involve publicly denouncing representative claims made on someone's behalf as false, skewed or otherwise objectionable. It denies the political theorists the role of adjudicator of legitimacy and instead leaves it to the appropriate constituency to accept or reject representative claims (Disch, 2015).

## 5.6 Conclusion

Our aim in this chapter has been to understand how Bangladeshi garment workers have been represented in the transnational governance process. We focused on the 'labour caucus' – signatory unions and NGOs – in representing workers and their interests in the creation and implementation of the Accord. To be sure, the Accord's focus on building and fire safety represents a very narrow representation of worker interests, which scholars have criticised as displacing represen- tation of other, more prominent, interests when asking 'actual' workers about fair wages, job security and other workplace conditions (Tanjeem, 2017; Kabeer et al., 2020) or even contesting the systemic asymmetries generated by neoliberal capitalist relations. Thus, we do not seek to present the Accord as the reflection of the 'authentic' preferences of Bangladeshi workers but as the contested outcome of the political processes of transnational representation, while neverthe- less acknowledging the Accord's role in protecting first and foremost the human right to life by significantly reducing the number of deadly factory accidents.

Thus, the case of the Accord suggests that representative alliances are highly effective in enhancing transnational representation. While previous scholarship has emphasised the multiplicity of actors involved in global governance arenas, it has not been quite clear how different types of actors contribute and create new opportunities for 'collabora- tive governance' (Rasche, 2010). Often, the Labour Caucus is seen as one homogenous actor, described under the broad heading of 'civil society'. Unions are not even considered as a relevant actor, as most focus is on consumption actors – those able to exercise pressure on the consumption relationship. However, the governance of labour rela- tions within supply chains must be viewed through the prism of both production and consumption relations and thus pay attention to both unions as the official representatives of labour within the sphere of the employment relationship and NGOs as self-appointed representatives of labour within the sphere of the consumption relationship.

As seen above, focusing on the different logics of representation also allows us to understand better the political dynamics of whose interests get represented and how representation is performed. Just as parties vie for the right to represent constituencies in electoral politics, trans- national representation is the outcome of political processes: competi- tion and collaboration among potential representatives who must demonstrate their legitimacy to represent. In the Bangladeshi case, due to the unions' weak local representative structures, representation tilted to where structures were strongest, namely GUFs' representative structures and their relationship with Western brands. For NGOs, the ability to make claims was strongest within a Western-media domin- ated global public sphere, where they could generate most attention.

The interplay between the two created representation where both were strongest. As a result, representation was targeted at Western brands and their consumers, rather than Bangladeshi employers. Thus, who got represented were manufacturing workers who produced for Western brands based on a union's structural relations across the supply chain and NGOs' ability to establish discursive links between consumers and workers evoked through claim-making. Not represented were garment workers who did not produce for Western brands or workers across the rest of the supply chain (cotton growers, weaving, transport workers, etc.). Nor were employers involved and represented. As we will explore in Chapter 7, the Accord's exclusion of employers was aimed at counterbalancing the extreme power asymmetries between unorganised workers and strongly organised employers in the BGMEA, which led to resistance to contestation.

# 6 | Creating Representation through Industrial Democracy versus CSR

## The Accord and Alliance as a Natural Experiment

The representation of interests has been the main focus of this book. Our central argument is that the independent representation of worker interests should be a core feature of transnational labour governance. However, with the exception of IFAs, there have been few such governance approaches where independent representation of worker interests has been a core feature. Many industrial relations activists and academics have shown scepticism about initiatives that claim to be socially responsible yet exclude democratic representation of workers. This is reflected in 'a degree of reluctance in both the HRM and IR communities to actively engage with CSR' (Preuss et al., 2009: 954), mirroring the reluctance of unionists to lend legitimacy to an approach that does not provide appropriate representation to labour actors (Preuss et al., 2015). In Chapters 3 and 5, we argued that industrial democracy carries with it important assumptions about who should represent workers and participate in governance systems (democratically elected worker representatives), where representation takes place (within the employment relationship) and what the content of labour governance (process rights) is. In contrast, CSR is typically advanced by actors who claim to act on behalf of workers without giving them an explicit say in governance instruments.

To understand better the role of worker representation in the construction of global labour governance, this chapter compares the two most significant private governance initiatives launched in response to the Rana Plaza disaster: the Accord and the Alliance for Bangladesh Worker Safety (the Alliance). Quite interestingly, the creation of the Accord and the Alliance provides the closest thing to a natural experiment in transnational labour governance as possible. On the surface, the two private initiatives appear very similar. Both are aimed at improving OSH in the Bangladesh garment supply chain and both pursued a similar course of action involving inspections and worker training. However, they were underpinned by very different logics of industrial democracy and CSR. The Accord was clearly designed to bring to the table those representing worker interests. The Alliance, based on a very traditional CSR approach, was often viewed as an initiative set up to mirror the Accord in all but two interrelated ways: the role of labour representatives in its governance and the extent to which it was legally binding. Their comparison allows us to understand what difference, if any, the role of labour representation makes in transnational labour governance.

The Accord is underpinned by principles of industrial democracy: Labour was represented based on the representative structures of workers. However, it deviates significantly from traditional industrial democracy in terms of engaging with brands, based on a CSR approach rather than the actual employers of workers. In the domain of supply chains, the emergence of CSR holds promise to contribute to promoting labour standards as transnational corporations assume quasi-governmental governance duties and fill regulatory voids left by the retreating state. Matten and Crane (2005; see also Williams, et al., 2017) observed forms of 'civil regulation', whereby corporations co-design forms of oversight of global employment relationships. This line of scholarship has somewhat 'mutated' the CSR concept in arguing for a more political conception of CSR in global supply chains where corporations take on the traditional functions of the state in supporting institutional frameworks (Scherer and Palazzo, 2011). Yet, even in this broader, more political conception of CSR, rather scant attention has been paid to the role of democratic participation of workers. Scholars have focused mainly on the role of NGOs and activists (Den Hond and De Bakker, 2007), while organised labour has generally been seen as excluded from the definition and practice of CSR. However, brands rarely engage directly with workers or representatives chosen by workers to defend their interests. That said, unions increasingly have engaged in complementary activities that induce brands to take responsibility for labour issues in their supply chains (Compa, 2004; Egels-Zanden, 2009). This has prompted a growing relationship between unions and NGOs in terms of building international alliances to leverage CSR commitments of brands and retailers (Preuss et al., 2015; Reinecke and Donaghey, 2015). Thus, the research question driving the chapter is to examine how differences in the logic of global labour governance translate into differences in design and implementation on the ground. What differences does the inclusion of worker representatives make in terms of the design and implementation of global labour governance in supply chains?

## 6.1 The Co-emergence of the Accord and the Alliance

While brands had no legal duty of care, pressure grew on them to take responsibility for the health and safety of garment workers after Rana Plaza. Two parallel initiatives emerged in response: first, as outlined in Chapter 4, the Accord was signed in May 2013, followed by the Alliance in July 2013.[1] On the surface, they appeared to be comparable, having as their central rationale worker safety in the Bangladesh ready-made garment sector. Yet, on closer examination, the initiatives represent paradigmatic cases of transnational co-determination (Accord) and industry self-regulation CSR (Alliance), differing considerably with regard to the role of labour representatives and governance dimensions, as outlined in Table 6.1.

Following the establishment of the Accord as outlined in previous chapters, pressure began to be placed on a number of brands that had not signed the Accord to join it. In particular, attention was placed on the US general retail giant Walmart and apparel chain Gap, due to their size but also because both were selling clothes produced in the Rana Plaza complex. It became evident very early on that Walmart, an aggressively anti-union retailer, would not sign a legally binding joint initiative with global union federations. Initially, many leading players from both the brand and union side of the Accord were hopeful that Gap would join. However, as time progressed, news emerged that Gap and Walmart were working together to establish an alternative to the Accord. The main reason attributed to Gap not joining the Accord was its legally binding nature. Thus, on 10 July 2013, the Alliance for Building and Worker Safety in Bangladesh was launched. Consistent with a CSR underpinning, the Alliance was essentially a voluntary approach by twenty-nine brands, all bar one (Australian brand Just Group) coming from North America. As will be explored in the remainder of the chapter, significant differences in approach were

[1] Assessments of factories not covered by the Accord and Alliance are carried out by engineering teams led by Bangladesh University of Engineering and Technology (BUET) and overseen by the Tripartite Committee in Bangladesh with the assistance of the ILO.

Table 6.1. *Comparison of the Bangladesh Accord and Alliance*

|  | Accord (as of May 2021) | Alliance (as of July 2018) |
|---|---|---|
| Governance model | Transnational co-determination | Industry self-regulation |
| Coverage | 1,646 factories | 654 factories (about 50% shared with Accord) |
| Unsafe factories reported to review panel | 34 | 26 |
| Duration | 5 years (2013–2018) + 3 years Transition Accord (2018–2021) | 5 years (2013–2018) |
| Legal commitments by signatory brands | 5 years' participation Membership fees Maintaining purchasing volumes Binding arbitration process in legal system of home country | Minimum 2 years' participation Membership fees |
| **Constituency** | | |
| Brands | >200 International brands from 20 countries. | 28 North-American retailers representing 90% of RMG exports to the United States from Bangladesh plus one Australian retailer. |
| Organised Labour | IndustriALL, UNIGlobal, 6 Bangladeshi unions (IndustriALL Bangladesh Council, BIGUF, BGWIF, NGWF, BRGWF, BGTLF, and UFGW) | None on board. Five members of Labor Committee |
| Other | Four international labour rights NGOs are 'witness signatories'. (Clean Clothes Campaign, Workers Rights Consortium, International Labor Rights Forum, Maquila Solidarity Network | 'Supporting associations': North American trade associations and the NGO BRAC. Li & Fung serves in an advisory capacity. |

**Table 6.1.** (*cont.*)

|  | Accord (as of May 2021) | Alliance (as of July 2018) |
|---|---|---|
| **Governance** | | |
| **Steering Committee** | 3 Brands + 3 Unions, chaired by ILO | 4 Brands + Bangladesh industry member + experts + elected chair |
| **Advisory** | Board of Advisors with Bangladesh industry associations BGMEA/ BKMEA | Board of Advisors with 12 multi-stakeholder industry experts Labour Committee of the Board |

linked to the nature of representation in the respective initiatives. This chapter focuses on three particular aspects in terms of comparing the Accord and the Alliance: their governance structures, their implementation and operation in Bangladesh and what replaced them in Bangladesh.

## 6.2 Governance Design

The governance design of the Accord and Alliance reflects the different commitment of each initiative to principles of industrial democracy and CSR: pluralist versus unitarist interest representation credible commitments versus flexible voluntarism and orientation towards input legitimacy.

### 6.2.1 Pluralism versus Unitarism in Governance Structure

A core difference between the industrial democracy and CSR approach is how they treat the role of interests and their representation. As outlined earlier, a central feature of the industrial democracy approach is its pluralist foundation, built on an assumption that the interests of labour and capital will often be divergent (Fox, 1975; Budd, 2004). There is thus an underlying understanding that this tension can never be fully resolved, but it is necessary to recognise its existence by the presence of the representatives of both interests (Edwards, 1986). In contrast, the CSR approach has generally been associated with a unitarist ideology that sees the interests of management and workers as shared. In this way, CSR responses are often driven by ideas of 'win–win' (Mintzberg, 1983) and justified in terms of the business case (Carroll, 1999); in other words, CSR interventions should take place because they are good for enterprise profitability rather than due to any idea of democracy. These differences were reflected in the Accord and the Alliance, with the representation playing a key role in the Accord with the Alliance adopting a more corporate driven approach.

### 6.2.2 Labour-Driven Governance in the Accord

The Accord presented a pluralist structure in which labour was recognised at the highest decision-making level and acted as an example of transnational co-determination. Central to such a pluralist approach was the recognition that employers and workers had differing interests and these interests needed to be represented in decision-making (Fox, 1974; for a discussion of recent developments in pluralism, see van Buren et al., 2021). As shown in Chapter 5, GUFs were heavily involved in the design of the Accord. IndustriALL and UniGlobal, representing garment workers in Bangladesh and retail workers in developed countries respectively, were at the forefront of negotiations with brands to push them to sign up to an agreement that labour actors had previously drafted but that had lacked sufficient commitments from brands to become live. Part of the rationale for GUFs to champion the Accord was the argument that traditional CSR initiatives, driven through social auditing, failed because they did not involve labour actors. As an experiment in transnational industrial democracy, the Accord presented an opportunity to integrate the principles of industrial democracy to develop more robust mechanisms of worker representation.

The Labour Caucus insisted on the Accord being not just a voluntary commitment but a legally binding agreement, previously unseen in transnational supply chain labour governance. Brand signatories were legally bound to contribute financially on a sliding scale up to US$0.5 million per annum, members agreed to maintain their purchasing volumes from Bangladesh for two years and disputes were to go to binding arbitration that could be enforced through the legal system in the home country of signatory brands. The fact that the ILO took on the role of independent chair of the Accord Steering Committee is indicative of the pluralist governance structure. Having both labour and business interests at the table, the Accord more closely resembled the ILO's tripartite governance structure than a CSR initiative, even if international brands rather than local employers of Bangladeshi workers represented business interests at the table. The Accord therefore sought to leverage the power of the brands via enforceable commitments, while minimising the degree to which the process was vulnerable to obstruction by local employers, who were excluded from the agreement. By leveraging brand power to constrain local employer behaviour, the Accord created space that previously did not exist for unions to play a meaningful role on safety issues.

The Accord's governance structure was designed to create a balance between the interests of labour and corporations. This created accountability and inevitably also rendered governance processes more conflictual. Ultimately, unions could attempt to hold companies accountable to the Accord's terms through binding arbitration, which rendered them powerful partners. As members of the Accord Steering Committee, unions raised controversial issues, such as brand responsibility for financing costly compensation and remediation. Unions were also the actors that handled complaints filed by Bangladeshi workers and raised them through the Accord, which otherwise may not have been addressed. The Accord was thus an attempt to create at least an embryonic form of transnational co-determination, where co-determination is understood as institutions that recognise 'labour's claim to a legitimate role in the running of companies and the economy' (Müller-Jentsch, 2003: 40).

### 6.2.3 Corporate-Driven Governance in the Alliance

Consistent with its CSR underpinning, the Alliance was essentially a voluntary business-led approach conducted by twenty-nine brands. Respondents described the Alliance as a 'me too' initiative that tried to make itself look like the Accord by adopting similar features. It was a collective approach by brands; shared broad commitments to workers' safety, training and voice; included specialised auditing for structural, electrical and fire safety; and published auditors' reports online. However, while on the surface the Accord and Alliance appeared similar, the Alliance did not include unions as signatories.

In fact, the prominent role of unions in the Accord was viewed as a key reason behind the emergence of the Alliance as an alternative to the Accord. The Alliance involved local unions only in an advisory capacity through the Board Labour Committee and workers had no formal voice in decision-making. Its board of directors was dominated by business interests: it included four brand representatives, three outside experts and an independent chair, and until July 2015, the president of the BGMEA as representative of local business interests. Described as learning from the 'shortcomings of the Accord' (Alliance.1), which faced strong criticism in Bangladesh for excluding local employers, the Alliance was instrumental in engaging with factory owners and the BGMEA. This explicit inclusion of local business actors rendered the Alliance more legitimate in the eyes of Bangladeshi employers and policy-makers. Nevertheless, the BGMEA president resigned his seat on the board in July 2015 over differences with the Alliance, which BGMEA interviewees highlighted was because he refused to be associated with a statement from the Alliance that was critical of the Bangladeshi RMG sector and it was made clear to him that all members of the Alliance Board were expected to sign it, leaving neither organisation having the BGMEA on its governing body. This approach by the Alliance was consistent with the 'dark side' of unitarism, where dissent from agreed approaches is generally not tolerated (Cullinane and Dundon, 2014).

## 6.2.4 Credible Commitments versus Flexible Voluntarism: Binding versus Voluntary Agreement

### 6.2.4.1 Credible Commitments in the Accord

A key difference was the legally binding nature of the Accord compared with the more traditional, unenforceable CSR approach by the Alliance. The rationale for requiring Accord signatory companies to maintain purchasing volumes from Bangladesh for two years was that employers could invest in developing workplace safety while having a steady stream of orders to fulfil. Thus, the Accord was designed to develop stability while employers made the structural adjustments necessary to fulfil the principles of the Accord. Commitment to a legally binding agreement and funding a five-year programme was described as assurance that brands would not 'cut and run' out of Bangladesh but were prepared to take responsibility.

#### 6.2.4.2 The Alliance's Flexible Voluntarism

In contrast, the Alliance was strongly aligned with Carroll's (1999) notion that CSR as 'soft' regulation is a voluntary commitment by corporations that is typically motivated by a business case. Voluntarism and the primacy of business interests were stressed in the deeds of the Alliance:

The Corporation [Alliance] is a voluntary association of business organizations the primary purpose of which ... is to further their common business interests by strengthening worker safety conditions at ready-made garment ('RMG') factories within the business organizations' supply chains in Bangladesh.

While the Alliance also emphasised that it was legally binding, this was limited to fee payments by brand members. Brands paid up to US$1 million per year, relative to their purchasing volumes, for an initial minimum of two years followed by a one-year notice period. Unlike the Accord, there was no commitment to maintain purchasing volumes or to legally binding arbitration. Where included, stakeholders were used in an advisory capacity rather than through a negotiated co-management approach. As such, worker safety was seen as an issue between the business interests in the supply chain, rather than an issue for both workers and business to solve. Thus, the Alliance resembled the legal construction of voluntary codes of conduct whose intended beneficiaries were companies rather than workers (Lund-Thomsen, 2008). This point about voluntary codes was clarified in 2007, prior to Rana Plaza, when the International Labor Rights Forum brought a suit in California against Walmart on behalf of workers for code prohibitions on overtime and non-payment of overtime wages (ILRF, 2015). Walmart admitted to the courts that its code of conduct was intended to protect it from reputational harm, which meant workers had no standing to sue.

### 6.2.5 Orientation towards Input Legitimacy

The Accord and Alliance were not simply competing initiatives, but their coexistence created strong legitimacy pressures to perform under the global spotlight, especially since comparisons were inevitably drawn (Labowitz and Baumann-Pauly, 2014). Thus, the coexistence of the Accord and Alliance led to a 'levelling up' effect. To begin with, input legitimacy was scrutinised from different sides. In the United States, student-led actions and protests were initiated against the Alliance and its member brands for having no worker representatives, while in Bangladesh criticism was levelled against the Accord for excluding employers. To placate local employers, the Accord introduced formal meetings twice a year between the Accord steering committee and the BGMEA but without offering a seat on the steering committee.

Overall, though, the Accord had established a high bar in terms of worker representation, brand commitments, inspection quality and transparency commitments. To be able to defend their program as credible, Alliance brands had no choice but to embrace some of the elements of the Accord (though not all of them), including commitments that no brand had previously made. For instance, by establishing a 'Board Labor Committee', the Alliance created quasi-representation for workers that it had previously excluded. However, this was criticised as a 'token' board with only an advisory function. Unions were not part of the Alliance board of directors and thus had no institutional power to hold corporate signatories such as Walmart, Target or Gap to account. Both IndustriALL and the ITUC made it clear they expected their affiliates to decline invitations to participate. This led to the ironic situation that a Walmart-led initiative drew legitimacy from the participation of unions affiliated with the Marxist-Leninist World Federation of Trade Unions.

Nevertheless, the creation of the Alliance Board Labor Committee created a slightly more pluralist approach that led to important changes: Nine months into its life, and following requests from the Board Labor Committee, an amendment to the by-laws introduced a clause to prevent reprisal against workers, which had hitherto been missing. However, while the Accord clause merely required a worker to believe the building was unsafe to benefit from its protection from 'undue consequences', the Alliance required 'an imminent and serious danger to his/her life'. In addition, under the Accord, a factory found to be taking retaliatory action against workers for raising safety concerns became ineligible to supply for all Accord signatory brands, while the Alliance declared the supplier as being in breach of the by-law but left the decision about whether to continue business to the discretion of individual brands.

In addition to pressures regarding input legitimacy, pragmatic and operational considerations placed pressures in terms of output legitimacy on both initiatives to harmonise their approaches. As Accord and Alliance brands often sourced from common factories, consistency necessitated common structural, fire and electrical standards. Harmonisation was achieved through an 'intense and ongoing period of coordination and collaboration' in which the ILO (2015: 9) played 'a central role in facilitating stakeholder cooperation in what have at times been complex negotiations'. Both initiatives agreed a common set of standards based on the Bangladesh National Building Code and a common reporting template to ensure consistency between inspection reports produced by the different initiatives, as well as mutual recognition of audits in factories that were shared between Accord and Alliance brands. Remediation plans followed the inspections and follow-up inspections were carried out at factories. Where these were not carried out to a sufficient level, both agreements had the capacity to declare factories non-compliant and ineligible to supply signatory companies. By May 2021, the Accord had inspected 2,280 individual factories, with 1,692 still under the Accord's remit. In terms of those no longer covered by the Accord, 190 factories had been declared ineligible to supply Accord firms, 173 were closed, 170 relocated and 72 declared out of scope. In addition, 33,242 follow-up inspections took place across the three areas covered: 12,941 in fire safety, 13,210 in electrical safety and 7,091 in structural safety. When the Alliance exited in 2018, it had inspected 714 individual factories with 654 still covered by the Alliance. Over its five years, the Alliance suspended a total of 178 factories, with factories eligible to reapply to be considered compliant by the Alliance when they believed they could be deemed compliant. In sum, the high bar set by the Accord created a strong motivation for the Alliance to engage in levelling up. Thus, governance competition with a high-level initiative led to a stronger programme than would likely have been the case had the Alliance existed alone. The Accord also faced comparison with the Alliance and thus was motivated to showcase the rigour of its approach. Yet, as outlined below, the implementation of the two initiatives also revealed the significance of the differences in their underlying logics.

## 6.3 Implementation: Capacity-Building versus Problem-Solving

The Accord and Alliance differed in terms of the extent to which they aimed to develop worker representation to solve problems on their own behalf. The Accord emphasised capacity-building because it was underpinned by an approach that workers need to be enabled to act on their own behalf and make safety self-sustaining rather than businesses taking care of their interests. Putting democratic worker voice at the core of safety processes, it took a proactive role in including workers in safety management and protecting them from retaliation. In contrast, the Alliance was very much driven by an approach aimed at putting right the faults in the Bangladesh RMG sector that had led to the Rana Plaza disaster. As such, the Alliance was driven by a more project-oriented, problem-solving approach.

### 6.3.1 Building Worker Voice under Unfavourable Conditions

Both the Accord and Alliance aimed to establish OSH Committees with elected worker representatives, in line with Bangladesh labour law and in recognition of the need to create an internal, workplace-based mechanism to address safety concerns. However, given that worker representatives were selected rather than elected in most factories, this proved to be a highly significant obstacle. Both initiatives established safety committee pilot programmes with the aim of rolling them out more broadly.

The immediate demands of carrying out factory inspections meant that for the Accord, establishing worker representation was initially placed on the back burner. In late 2015, however, the Accord started working with approximately seventy unionised factories to establish OSH representation. While this picked the low-hanging fruit, as these factories did not require the organisation of elections, the fact that these OSH committees were overseen by the Accord meant that worker representatives enjoyed additional protection from retaliation over safety-related issues. Over the next five years, from 2015 to 2020, the training of workers for membership of occupational safety and health committees became a major focus of the Accord's work. Realising this, unions leveraged OSH committees as a protection mechanism for the union officers they placed on the committees. In particular, a change was made to the 2018 Accord to guarantee freedom of association in relation to OSH issues. By framing the Rana Plaza disaster as an issue of worker disempowerment and lack of voice rather than just poor infrastructure, the Accord attempted to harness international pressure on Bangladesh to accept the need for effective industrial relations against resistance from local industry. By May 2021, of 1,581 factories expected to complete the OSH requirements, 1,022 (64.64 per cent) had completed the training, 76 (4.8 per cent) had completed the 2013 Accord requirements but not yet the 2018 update and 230 (31.6 per cent) had less than the required training. By the end of its term, across the 654 factories covered by the Alliance, it reported a total of 181 active safety committees – that is, in 28 per cent of factories covered. These committees covered 238,809 workers in total and trained 30,000 safety committee members.

While both the Accord and the Alliance granted unionised workers – or representatives in non-unionised workplaces – the right to be present during inspections in principle, the Accord offered active intervention, which was necessary as implementation proved challenging in practice. In the social auditing model, workers are excluded from inspections and reports are proprietary to corporate clients. Participation of worker representatives required the Accord to work closely with unions to overcome resistance from factory managers, as well as to be willing to address violence and threats to union members. The Accord employed field workers who trained and worked proactively with union leaders of all fourteeen IndustriALL affiliates in Bangladesh to inform them about their rights under the Accord to participate in inspections and obtain copies of inspection reports, made available in the local language. In cases where management refused to let unions participate in inspections, informed workers were able to get Accord case handlers to intervene and ensure their participation.

While inspections with the input of genuine labour voice occurred in relatively few factories, where they did occur, they represented a powerful mechanism to strengthen workers' voice by legitimising their representation. In the societal context of factory hierarchies where workers enjoy very little respect, interviewees highlighted the symbolic importance of workers seeing union leaders participating actively in factory inspections. A local union president 'to be seen walking through the factory with those inspectors' (BD Unionist.1) was considered a powerful demonstration that workers were eligible to speak on the same level with outside authorities and managers. In sum, the Accord realised it had to invest in longer-term capacity-building to support and defend workers facing threats, violence and intimidation to enable and sustain their genuine participation beyond one-off external interventions.

## 6.3.2  Workers' Compensation and Factory Closures

The way the Accord and Alliance dealt with the issue of workers' compensation for loss of earnings in cases of (unsafe) factory closures revealed key differences in their approaches: brand-benevolence versus labour-negotiation. While closures following the initial inspections only affected a small proportion of workers, it was heavily politicised. Out of 1,454 Accord and 662 Alliance inspections, 34 Accord and 26 Alliance factories went to the Review Panel, established under the Bangladeshi National Action Plan, to decide on factory closures. These were factories that potentially posed immediate threats to life. This led to sixteen closures under the Accord and eight under the Alliance, of which four were shared. Bangladeshi law (Labor Act, 2006, Art. 20) requires that when workers' employment is terminated due to retrenchment (akin to redundancy), the affected employees must be paid compensation in the amount of thirty days' wages for each year of service. In practice, though, it was often difficult for workers to pursue their rights. Thus, both the Accord and Alliance put in place different compensation mechanisms to deal with the employment implications of factory closures.

### 6.3.2.1  Alliance: A Brand-Benevolence Approach

The Alliance pursued a 'brand-benevolence' approach that relied not on workers to pursue their interests but on brands to act benevolently on behalf of workers. The Alliance required both employers and brands to pay two months' compensation each. The contribution by brands was paid directly from the Alliance member–funded Worker Safety Fund, which reserved 10 per cent of its resources for the support of temporarily displaced workers. This provided a quick response mechanism to make interim payments of up to two months' salary paid directly by the Alliance. However, once this payment was made, the remaining two months' severance was an issue to be dealt with by the employer. The extent to which this was paid was unclear, as workers often moved onto other jobs quickly and legal enforcement in Bangladesh is limited.

### 6.3.2.2  Accord: A Labour-Negotiation Approach

Under the Accord, workers were entitled to six months' compensation if the factory was temporarily shut and four months, in line with

Bangladeshi law, if the factory was permanently shut. Out of eight factories that were shut (with eighteen reopening after remediation and eight factory relocations) in the early rounds of inspections, workers received full benefits in one, and two to three months' compensation (i.e., short of the legal requirement) in only three cases. In four cases, compensation was never fully finalised. Where a need for compensation arose, the Accord pursued a negotiation approach premised on the principle that compensation should be negotiated between employers and workers, that workers should be enabled to pursue their own interests and that employers, rather than brands, should be made to take responsibility. Both brands and unions agreed that it was important to create a strong expectation of employer responsibility within the Bangladesh context and to end a culture in which factory owners could 'cut and run' with the profits while abandoning their legal responsibilities towards workers.

In the few cases where workers were only paid a lump sum severance, the Accord heavily relied on workers to raise the issue and put pressure on employers and brands. While some brands were responsive, overall the minutes of the Accord Steering Committee meetings recorded general criticism of brands not making adequate efforts. 'This was the most frustrating part . . .. They were really slow to step in and put pressure on the suppliers', said one labour rights activist (NGO B.3). GUFs took an active role in supporting negotiations across the supply chain. IndustriALL employed one staff member in Europe and two in Bangladesh to facilitate conversations among workers, unions and brands. Where needed, they put pressure on the brands sourcing from closed factories by documenting non-compliance with the Accord, which opened the road to legal arbitration. Working in collaboration with IndustriALL and other international partners such as the Worker Rights Consortium provided local unions with an important opportunity to build capacity in pursuing negotiation skills, which were often absent due to a confrontational tradition of union–management relations. Moreover, once compensation payments were achieved, it allowed local unions to showcase their capacity to pursue workers' interests.

However, in the context of low-paid, female migrant workers with low literacy from rural areas, the Accord's negotiation approach was perceived as a cumbersome and 'very slow process'. Delays in compensation payments were seen as inadequate help to low-paid workers who needed the money immediately to sustain their livelihoods. In one case, the negotiation of compensation took almost three years to finalise. The case was one where multiple buyers, who were both Accord members and non-Accord members, were sourcing from the factory. In addition, a notorious 'yellow' union (that was not a signatory to the Accord) agreed a compensation deal that significantly undercut both the legal and Accord minima. In this context, it required reopening negotiations and a significant amount of pressure over a period of more than year after the 'compensation deal' with the yellow union to deliver workers an improved deal. In addition, negotiating in permanently closed factories was difficult as neither unions nor brands had much leverage where factory owners decided to discontinue all work in the enterprise. Yet the Accord provided a platform for negotiations to take place: without the Accord, the pathway for workers to receive any payment would have been shut off on closure.

Trade unionists interviewed, including some Accord signatories, expressed greater satisfaction with the Alliance on the speed of compensation, which workers often received in part within days, which meant they could seek alternative employment. Even though the Accord required an extra two months' payment, in taking a principled position that the employers pay compensation, it was much more difficult to enforce. However, while the Alliance provided a straightforward solution in the short term, it did little to develop longer term associational capacity and negotiation skills for union federations to address other employment-related issues. In sum, the Alliance's focus on problem solving for, not by, workers proved more effective in terms of compensation speed, leading to more immediate income payments for workers in need. In contrast, the Accord relied on the active role of labour actors in demanding compensation, thus trying to develop capacity, even if this was seen as slow and insufficient to serve workers' immediate needs.

### 6.3.3 Dealing with Complaints: Utilisation of Workers' Voice

Both the Alliance and the Accord emphasised the need for workers to be able to voice safety concerns, yet they pursued different mechanisms – an individualised versus a collective mechanism of voice. The focus on worker voice grew out of the recognition that Rana Plaza could have been prevented if workers had had a voice to refuse unsafe work conditions. But given low union density – with a union registered in only 21 out of 598 Alliance and 65 out of 1,500 Accord factories at the time of the disaster – facilitating worker voice was a challenging task.

### 6.3.3.1 Alliance Helpline 'Amader Kotha': Utilisation of Individual Voice

The Alliance set up a toll-free worker helpline (Alliance, 2015) to provide workers with an independent reporting channel to raise safety concerns anonymously. The local Bangla name 'Amader Kotha' ('Our Voice') implies a collective approach. But the helpline was designed as an individualised channel helping the Alliance to trouble-shoot problems where they occurred. The Alliance (2015) marketed this mechanism as a 'new, innovative approach to workplace problem solving' that aligned with the interests of factory managers as it 'can be used to boost worker morale', consistent with a more unitarist approach. Under this approach, each worker in the 1,017 factories covered by the scheme was required to wear the 'Amader Kotha' helpline card on their badge. In its final report in 2018, the Alliance reported that the hotline was operational in 1,017 factories with 1,508,007 workers, covering almost all Alliance and some non-Alliance factories. Given the lack of collective representation and functioning worker–management dialogue, the helpline was easily accessible to workers with low levels of education. Cooperation with the Bangladeshi NGO, Phulki, which had a long-term presence in factories as a childcare provider, was an attempt to gain workers' trust. When a complaint was received, issues were passed onto factory managers and where serious safety concerns were raised, Alliance technical experts become directly involved.

Statistical diagnostics provides a tool for the Alliance to analyse caller trends. From its inception in July 2014 until the end of the Alliance in 2018, approximately 233,000 calls were made with the Alliance reporting 600 calls per month in 2018. Some 17 per cent of reported issues were categorised as 'safety' issues, while 83 per cent were 'non-safety' issues. Curiously, the Alliance included 3 per cent of issues raised around physical abuse of workers and worker unrest under the 'non-safety' heading. Urgent safety issues included factory fires, locked exits, cracks in beams, columns and walls, shaking walls or windows and sparking or short-circuits. This indicates that the hotline served as a useful mechanism to report life-threatening issues such as locked fire exits, the cause of 117 deaths in Tazreen in November 2012. However, the crude classification system of worker concerns into what counts as 'safety' or 'urgent safety' raises questions over how workers, who were routinely silenced and punished for raising concerns by factory management, could voice complex grievances that may not have been easily classifiable. The fact that most calls were made from outside of the workplace indicates that the helpline was used as a one-way communication channel for individual voice that workers found easier to access away from the workplace, rather than a mechanism to raise grievances collectively in the workplace where they occur. With 67 per cent of helpline users being men, the helpline also suffered from the under-representation of women, potentially perpetuating the existing silencing of women's voices in the workplace. In sum, the Alliance Worker Helpline illustrated a problem-solving mechanism that offered speed and scope in implementation but relied on brand-sponsored external intermediaries rather than utilising or developing workers' own capacities to solve such problems.

### 6.3.3.2 Accord Complaints Mechanism: Utilisation of Collective Voice

The Accord sought to develop a mechanism of collective voice alongside the capacity for individual complaints. The Accord developed a complaints mechanism through which workers, unions or brands could collectively bring a complaint against a factory for unsafe workplaces or worker victimisation. After hearing the facts, the Accord took on an arbitrator role and produced a 'Resolution' that decided the Accord position on the case. Complaints received by the Accord are outlined in Figure 6.1. What is particularly interesting here is that the number of complaints, and the rate at which they were received, increased even though compliance also increased at the same time. This period also coincides with the establishment of OSH Committees in the factories. One plausible inference is that as the Accord became embedded, particularly in the form of the OSH Committees, workers exercised these institutions of voice. Such complaints, from a pluralist perspective, should be regarded as a positive achievement for the Accord rather than a failure: while the complaints may indicate worker safety issues, the fact that people felt able to voice their concerns to initiate a complaint is in itself a successful outcome.

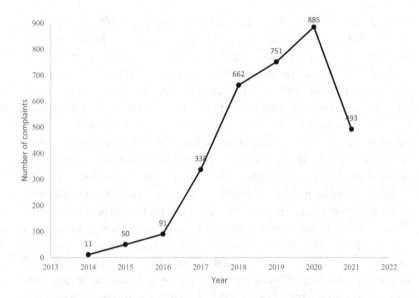

Note: 2021 figures only run to May 2021

**Figure 6.1** Complaints filed to Accord signatories, 2014–2021

The strengths and the weaknesses of this approach have been demonstrated in two cases. The first time the Accord complaints mechanism was truly tested on a freedom of association issue involved the Dress and Dismatic factory in Rampura, Dhaka. Management was resistant to allowing worker representatives to accompany a factory inspection in 2014. This escalated six months later when union members, using the Accord inspection report, reported weight overload to the Accord. This prompted an unannounced visit by the Accord. When the factory management retaliated against nine workers by forcing their resignation, they complained to the Accord. Despite it being a rather long, drawn-out process, the workers decided to keep fighting with support of their union. After six months of investigation under the official complaints procedure, the Accord drew up a resolution ordering the reinstatement and back-payment of wages for the nine workers and made clear that the factory had to comply if they wanted to supply Accord brands. In December 2015, this was implemented by management.

The second case involves BEO Apparel, a supplier to the German discounter Lidl, which employed approximately 1,000 workers in

Gazipur, a suburb of Dhaka. The factory-level union complained to the Worker Rights Consortium about a number of workplace issues in September 2014. One was related to a boiler explosion, making it an Accord-related issue of worker safety. When the Accord got involved, BEO management first retaliated against the unionised workers who complained, claiming it was over performance issues, and later sacked forty-eight workers who had participated in an Accord-convened meeting. Acting on the complaint filed on the grounds that BEO fired workers in retaliation for raising safety issues, the Accord subsequently issued a resolution against the factory and ordered reinstatement of the workers. Despite numerous meetings and negotiations between management, owners, unions and the Accord, with the involvement of the Worker Rights Consortium and UNI Global, the factory management refused to reinstate the workers. The conflict erupted in violence on 16 February 2015, when Accord negotiators and staff from Lidl importers Distra and Chicca witnessed the beating with sticks and iron bars of the union general secretary and employees and were themselves only able to leave factory premises after summoning the police. Fifteen days later, the factory owner decided to close the factory, as well as another factory, as Accord brands were required to refuse to source from a factory under the same ownership. Workers were paid the legal severance payment and back-payment to the union members who were sacked.

In both cases, workers went for over six months without pay but eventually received it, even if factory closure was a highly unsatisfactory outcome in one case. However, such cases set important precedents in terms of the Accord enforcing standards including freedom of association. Both cases contributed to capacity-building as the unions had to develop skills to make claims supported by evidence, negotiate with employers and leverage brand relationships to exert pressure.

In comparison, the Alliance's approach was primarily one of identifying individual voice first. This approach viewed safety as being an issue for the Alliance and factory management to solve rather than being an ongoing capacity issue for workers to negotiate. External support can provide effective and immediate intervention but lacks a longer-term mechanism when funding is withdrawn. In contrast, the Accord focused on developing collective worker capacity to create a self-sustaining mechanism. However, the complaints mechanism was a long process and difficult for non-unionised workers to access. In addition, developing collective processes requires a favourable institutional framework supported by legal enforcement and the willingness of management to support, both of which are lacking in the Bangladesh context.

## 6.4 Institutional Legacy

Both the Accord and the Alliance were established for an initial period of five years, with both due to expire in mid-2018. However, in retrospect, the extent to which these arrangements could overhaul the sector in Bangladesh and achieve their goals in five years was overly optimistic. This was particularly the case for the Accord, due to its underlying principle of being built upon foundations of worker representation with its dual goals of both improving the state of factories in the immediate term but also building systems of representation in the area of OSH within its timeline. While the Alliance always took the position that it was a five-year book-ended programme, by the midway point of the Accord from late 2015, discussions had already begun about extending the Accord as the Accord view was that it was necessary to build institutions for the future. This was summed up by one interviewee who stated that 'the real difference between the Accord and the Alliance is . . . that the Accord is trying to build something for after 2018 [when it was initially due to expire], while the Alliance is just trying to solve a problem in the short-term' (Accord.2). The next section will examine each in turn in terms of how they came to an end and what was ultimately to replace them.

### 6.4.1 The Accord: Building Institutional Offspring

Very early in its life, it became apparent that the Accord would struggle fully to reach its dual objectives of remedying all existing safety issues in factories and building a system of employee representation as a means of preventing future safety issues from developing. For this reason, negotiations started about what would come after the Accord was due to expire in 2018. It was clear that it could not just dissolve. Participants were eager to complete the outstanding work: however, they were equally eager to ensure that something with equal strength was in place that would ensure worker safety going forward. It was recognised though the Accord could not regulate the Bangladesh RMG sector ad infinitum: on the one hand, given its focus on democratic input, there was a recognition from parties across the board that having a largely transnationally driven system of governance was not sustainable in the long run and instead a system with key input from Bangladeshi actors was deemed necessary. On the other hand, actors in the Accord believed that there was a significant lack in capacity within Bangladesh for this function to be handed over in 2018. In addition, following their exclusion from the Accord and their withdrawal from the Alliance, a moderate faction of the BGMEA started to work on a proposal to develop a Bangladeshi alternative to the Accord and the Alliance, which will be discussed in Chapter 7. In early 2018, the parties agreed to extend the Accord to gain more time to complete the work but also to ensure that some regulatory system would be in place afterwards. In this context, a 'Transition Accord' was concluded – to the shock of the BGMEA, which had lobbied for an earlier transfer of regulatory power.

The Transition Accord took with it the principal institutional features of the original Accord. In terms of signatory companies, while 221 companies signed up to the original Accord, 205 signed up to the 2018 Transition Accord. While this was fewer signatories than to the original Accord, this was not something of concern to either corporate or union signatories interviewed, as more workers were covered by the 2018 agreement and it also meant some of the smaller brands with less implementing power were not involved. A number of operational changes were introduced. The most controversial was a change made with a new clause 12.b, where OSH Committee representatives were to receive training that included issues around 'freedom of association' in relation to individual OSH. This caused particular consternation with Bangladesh employers who believed it was a means of forcing freedom of association on them in all areas. Resistance from national actors meant that legacy building was less than straightforward. Following the launch of the Transition Accord, pressure increased from the Bangladeshi government and employers to stop the Accord operating in Bangladesh. As will be outlined in Chapter 7, from 2018 through to the end of August 2021, protracted legal and political exchanges occurred around the Accord. Yet it is significant that, in addition to the Accord itself, two direct institutional offspring emerged from the Accord.

First, participants tried to replicate the success of the Accord governance model in other supply chains and extend it beyond health and safety. In this spirit, Action. Collaboration. Transformation (ACT) was launched in 2015 between twenty global brands and IndustriALL, with the aim of developing structures of sector-level collective bargaining in eight garment-producing economies, including Bangladesh. The task itself is a considerable one and IndustriALL interviewees recognised this. As in the Accord, Inditex and H&M are key actors on the brand side. While the scope and operation of ACT are beyond this book, it is important to highlight that ACT emerged as a 'spillover' (Ashwin et al., 2020) from the work of the Accord.

Second, throughout the three years toing and froing over the future of the Accord, the Accord also worked closely on the transition towards the Ready-Made-Garment Sustainability Council (RSC) in Bangladesh, agreeing to hand over its regulatory capacity held in its Dhaka office (trained inspectors, systems, equipment, etc.) to the RSC. It bargained with the BGMEA over representation of actors in the governance of the RSC with the aim of carrying forward the legacy of equal worker representation. Initially, IndustriALL, UNI Global and local unions in Bangladesh were to be part of the RSC and its board of directors. However, in May 2021, IndustriALL and UNI Global, the labour signatories of the Bangladesh Accord, gave notice to withdraw from the RSC. The unions' threat to refuse to participate in what they saw as an ineffective approach raised significant questions about the credibility of the RSC as an effective worker safety organisation.

In August 2021 the Accord constituents – brands and unions – announced that it was to transform into the 'International Accord' – a twenty-six-month legally binding agreement to make ready-made garment (RMG) factories safe with an initial group of seventy-seven brand signatories (growing to ninety-one as of September 2021). Its stated aims include working alongside the RSC in Bangladesh to ensure worker safety and also to extend the approach to at least one other country within two years. While at time of writing it is too early to analyse this initiative, it is notable that the positive experience of the Accord and the fact that serious work remains to be done in relation to safety in Bangladesh have led to a situation where some of the most significant global brands have decided to extend their working relationships with IndustriALL based on the experience of the Accord.

### 6.4.2 Alliance: Fading Out in the Background

In contrast, in 2018 the Alliance ended its operations in Bangladesh and declared that its work in transforming the sector was done. Unlike the Transition Accord, Alliance brands created a new initiative, called Nirapon, as the Alliance's nominated successor. Twenty-one of the twenty-nine Alliance brands signed up to work with this initiative, yet Nirapon marked a substantial move away from the approach previously adopted by the Alliance back towards the previous social auditing approach. This was a very typical certification approach: factories that wished to supply these brands were expected to be certified under Nirapon by international engineering company Elevate. What it retained was the use of the individualised voice mechanism of the Amader Kotha safety hotline.

Under the new approach, a major change that proved very unpopular with factory management in Bangladesh was a switch in the financing model from one of 'brand pays' to that of 'supplier pays' for inspections and auditing. This approach also shifted the risk away from brands and onto factories, as factories had to have certification to compete for contracts. One irony was that factory owners who had extolled the positives of the more 'flexible approach' of the Alliance now expressed extreme frustration with its successor, the Nirapon approach, by saying:

> So they want us to pay them a fee, then they want us to go to one of their six recommended people and then ask these people to come and further evaluate us. We have to give them air tickets, we have to give them transportation, and we have to pay for accommodation if they want it, and on top of that we have to pay them a fee to come and actually carry out the work.... And why am I supposed to pay all these charges and go to all these recommended people and pay more? I mean, who's giving me this money? (Factory Owner 1)

This point proved to be highly contentious and a Bangladeshi factory owner began a lawsuit against Nirapon based around the fee structure that was being imposed. In October 2019, the Bangladeshi High Court imposed a six-month ban on Nirapon conducting factory inspections and training, which was upheld on appeal to the Supreme Court in December 2019. The Supreme Court asked Nirapon to return to explain why its operations could not be carried out by the Bangladeshi RSC. On 29 May 2020, a week in advance of the judgment being made and just as the six-month period was ending, Nirapon announced it was 'streamlining' its processes, withdrawing from operating directly in Bangladesh and that it would operate as 'Nirapon 2.0' from the United States instead with effect from 31 May 2020, two days later. On 3 June 2020, the Bangladeshi court announced its decision to impose a court order to stop Nirapon from operating within Bangladesh. At the time of writing, approximately twenty-one months after this date, there have been no updates to the Nirapon website, though Elevate published a story in August 2021 claiming it was carrying out the work. In sum, there was no attempt at building a legacy or to utilise the governance capacity from the Alliance.

## 6.5 Conclusion

While there are tensions between the industrial democracy and CSR approaches to transnational labour governance, this chapter highlights that the two approaches are not mutually exclusive: the Accord, as a form of transnational co-determination, was rooted in the organising principles of industrial democracy but with elements of CSR as well. The Alliance, as a form of industry self-regulation, was rooted in the principles of CSR. These underlying principles played important roles in how the programmes respectively rolled out and in terms of what they sought to achieve in the longer term.

The Accord demonstrated a strongly pluralist orientation with inclusion of worker representatives in its core governance structure, while the Alliance demonstrated a more unitarist approach but with the addition being made of worker representatives in an advisory capacity. This shift in the Alliance towards some, if limited, representation of labour illustrates the pressures for input legitimacy it faced – especially following its comparison to the Accord. In terms of input legitimacy, the Accord contains significant institutional actors in transnational employment relations. However, it must be noted that in terms of both density and coverage in Bangladesh, the unions are far from being encompassing groups (Olson, 1965) that can genuinely claim a wide span of representation. In addition, the exclusion of the actual employers, which will be picked up in Chapter 7, diverges somewhat from the industrial democracy ideal. In terms of output legitimacy, a key feature of the work of the Accord was to develop a context where workers become agents for their own interests, which is aligned with the under-pinning logic of industrial democracy.

Without doubt, this was one of the most difficult tasks that the Accord set itself, as there was little existing institutional support or political appetite for worker agency in Bangladesh. The CSR approach of the Alliance favoured external intervention – with, for example, an external contractor providing its helpline and then intervening rather than assisting workers in bringing and processing threats collectively. Similarly, in the area of worker compensation for factory closures, providing quick and efficient recourse for workers comes at the expense of developing worker agency. In terms of credible commitment versus flexible voluntarism, the Accord's legally binding nature in three areas meant that brands were legally accountable in terms of ensuring that contracts with non-compliant factories were suspended or termin-ated. This level of enforceability was a major departure from voluntary social auditing, where credible sanctions are rarely applied. The Alliance followed this approach and, while legally binding in a narrower sense, the coexistence of the Accord has helped to ensure that inspection standards remain high.

While CSR alone does not bring about meaningful institutional change (Bartley and Egels-Zandén, 2015), a key advantage of the CSR approach is that it can bring about immediate problem-solving when there is a lack of an institutional framework in global supply chain contexts, demonstrating the need of external intervention through market power. By using brands' financial resources, the Alliance was able to make short-term effective interventions by paying compensation directly out of a central fund. In doing so, while workers may not have received as much as they would have been entitled to under the Accord, the speed at which payments were made enabled workers to move into new jobs more quickly and with less financial precarity.

The industrial democracy approach offered lessons in terms of the need to build a participatory mechanism for labour involvement to allow labour actors to pursue their own interests in the long term by building mechanisms of worker voice. The Accord placed significant stress on building capacity to enable workers to develop meaningful collective representation in the area of health and safety as a preventa-tive mechanism, but also in the area of workers' rights more generally, such as compensation and complaints. However, capacity-building for worker representation is contingent on embeddedness within functioning institutional frameworks, both at the national and international levels. The absence of collective worker representation capacities and weak legal support test the ability to develop meaningful collective, representation mechanisms. Unions are thus more dependent on collaboration with other governance actors. By bringing together actors from along the global supply chain, the Accord demonstrated an effort to build effective processes of 'transnationally coordinated global labour solidarity' (Wells, 2007: 577). While much of the mainstream CSR literature tends to downplay tensions between corporate interests and those of other stakeholders, including workers, transnational co-determination based on industrial democracy affords a more open acknowledgement and accommodation of diverging interests. CSR-based self-regulatory initiatives often seek to 'look like' more socially controlled initiatives, and are thus 'remarkably similar in their organizational design, processes and rhetoric' despite lacking pluralist control (Dingwerth and Pattberg, 2009: 708; Fransen, 2012). But the risk is that diverging voices are marginalised and resulting policy instruments deviate significantly from those preferred by beneficiaries (Khan et al., 2007; Koenig-Archibugi and MacDonald, 2013). This underlines the importance of structural representation where recognised labour representatives participate in both the design and implementation of global labour governance.

# 7 | When Transnational Governance Meets National Actors

## The Politics of Exclusion in the Bangladesh Accord

Without doubt, the Bangladesh Accord, with its brand-labour governance structure, has been innovative in terms of transnational labour governance. That said, the Accord departed from the norm of industrial democracy in one important area. A central feature of the industrial democracy approach is the idea that capital and labour engage with each other and make mutual commitments about their future behaviour, generally in the form of employers making commitments on wages and other terms and conditions, with labour agreeing not to carry out strike action in return. The Accord differed in this important aspect in that, on the side of capital, the subject of governance differed from the object of governance: brands were involved in rule-making processes for employers and the employers did not have a seat at the table. Inevitably, this created tensions since, to use legal terminology, the employers who have what can generally be viewed as the property rights were excluded from the process. This chapter will discuss the effects of these politics of exclusion and their significance in terms of the Accord as a model of industrial democracy.

## 7.1 Associational Governance, Exclusion and the Accord

As outlined in Chapter 3, closely aligned to the ideas of industrial democracy and industrial citizenship is the concept of private-interest government. Central to private-interest government is that non-state actors take on the functions and authority of the state to engage in rule-making processes. Such authority is viewed as being legitimate, as members of communities affected have the opportunity to engage in their functional hierarchies. In the private-interest government approach, parties with differing interests engage in political exchange, where they agree to exercise voluntary restraint over their potential power resources in exchange for commitments made by others. The idea here is that peak-level bodies make commitments that are binding on their lower-level relevant constituencies because they are devolved the authority to do so by the state (Cohen and Rogers, 1992). Rather than exercising state authority for actors who fail to follow rules that are set, private-interest government thus depends on associations having the ability to reward and sanction members through incentives and penalties for those who both follow and fail to adhere to processes.

One implication of such an approach is that organisations engage in such a system as both subjects and objects of governance. While, on the one hand, it may be thought that such a system creates conflicts of interest where parties are setting rules that have the effect of limiting their action, while on the other hand, in terms of being subjects of governance, by participating in rule-making processes parties are actively involved in creating the rules. However, by also being subjects, parties are aware that any such agreements must be possible to deliver in their constituency and must also be politically palatable to their membership. Within such systems, the peak-level organisations thus must make a political calculation about the extent to which their membership sees the benefit of participation in rule-making in return for imposing constraints on behaviour to which the organisation is party. A key focus of this approach is that it is meant to move away from 'command and control' forms of governance and instead to encourage participatory democracy between levels in the organisation (Baccaro, 2006). In this way, representatives are expected to be held to account by their membership and to only make commitments through which they are authorised by those they represent. Baccaro (2006) highlights that such systems carry with them the sometimes-conflicting outcomes of social control versus problem-solving. The state in such an arrangement is considered to be a core actor, which enables the participation of actors and sets the boundaries of the governance arena in terms of the nature and scope of the authority it devolves.

The central feature of this book to date has been to explore the development of efforts to create institutions of transnational industrial democracy. Undoubtedly, a core aspect of the Accord was the idea of establishing institutions for the representation of workers' interests in the Bangladesh RMG sector. However, two of the most controversial questions were who represented the capital side of the employment relationship and what role there was for the elected government of Bangladesh? In these terms, the Accord differed in three significant ways from what has generally been regarded as the model of industrial democracy at the national level.

First, rather than being based on national-level institutions and industrial relations actors who work out governance among them, our findings highlighted the important role that transnational-level actors played in creating representation and governance for workers. This contrasts with industrial democracy at the national level, where workers engage with employers often in a context of institutional support from government. The extreme power asymmetries in Bangladeshi industrial relations meant that hitherto the interests of workers had been excluded. Representation of worker interests at the transnational level therefore became necessary to balance out the lack of worker representation at the national and organisational levels. While much of the effort was focused on managing the politics and establishing the structures at the transnational level, the relationship to the national system into which it was being developed was a secondary focus at the start of the Accord.

Second, the approach to transnational industrial democracy is based on transnational labour actors engaging brands as lead actors in global supply chains and leveraging their economic power over employers. Across most of the literature, the approach adopted has been to examine the actions of 'lead firms' (Gereffi, 1994) and to assume a fairly passive approach by other actors. This has also occurred in much of what has been written in relation to regulation in the apparel sector within Bangladesh post–Rana Plaza (Schluessler et al., 2019). In this way, a core feature of the approach in the Bangladesh case has been that, following Rana Plaza, employers have become the objects of governance through both worker-driven initiatives, such as the Accord, and CSR-type initiatives without any substantial input into the design of this governance. This matters because the supporting institutional framework that allows workers to develop a counter-weight to capitalist power is lacking or undermined in host countries for reasons explained in Chapter 2. In such an arrangement, the lack of power of local labour actors is instead partially compensated for by the power of brands. The rationale for this is as clear as it is paradoxical: even though brands benefit from labour exploitation, their economic power in the supply chain coupled with potential reputational vulnerability makes them the most likely actors to exert their power over employers. Yet brands only did so when compelled by the global Labour Caucus and its threat to disrupt consumption relations.

Third, and most unusually in this case, transnational industrial democracy includes brands and not employers as governance actors. This is a significant difference because it means the relationship between the peak level representation, the brands and the employers is a contractual/market-based relationship rather than an associative one. Effectively, the Accord introduced contractual terms for those factories that were seeking contracts to supply brands. In contrast to the annual membership fees for the brands, which were capped and defined according to the terms of the Accord, the Bangladeshi employers shouldered the risk in terms of bearing the cost of any remediation required by the Accord – employers were expected ultimately to pay the cost of remediation to the standards required in the Accord. This also led to a situation where the Accord wielded significant power over Bangladeshi manufacturers without the employers or state actors being represented in its governing body: the national actors who would typically be part of regulating employment relations – employers and the state – were largely left out of governance arrangements. As a result, the power to constrain employer interests in transnational industrial democracy was largely driven by transnational actors, so private governance was de facto imposed on reluctant employers without their representation.

This chapter thus focuses on the implications of this unusual and asymmetric set-up of industrial relations in the Bangladeshi supply chain in terms of the relationship between transnational industrial democracy and national actors. We raise questions about the nature of transnational democracy and its interaction with national-level representation. What is the role of national actors – Bangladeshi employers and the government – in transnational industrial democracy, particularly in terms of those who are the objects of the governance? Is it democratically legitimate to create more worker-driven forms of governance from 'the outside', like the Accord, if this excludes some of the traditional governance actors at the national level? What was the response of national actors to transnational structures and to what extent did it lead to changes at the national and/or transnational levels?

## 7.2 Employers and the Regulation of Worker Safety in the Bangladesh RMG Sector Following Rana Plaza

Empirically, we focus on how these questions play out when considering the contentious relationship between the Bangladesh Accord, and Bangladeshi employers and the government of Bangladesh. Despite their failure to ensure factory safety themselves, Bangladeshi employers, as well as state actors, contested the quasi-regulatory authority assumed by the Accord, widely seen in Bangladesh as a 'foreign' inspection body. For them, the imposition of private labour governance through the Accord undermined local ownership of regulatory authority. On the upside, it also spurred national actors into competing for regulatory authority. The core argument developed in this chapter is that while resistance to the Accord's 'foreign' regulatory takeover prevented the institutionalisation of a transnational governance regime, it also stimulated regulatory capacity-building efforts on behalf of national actors. This would have been unlikely without the existence of the Accord and, to a lesser extent, the Alliance. While the jury still is out on the efficacy of these nationally based initiatives, it is highly unlikely that they would have emerged without the transnational level initiatives.

Much of the hostility shown towards the Accord, and one of the key strains of criticism in Bangladesh, was grounded in the exclusion of Bangladeshi factory owners/employers from the process. The question is thus why employers, who are generally central actors in employment relations governance, were excluded from the Accord? In interviews with brand actors, it was made clear that the decision to exclude employers was done at the behest of the Labour Caucus – that is, the unions and NGOs. It is interesting that two very different rationales were conveyed by members of the Labour Caucus regarding why the employers were not represented in the Accord governance structures. First, trade unionists interviewed put forward the view that the problems arose from the mismanagement of factories in Bangladesh, and therefore the management of these factories should not be included in the governance. One trade unionist to the forefront of the Accord governance stated, 'We can't put the fox in charge of the henhouse' (GUF A.1). Another stated, 'They [Bangladeshi employers] have proven to the world that they are not capable of protecting their workers [as demonstrated by the Rana Plaza disaster] and so the world had to step in' (GUF B.2). This meant that Bangladeshi employers were viewed as being the primary cause of the series of industrial disasters that had killed workers in the sector. In this way, they were being viewed as the primary targets for regulation by the unions and there was a view that they should not be included due to their failure in creating the massive problems. This is a significant departure for unions – even those at the global level.

In contrast to the position of the unionists involved, a leading NGO activist involved in the Accord governance took a very different view:

The Accord is based on a recognition of an unavoidable reality, which is that garment factory owners in Bangladesh don't operate independently of brands. They are beholden to the brands. The brands are controlling the purse strings and decide what is and isn't possible. (NGO B.3)

This interviewee explained the exclusion of the employers as being down to the brands being the 'real' employer who exerted the power and who thus needed to be engaged. Another NGO interviewee expanded on this mentality, explaining:

These kind of things had grown up and they had actually occupied quite a lot of the space that should really be the space that is for negotiation between the unions and the employers. But what that negotiation looks like on a global supply chain level is very different to kind of old traditional unionism where you've got one workplace and one union negotiating at a local level. It's not a model that necessarily works for a supply chain like the garment industry which is so mobile. (NGO A.2)

In this instance, the interviewee again highlighted that in garment supply chains, where brands have huge power and choice in terms of who they chose to supply them, the focus of governance needs to be placed on the brands. In this approach, though, it can be argued that the Bangladeshi employers are viewed as generally passive actors who have little agency of their own to determine a direction, and thus their inclusion is not viewed as paramount.

While the competing rationales seem somewhat contradictory, they also provide important insights into the power relations and the political nuances of the relationships involved. Without doubt, and consistent with the position of the NGO interviewees, the most powerful actors in the supply chains are the multinational brands. In addition, as we develop in Chapter 5, within this supply chain the key power-based lever comes from the potential reputational association of brands with serious labour abuses. In this way, the concentration on the actions of brands and focusing on them to harness their power to regulate and govern the actions of Bangladesh-based employers is logical.

## 7.3  BGMEA: Political Power and Self-Regulation

The Bangladesh RMG industrial relations landscape is characterised by extreme power asymmetries. While workers are largely unorganised and offer a replaceable source of low-skilled labour, garment business interests are strongly organised into the country's most powerful economic institutions: the BGMEA alongside its smaller but still significant sister association, the Bangladesh Knitwear Manufacturers and Exporters Association (BKMEA). The BGMEA is a particularly highly influential private trade association that 'wields extraordinary power and political influence in the country', as a 2020 US Senate minority report noted (US Government Publishing Office, 2020). The BGMEA, employing 357 staff, was initially established in 1983 and is headquartered in Dhaka, Bangladesh with a regional office in Chittagong, the country's port and home to another garment hub. The BGMEA covers, to use the term of Schmitter and Streeck (1981), both the functions of a business association and those of an employers' group. As business groups, the BGMEA and the BKMEA have the capacity to license businesses to export their goods. Thus, it is necessary to belong to one of these associations to become involved in the lucrative export market. In addition, the BGMEA formally represents employers in the RMG sectors through membership, amounting to 4,621 garment factories in 2019 (BGMEA, 2020). Its members are influential in the national economy and political landscape: a number of BGMEA members (or their relatives) are also members of parliament, as well as owners of television stations and newspapers and other commercial enterprises.

The immense power wielded by the BGMEA has led to hotly contested elections for positions in many years, with slates of candidates being organised by competing factions within the organisation, ironically fulfilling the democratic function of factions that Lipset (1952) recognised for factions within unions. For example, in the period following 2013, a key dividing issue between candidates and factions in the BGMEA elections was the extent to which candidates proposed outright opposition to the type of regulation operated by the Accord or the extent to which the BGMEA should seek to engage with the Accord while simultaneously developing an indigenous approach to regulating workers' safety and health. In line with its secondary function as an employer association, the BGMEA also claims oversight over employment rights more broadly, such as monitoring to ensure healthcare and parental leave are implemented in accordance with the Bangladesh Labor Act 2015 and that factories do not discriminate against workers on gender, health condition, pregnancy, religion, caste, region and other grounds. It collects data on worker recruitment and turnover and maintains a database where workers are identified with their national ID number, keeping a job history of each worker. As a self-proclaimed watchdog, the BGMEA also claims to provide 'arbitration facilities to workers' by its Conciliation-cum-Arbitration Committee, which seeks to solve disputes between factory owner and employees outside of the court. It receives over 1,000 applications per year on issues such as unpaid wage and overtime (52.9 per cent), salary and benefit increase (18.8 per cent), employment contracts (12.1 per cent), lay-offs (7.1 per cent) and freedom of association (0.7 per cent) (BGMEA, 2020: 8). This dual function of being a trade association and an employers' group in an industry that dominates the national economy meant that prior to 2013 the power of the BGMEA generally went unchallenged.

### 7.3.1 Employer Response to Being Excluded from Representation in the Accord

There is no representative stakeholder from the manufacturers. And from the owners. You are coming here to inspect my house but nobody is in that steering committee. (BGMEA.1)

Even if Rana Plaza was widely seen as a 'wake-up call' for the industry, which created a shift in mindset towards the need to ensure building safety, Bangladeshi employers contested the regulatory role and power of the Accord to ensure safety. As illustrated in the quote above, the BGMEA's lack of a seat on the Accord Steering Committee cemented the view that the Accord represented foreign interference in national labour relations. In protest to being excluded from the Accord's governing body, the BGMEA refused to take the seat the Accord offered it on its advisory board (whereas the BKMEA and government took them). The analogy that foreign actors 'come to our house' as a guest but then tell the host what to do was repeated over and over in interviews with employers and factor managers. Rather ironically, despite bitterly contesting the very need for the existence of the Accord and opposing much of its activities, from a few years into our research, multiple BGMEA officers, staff and members interviewed often highlighted that the work of the Accord and the Alliance meant that Bangladesh had the safest factories and that Bangladesh was 'now known to the world as a model for workplace safety in the garment industry' (BGMEA, 2020: 31).

The global governance actors were acutely aware that the lack of employers' representation in the Accord's governance was an issue from the start. This was particularly the case for brand actors. One Accord brand representative highlighted that:

The difficulty of course that we had was that the local stakeholders, BGMEA in particular, wanted to have a seat on the steering committee of the Accord ... we explained to them why they couldn't be because, you know, they were not one of the signatories to the Accord as it had been set up, but that it was essential that they were part of the process and we offered from the start to involve them in pre-steering committee meetings ... and a seat on the advisory board. (Brand C.1)

As outlined in Chapters 5 and 6, this offer was declined by the BGMEA. The lack of representation increased and was perceived as a 'heavy-handed' regulatory regime of standards, inspections and the tangible sanctions of escalation and suspension from the Accord. Employers repeatedly expressed frustration over being forced to upgrade factory safety, while their competitors in other garment-exporting countries did not face the same level of scrutiny and regulation. 'Why is there no Accord in Cambodia?' and 'Nobody tells Pakistan what to do' were complaints that emerged again and again. The obvious answer – that the Accord was in Bangladesh and not Cambodia because Rana Plaza, Tazreen and the other disasters had happened in Bangladeshi factories – did not alleviate their anger over being more heavily scrutinised than their competitors.

### 7.3.2 Forcing Labour Governance on Employers

The Labour Caucus knew that in the Bangladeshi garment sector, unions could not leverage worker power to force employers to the negotiating table. But they could force employers through the existence and exploitation of buyer power. A Bangladeshi union leader summed this up:

Our manufacturers are not afraid of the local unions due to their weaknesses in this chain, they are not even afraid of the government because the government mechanism is in favour of them: in the parliament they have a lot of parliament members, they have a lot of ministers. But they're afraid of the brands because they are the heart of their business. (BD Unionist.1)

Indeed, most factory owners with whom we spoke readily admitted that they were dependent on orders from brands: 'We are petrified of the brands. That they might pull out. If they pull out, I will have no factory' (Factory Owner.1). If trade unions did not want to 'put the fox in charge of the henhouse', then it might have seemed contradictory to put those brands who benefit most from the power asymmetries and cheap labour in charge of regulating worker standards. But they knew they could effectively leverage the economic power of brands to force employers to accept what had been negotiated between labour and brands. A respondent from an NGO explained, 'If you want to affect working conditions in a meaningful way you need to constrain the behaviour of the brands and retailers, they are the de facto employer' (NGO B.3).

Moreover, this existing power asymmetry between brands and employers was exacerbated by the Accord's ability to pool the resources and influence of over 200 signatory brands to pressure factory owners to participate in the Accord inspection programme and invest in safety upgrades. In other words, the Accord's quasi-regulatory authority was based on its ability to drive employers to remediate life-threatening safety hazards through the leverage of concerted buyer power: the Accord bundled the economic dominance of an economically significant group of buyers, translated it into regulatory power to govern, and potentially disrupt, the Bangladeshi supply chain by effectively withdrawing orders from unsafe or non-cooperative factories. With over 1,600 factories covering over half of all workers employed in the sector, the Accord controlled the buyer power of a very significant share of the RMG sector. This consolidation of demand meant the Accord wielded substantial economic power in enforcing standards on behalf of its signatories. For this reason, employers were unable to refuse the Accord outright.

Facing such concerted buyer power, Bangladeshi employers largely resigned themselves to the regulatory role of the Accord. Nevertheless, Bangladeshi factory owners resented being forced to accept the Accord's 'rigid' safety standards and invest in safety upgrades or else risk losing business with all Accord signatory brands. A GUF described the resentment:

In Bangladesh the pushback is extraordinary. There is an incredible amount of pressure and we had it at every stage. Before it was the [safety] standards: The sprinklers and fire doors, those were the crucial elements in the standard they didn't like, also the two most expensive things in the standard. Then now it's the factory closures. It's always something and there is a lot of pushback on this. And it, they don't like it, they don't feel like they have ownership on that, the BGMEA is not in the Accord. (GUF B.2)

The results of the first round of Accord inspections led to starkly competing narratives about the state of factory safety in Bangladesh. Many employers celebrated that 'only' seventeen factories had to be shut down because of safety issues – less than half a percentage of the total factories. Employers interpreted this as meaning that the vast majority of Bangladeshi factories were safe to operate. This narrative was reinforced by the government. For instance, at the Safety Expo in 2014, Sheikh Hasina concluded about the initial round of inspections of over 2000 factories under the Accord, Alliance and National Action Plan: 'They found most of the mills and factories running in trouble-free manner.' One year later, at the 2015 Safety Expo when the bulk of remediation work had not even started, the Bangladeshi commerce minister Tofail Ahmed repeated these claims:

Initially, I was also irritated with the presence of Accord and Alliance in Bangladesh. But after the completion of the preliminary inspections I am very happy, as they found that less than 2 percent of the factories are risky .... Now, we can say that most of our factories are compliant.

The Accord contested this interpretation and did not view non-closure as an endorsement of safety standards. It insisted that it found serious safety issues in 100 per cent of factories inspected and immediately closed those factories where they believed another Rana Plaza disaster was imminent, with all others requiring significant remediation.

In the light of these diverging interpretations, Bangladeshi factory owners complained about the Accord applying overly strict standards, pressuring them into remediation, and about Accord engineers not accepting remedial action as acceptable and identifying new issues while factory owners felt the work was near-complete. The cat-and-mouse play of social auditing had become serious, being replaced by hard sanctions for non-compliance. Depending on their business size, owners reported spending between Tk5 crore and Tk20 crore (approximately between US$500,000 and US$2.25 million) on remediation of each factory, according to the BGMEA. One frustrated factory owner claimed that he spent Tk38 crore (approximately US$4 million) on remediation: 'Accord engineers often threaten to cut business ties if the problems are not fixed and re-fixed in line with their recommendations. I do not want the Accord anymore' (Daily Star, 2018). Of course, there are two sides to the issue. The factory owner quoted above also claim that his annual exports are worth more than US$135 million, meaning that this [one-off] investment in worker safety amounted to only a bit more than 3 per cent of his annual export value. In another instance, a factory owner complained to us that their fire safety remediation was not accepted: the owner claimed the Accord inspector would not verify the supply route that had been built to a natural pond as firefighting water supply. When questioned about this, Accord staff had a different version: the natural pond was inadequate as a water supply for fire protection not least because its muddy water was infested with snakes that were likely to clog up the supply pipes. Staff showed us a video of a large python in the muddy pond, which they claimed was from the factory in question, that would potentially block fire hoses.

The strict implementation of standards by the Accord can be seen in one of two ways, which are not entirely contradictory. One the one hand, as Anner (2019) highlights, the downwards pressure by brands can be viewed as an unfair tightening of the squeeze on employers by brands. On the other hand, it can also be viewed as a necessary squeeze to prevent standards being driven down by employers without the economic ability to maintain basic safety standards. During the fieldwork in Bangladesh, in addition to interviewing individual factory owners, we visited eight different factories in the greater Dhaka area. These included a wide variety of different factory sizes and forms, ranging from a high-end factory situated on a purpose-built site at the edges of Dhaka with its own fire service, ambulance and water supply to cater for thousands of workers, to a relatively small factory with a few hundred workers based in inner-city Dhaka. The contrast between factory owners and their attitudes was also often stark. In one of the larger operations we visited, management explained to us that its supply strategy was to concentrate on fulfilling the orders of two particular large European brands, which were both significant players in the Accord. For both, they were officially 'gold-level' suppliers, signifying the quality, price and punctuality of delivery, and had been supplying each for in excess of five years. Management outlined that it had carried out all remediation required by the Accord, with the exception of installing fire doors of the standard required by the Accord. The owner explained that they had installed new fire doors after Rana Plaza and that these new fire doors were compliant with the standards required by the Bangladesh Building Code but not the Accord (fire doors was the one area where the Accord standard diverged from the Bangladesh building code). The owner was adamant that he would not be purchasing the fire doors required by the Accord and when asked about the risk of losing the opportunity to supply these two suppliers, he simply responded 'let's see' in a relaxed manner.

This was a stark contrast to another Accord factory we visited based in inner Dhaka, housed on the fifth to eighth floors of a multi-purpose building on a rental basis. The factory owner explained that he was a relatively new entrant to the sector. In terms of supply relationships, the factory did not have direct relationships with brands and instead supplied through buying houses based in Hong Kong and Turkey. At the time of visiting, the factory was undergoing retrofitting and strengthening of load-bearing columns. Under Accord rules, if the factory wished to continue operating from this building, the factory owner would be responsible for fire, building and electrical safety on all levels, not just those of the factory. Because the owner was renting the factory space, this placed a huge risk on his shoulders should the building owner decide to change tenants. The anxiety of the factory owner was palpable: at several points in the interview, he asked us if we had any ideas on how he could get financing and even if we could intervene with brands on his behalf. He also made it clear that the only choice for him was to implement the Accord requirements in full or to lose his business. While it was hard not to feel empathy with this factory owner and frustration with the previous owner, the entire lack of regulation in the sector where barriers to entry were so low was certainly at the heart of the safety problems bedevilling the industry in Bangladesh.

## 7.4 The Bangladeshi State: Lack of Regulatory Capacity

In the Bangladesh context, the position of the government in relation to the Accord was problematic. Many interviewees (consistent with prior research) viewed the government and state apparatus as essentially being captured by the RMG industry, which was seen to mobilise state actors in pursuit of their interests. Facing conflicting pressures from domestic manufacturers, on the one hand, and international actors, on the other, the government of Bangladesh only reluctantly tolerated the Accord. In fact, it was pressured into allowing the Accord to operate by the threat of losing business from brands and diplomatic pressure from its most important trading partners. The United States sent a warning shot when it suspended trade benefits of its Generalized System of Preferences (GSP) for Bangladesh over safety concerns following Rana Plaza. While the GSP did not cover RMG exports to the United States, it nevertheless was seen as a strong signal that Bangladesh could not take its trading privileges for granted. Bangladesh's RMG sector could not risk losing its trading benefits under the EU's Everything But Arms trade arrangement, which granted least developed countries such as Bangladesh quota-free and duty-free access to EU markets on all products including garments. While this was never revoked, it is fair to assume that trading privileges gave weight to the international diplomatic efforts that were made to lobby the Government of Bangladesh into improving its public labour governance. For instance, the Sustainability Compact, a meeting between Bangladesh and its most important trading partners – the European Union, United States and Canada, representing 85 per cent of Bangladeshi garment exports – and with technical support provided by the ILO, was created 'to promote continuous improvements in labour rights and factory safety' (European Commission, 2018).

Major efforts were made to improve the state's abysmal regulatory capacity. At the time Rana Plaza occurred, only ninety-two labour inspectors were employed by the government to oversee compliance across all of Bangladesh's factories, shops, industries and commercial establishments. Under the National Action Plan, which was drawn up in the aftermath of Rana Plaza, the government had committed to enhance the capacity of its regulatory bodies to ensure worker safety and labour rights and amend the Labour Act, particularly regarding freedom of association and collective bargaining as well as factory-level participation committees and OSH committees, to provide a better legislative environment for industrial democracy. In early 2014, it upgraded its inspection body to a full department – the Department of Inspection for Factories and Establishments (DIFE) – which operates under the Ministry of Labour and Employment (MOLE). DIFE slowly increased its capacity to 639 occupied positions by July 2020 (DIFE, 2020). DIFE's responsibility includes the inspection of factories, shops, industries and commercial establishments to establish terms of employment, safety and health, and labour welfare as defined by the Bangladesh Labour Act of 2006 (and its subsequent amendments), the Bangladesh Labour Rules (2015), and the ILO's International Labour Standards. In May 2017, the Government of Bangladesh, BGMEA and BKMEA, with technical support from the ILO and funding from the United Kingdom, Canada and the Netherlands, established the Remediation Coordination Cell (RCC) with the aim of building up capacity to oversee factory safety for a post–Accord and Alliance industry.

However, there was ongoing concern about DIFE's commitment and capacity to inspect RMG factories. Ironically, capacity-building was undermined by poor working conditions at the department itself. Industry insiders noted that by 2017, out of the 450 new labour inspectors hired by the MOLE, 300 had already left. An ILO interviewee explained the reason for this high turnover:

The turnover there is huge and they [labour inspectors] often get attracted by the companies, who are hiring them. If you're a good labour inspector the factory hires you as an HR person or compliance officer. They are like 'You are making what? I'll pay you double that.' (ILO.1)

In addition, a lack of funding and basic equipment such as computers and cars were highlighted as complicating government oversight. Labour inspectors often lacked basic IT equipment to perform their jobs. Even getting to the factories was described as a challenge. Visiting a factory was a tiring and challenging journey that could take several hours even in a chauffeur-driven car, a relative standard arrangement for most mid-level private sector workers in Bangladesh. Yet public labour inspectors were given motorcycles and expected to visit several factories a day.

Given these basic challenges, industry insiders were thus highly sceptical about the government's ability to take over from private regulators to perform regulatory oversight:

I still find it difficult to imagine how Accord and Alliance will want to transfer their work to the government. It sounds great in practice but Accord and Alliance will also realise that this is very difficult. (ILO.1)

However, notwithstanding these operational issues, the government was keen to take over the role from the Accord. When the Accord signatories agreed to extend the commitment for another three years from 2018 to 2021, the intention, as stated publicly by the general secretaries of IndustriALL and Uni Global, was to hand over the Accord's work 'to a national regulatory body' on the condition that 'there is a national regulatory body ready to take over this role' (Sanches and Hoffman, 2017). Thus, the government's regulatory 'readiness' was an explicit term of the agreement.

As the expiry date of the first Accord's tenure drew closer in 2018, the government claimed that its national labour inspectorate responsible for the inspections of structural integrity, fire and electrical safety in factories was capable of taking over the Accord's and Alliance's job. But joint research by the Accord's witness signatories (Clean Clothes Campaign, International Labor Rights Forum, Maquila Solidarity Network, and Worker Rights Consortium) contested the government's claims to be ready and instead revealed 'a shocking level of unreadiness' (Clean Clothes Campaign et al., 2019). The European Union Sustainability Compact's 2018 (European Union, 2018) report also concluded that DIFE was still not fully operational. In defending the need for the Transition Accord to come into effect, the Accord witness signatories compared progress in Accord remediation with that in the government-run programme for factories not covered by either the Accord or Alliance. They highlighted that, in early 2019, at the time when 89 per cent of renovations required at all 1,600+ factories covered by the Accord were completed, the factories covered by the government's inspection agencies lagged far behind in completing the remediation work and cited one government database as indicating that in 346/400 factories, progress was less than 20 per cent. In addition, many of the factories deemed unsafe for any work to be carried out in by the Accord and Alliance were listed as operating under the government database. Nevertheless, despite the lack of capacity compared with the Accord (as will be developed), when the Transitional Accord was signed, it intensified activity by both employers and the government in Bangladesh to develop a nationally based system of factory safety.

## 7.5 Employer and State Resistance against Transnational Labour Governance

Through the eight years of the Accord's existence, the Bangladeshi government and employers enacted a struggle against the Accord. Initially, employers and particularly the government waged very public opposition to the Accord's existence, with the Accord being likened to an invasion. One feature of the early approach of the Accord focused upon was that the initial building surveys were undertaken by engineering consultants brought in primarily from Europe to inspect and survey the factories. At this stage, there was significant rhetoric against the Accord, particularly by the government in the form of the Prime Minister and the Minister for Commerce, as illustrated when Bangladesh's Prime Minister Sheikh Hasina inaugurated the three-day 'Dhaka Apparel Summit – 2014', organised by the BGMEA, and stated:

Bangladesh is the second largest RMG exporter of the world. Perhaps several quarters do not like this and that's why they're engaged in conspiracy against this apparel sector.

I'm urging the owners, workers, foreign buyers and consumers to beware of local and foreign conspirators.

However, in terms of meaningful pushback from actors in Bangladesh, this was short-lived and confined largely to the rhetorical from the government. Very quickly, though, attention shifted from outright opposition to limiting the lifespan of the Accord to its initial five-year term.

From 2015 onwards, it was well known that the parties to the Accord were engaging in discussions about extending its work. This was justified because it was felt that the resources necessary for an effective Bangladeshi-led system were not a realistic possibility within three years. Having reluctantly tolerated the Accord's introduction, the Government of Bangladesh and the BGMEA were adamant about resisting any extension of it. When speaking at the 2015 Fire Safety

Expo in Dhaka, the Bangladeshi commerce minister and outspoken critic of the Accord, Tofail Ahmed, pledged publicly that the government would not allow the Accord and Alliance to operate 'one second longer' after their tenure was due to end in July 2018. And as the expiry date of the first Accord's tenure drew closer, the government claimed that its national labour inspectorate responsible for the inspections of structural integrity, fire and electrical safety in factories was capable of taking over the Accord's and Alliance's job.

While the BGMEA had initially adopted a highly adversarial stance towards the Accord, opposing all forms of regulation, in about 2016 what was viewed as the more progressive faction, based around second-generation factory owners and headed by Siddiqur Rahman, Rubana Huq and Miran Ali, started to exert more influence on the organisation. Central to their approach was that regulation of the industry was necessary to preserve it, but that Bangladeshi actors had to play central roles in any future regulatory system. As part of this approach, in August 2017 these BGMEA leaders announced plans for an initiative, pointedly called 'Shonman' (Respect), which was to be a Bangladeshi-based safety initiative. Its steering committee was to be composed of representatives from the BGMEA, BKMEA, government and trade unions from Bangladesh, as well as international actors in the form of the ILO and brands. Factories that had achieved 85 per cent remediation levels from the Accord and Alliance were proposed to be placed under its supervision, with remaining remediation to be overseen by the DIFE Remediation Coordination Cells. The proposal also included a provision for effectively a transitional period from 2018 to 2021, where brands would be involved from both a technical sense and to provide finance but that the initiative would be self-financing from 2021. The proposal marked a considerable shift in thinking from the BGMEA as it both recognised the need for oversight and included international actors as well as unions. That said, in many ways the proposal was effectively left dead on arrival when the Accord announced its extension in 2017. What was viewed as particularly problematic for brands and unions was that essentially the proposal amounted to the BGMEA taking the lead in regulating occupational safety and health in the sector.

When the extension to the Accord was agreed, the state and employers were angry. BGMEA officials openly expressed their frustration and anger to us: 'They didn't even consult us on that!' (BGMEA.1) and ignored efforts being made by the BGMEA to develop its initiative. The timing of announcing the agreement was also seen as culturally insensitive since it happened on the day of Eid, the most important Muslim holiday:

It is a surprise to us! ... We used to have regular meetings with the Accord and the person who is responsible for the Accord in Bangladesh and also the Steering Committee when they visited Bangladesh .... But very surprisingly, I mean, when we're in the Eid Festival that time, and all of a sudden they just came up with a draft adopted agreement [of the Transition Accord], it was so surprising to see. They didn't even consult us when they were making the draft or anything! (BGMEA.1)

Despite its weak power, the BGMEA scapegoated IndustriALL for pressuring brands into extending the Accord:

What we found is, this is very dominated by the trade union federation, IndustriALL. The brands are, I am sorry to use that word, the brands are almost blackmailed on that. (BGMEA.2)

Employers and government were both determined to prevent an extension of the Accord beyond its original tenure of May 2018. There was a widespread view that the government and industry worked hand in hand to protect the interests of the RMG sector. Over the next two years, interaction between employers and the state in two areas created the dynamic that effectively brought the operation of the Bangladesh Accord to an end.

### 7.5.1 Building the Capacity of Regulatory Institutions: The Ready-Made-Garment Sustainability Council

The resistance to the Accord and creation of the Ready-Made-Garment Sustainability Council (RSC) can be seen from two perspectives. On the one hand, it prevented the institutionalisation of an independent, transparent and legally binding inspection body; on the other, it spurred national actors into developing governance capacity themselves. When the Accord was extended for an additional three years in 2017 (covering 2018–2021), it was meant to operate as a 'Transition Accord' 'until a set of rigorous readiness conditions are met by local regulatory bodies'. The intention was to put the onus on local regulators to build regulatory capacity and show willingness to regulate the industry. Without the 'foreign interference' by the Accord and Alliance, and pressure from Bangladesh's trading partners, it is unlikely that competing for regulatory authority would have been a priority for employers at all. Now the BGMEA made it its mission to take ownership of regulation.

When Rubana Huq was elected BGMEA president in April 2019, a key priority of hers became the establishment of a Bangladeshi regulatory body that ultimately took the form of the RSC. Legally the RSC was established as a not-for-profit independent organisation based on a licence from the state to operate. In many ways, the RSC shared much of the architecture of the earlier Shonman initiative but, crucially, licensed by the state, rather than the BGMEA directly. What was viewed as being of utmost importance for Bangladeshi actors, however, was the increased role for national actors in the system. This was highlighted by one BGMEA interviewee, who stated, 'We had no voice in the previous organisation and now we will have a voice, it's going to be coming under the aegis of our laws and regulations' (BGMEA.2). While the RSC would retain all safety and health inspections, remediation, training and complaints-handling functions maintained by the Accord, it also departed from the Accord's governance model in significant ways. First, the RSC is governed by a board of directors that includes equal numbers of representatives of brands, factory owners via the local employers' organisations, the BGMEA and BKMEA and worker representatives. This means that, unlike the Accord, it is predominantly controlled by industry representatives – brands and BGMEA members. Second, even if brands remained contractually obliged to keep their factories safe until the Accord expires in 2021, the RSC itself was a voluntary initiative for the brands. Thus, unlike the Accord, commitments are non-binding and lack a mechanism through which labour representatives can enforce them.

Labour groups were sceptical towards the RSC. For instance, the Accord's witness signatories criticised the transition to the RSC as 'hasty and ill-advised', leaving worker safety 'in the hands of an RSC that is woefully unprepared to fulfil its immediate responsibilities' (NGO B.2). They raised questions about whether the RSC's chief safety officer would retain the same level of independence and autonomy to recommend that non-compliant factories be restricted from selling to brands, whether the RSC would retain the same level of transparency to disclose publicly inspection reports and CAPs to workers, buyers and consumers, whether it would retain the Accord's independent complaints mechanism and whether it could maintain the Accord's funding levels (US$5 million to US$6 million per annum), as well as technical capacity and staff integrity. BGMEA President Rubana Huq rebutted these criticisms: 'If Accord could be a meeting ground for brands and labour, why would a national initiative, which has Accord reps on board, be questioned?'

An interesting contrast of perceptions of alliances within the RSC emerged from interviews. For Bangladeshi actors, the RSC governance structure was viewed as balancing the national and international actors in terms of power relations. In contrast, labour representatives saw the structure as being one that reduced labour actors to one-third of the steering committee, compared to capital, in the form of employers and brands, taking two-thirds of the seats. By including employers in the governance of labour market institutions, the RSC had the potential to overcome the global–local tension that was built into the Accord model of transnational industrial democracy. But constraining the power of labour to hold firms and employers accountable also raises legitimate concerns as to whether brands and the BGMEA would be willing to regulate the industry from which they profit. Thus, whether the RSC can retain the key functions that ensured the effectiveness of the Accord remains to be seen. While the extent to which the international actors would buy into the work of the RSC was initially questionable, the termination of the Accord as an ongoing body was catalysed by a court case described below.

### 7.5.2 Fighting the Accord's Extension: The High Court Case

In 2017, Mostafizur Rahman of Smart Group, a significant Bangladeshi manufacturer that produced 25 million garments at an estimated export value of between US$130 million and US$160 million per year, filed a court case challenging the Accord's decision to terminate business relations with his group, Smart Jeans Ltd. This legal case contested the jurisdiction of the Accord in Bangladesh and brought the greatest challenge to the tenure of the Accord. One of the group's factories was initially inspected by the Alliance and the Alliance suspended all the factories owned in the group due to the Alliance finding that concrete strength tests were falsified in one factory. As the factory fell under both the Alliance and the Accord, the Accord terminated the group's certification as outlined under the Accord–Alliance cooperation agreement. The Accord's ability to place the entire business group of a noncompliant factory into the multistage escalation procedure and eventual termination was the Accord's most powerful means of pressuring reluctant manufacturers into making safety upgrades. For this reason, it was also the most contested. In response to being excluded by both the Accord and the Alliance, the factory owner, having carried out some remediation activities, applied to the Alliance to be reactivated, a request that was granted. However, the Accord then inspected the factory and reactivated its termination notice, as it was not satisfied with the work. In addition, the factory owner asked for his factory to be inspected by the national initiative under the National Tripartite Plan of Action on Fire Safety and Structural Integrity implemented through the Bangladesh University of Engineering and Technology (BUET), which found the building to be compliant. The owner claimed in his case, and was supported by the court, that as all three were operating under the National Tripartite Plan, the Accord had no right to terminate his factory supplying to their brands and claimed the BUET approval should be sufficient in this regard.

Arising from the case, the judge initiated a *suo moto* case – that is, a case considering a legal issue that was not raised by parties to the case. The court went on to make a ruling on the wider role and activity of the Accord. In its decision, the court both legitimised the work of the original Accord but prevented the Transition Accord from continuing. In terms of legitimising the Accord, the court argued that both the Accord and the Alliance were working to implement the National Tripartite Plan, rather than operating as independent governance regimes in their own right. The court determined that this temporary exercise of state authority was necessary in the national emergency after Rana Plaza but that, five years on, this was no longer the case as national institutions were now established to carry out the task.

In April 2018, the Bangladeshi High Court put a restraining order on the Accord's inspection programme, meaning that the Accord would have to cease operations and leave the country one month later after 30 May 2018. Labour groups widely believed that the 'government of Bangladesh is using proceedings before the Supreme Court of Bangladesh to prevent the Accord on Fire and Building Safety from operating' and that this was motivated by lobbying from the BGMEA (Clean Clothes Campaign et al., 2018). Various international diplomatic relations were mobilised in support of the Accord, such as by the Sustainability Compact. In addition, brands themselves voiced their support for the Accord. In August 2018, a number of German brands that were members of the German Textilbuendnis signed a statement addressed to the Bangladeshi Prime Minister, urging her to support the Transition Accord and stating:

It is of utmost importance for the safety of millions of employees in the garment industry of Bangladesh and in our firm interest that the agreed terms to hand over the Accord's responsibilities are met. (Textilbuendnis, 2018)

Similarly, in a letter to suppliers, Esprit's head of global supply, Luis Gonzaga, was quoted in *The Guardian* as saying, 'Activism in key market countries could make the Bangladesh brand toxic to consumers in spite of the tremendous improvements that we have achieved in recent years' (Safi, 2018). Because the Bangladeshi industry was essentially wholly dependent on brand retailers, this dependency on brands was a considerable counterweight to that of the government. Supported by the collective muscle of its signatory brands, the Accord remained confident that the government would not make good on its threat to kick out the Accord and aggravate the brands. As described by one Accord interviewee:

We got a lot of kick back from the BGMEA as well as from the government but it was fuck you, you're not going to have the brands leave. The brands have invested in this process, it's a brand initiative, we will get registration. (Accord.2)

The simultaneous pressure to end the Accord's reign, on the one hand, and to extend the Accord to appease international trading partners and brands, on the other, led to a series of deadlines and subsequent extensions from the state for the Accord to leave the country. At the request of the Bangladeshi government, the High Court postponed the date to 30 November. The Bangladeshi Commerce Minister, Tofail Ahmed, explained to the press: 'Following much pressure and persuasion, we extended its [the Accord's] tenure for six months. But we shall not extend the tenure anymore.' He further insisted that

there is no Accord-Alliance in any country in the world. Cannot go to Vietnam, cannot suggest that the Accord-Alliance will come. Not in China, not in Pakistan, even not in India, so only in Bangladesh .... We are a self-respecting nation, there's no more need for the Accord-Alliance.

He argued that the absence of fatal accidents since Rana Plaza was evidence that Bangladeshi factories were now safe and that the government's new domestic inspection agency was prepared to take over:

Last 5 years, there was no accident at this time that means our factories are complained .... After leaving the Accord-Alliance from Bangladesh, the Labor Ministry's Remediation Coordination Cell (RCC) will take responsibility for whatever the two organizations did.

Nevertheless, local voices became louder in criticising the Accord while demanding that brands pay higher prices for garments. When the Accord proceeded to escalate factories for not having made sufficient progress in remediating safety issues in 2018, government ministers publicly aligned with BGMEA leaders in condemning the Accord. Some of the 532 factories in question were large factories that were owned by BGMEA leaders. At an industry event in Dhaka attended by government and industry leaders, commerce minister Tofail Ahmed condemned the Accord's approach: 'There is no chance to extend the tenure of Accord in Bangladesh anymore. The Supreme Court also said that the Accord cannot stay here after November 30.' Shafiul Islam Mohiuddin, a former president of the BGMEA and then president of the Federation of Bangladesh Chambers of Commerce and Industry, claimed:

We have done a wonderful job, but still we have to see the reckless authoritarian attitude of their initiative. We condemn them. The reality is very crude and difficult. So, we are requesting our buyers not to show your muscle power.

The court repeatedly extended a stay on the order to allow for a negotiated agreement between the Accord signatories, the Government of Bangladesh and the BGMEA. Such an agreement was finally made in the form of a memorandum of understanding, which was reached just before the Appeals Hearing was scheduled in May 2019. The memorandum of understanding outlined that the Accord would be replaced by the RSC. The court decided that the Accord could continue operations for 281 days to transition to the RSC, rather than be based on conditions of readiness, which the government had agreed to previously. Under the agreement, the Accord agreed to close its Bangladesh office and hand over all major functions and operations of its Bangladesh office to the RSC by 1 June 2020. Uncertainty over the future of the Accord resulted in factories delaying repairs from November 2018 and progress slowed down even more after the memorandum of understanding was signed. This left the most difficult, expensive and/or time-consuming remediations such as structural renovations undone, as factories hoped to sit out the Accord until the new body was in place.

## 7.6 Conclusion

As outlined in Chapter 3 and at the start of this chapter, ideas of private governance, industrial citizenship and industrial democracy draw heavily on the associative logic of organisation. Central to this logic is the idea of cooperative and non-competitive relations between organisational hierarchies and licensed through governmental authority. Yet the supply chain model diverges from this approach in that governments are involved in competition for brand contracts and employers are linked to brands through cost-competitive contracts. As such, central actors to the employment relationship were excluded from representation in the Accord and this limited its potential to achieve local buy-in (Kang, 2021). Without doubt, there were certainly good grounds for this exclusion, but nevertheless it was an Achilles heel in terms of the democratic credentials in the Accord.

Central to the operation of the Accord (Chapters 5 and 6) and other initiatives such as developing workplace social dialogue, as will be outlined in Chapter 8, was the idea of increasing the democratic participation of workers in the Bangladeshi garments sector by giving those who represented the interests of workers a central role in the governance of the Accord. This compensated for the huge power asymmetry that Bangladeshi workers suffered vis-á-vis their employers. That said, Bangladeshi factories were certainly subject to asymmetric power relationships with the brands. There is little doubt that the intention of all the actors in the Accord was to use the power of the brands to regulate the activities of the Bangladeshi factories, with the rationale that the national actors in the form of the BGMEA and government had failed for years to raise standards – and in fact standards had deteriorated significantly.

Without doubt, the issue of excluding the employers and the government was the most controversial aspect of the Accord. As outlined, it also marked a significant departure from what can be thought of as industrial democracy and private-interest governance. In excluding these nationally based actors, a decision was taken by Accord actors that, in the context of the Rana Plaza disaster, effectiveness of governance was more important than inclusion in governance, as the Bangladeshi actors were considered to be a potential roadblock to increasing safety rather than ingredients for an all-encompassing governance system. That said, as objects of governance, neither the employers nor the state were content to accept the regulation without pushback.

The transnational governance logic, however, does to a large extent turn a blind eye to the actions of the brands, which have driven the race to the bottom. In many ways, the success of the Accord was based upon use of brand power against employers whose standards had been driven down through the ultra-competitive actions of the brands. Even though some factories had well-established and long-standing contact with large brands, each contract was short-term in nature, separately negotiated and based on factories bidding against others as to who could supply to the brands at the cheapest rate. In addition, several recounted stories of brands using their power to renegotiate the price during the production process or due to factors outside the control of employers. The factory owners viewed the Accord in similar ways: brands, through the Accord, were raising the production cost on employers by requiring the installation of what was claimed to be expensive equipment such as particular brands of Western sprinkler systems and yet were unwilling to commit to paying the price for such systems. By not including the employers in the formulation of the Accord, such action by the brands was viewed as going unchallenged.

The exclusion of the Bangladeshi actors unleashed a double dynamic in terms of their response to the Accord. First, both the government and employers opposed the Accord. In this regard, during the original Accord there was a lot of rhetoric, particularly led by the government, in opposition to the Accord. This focused on the fact that only Bangladesh was singled out and often claimed it to be a mechanism to undermine their international competitiveness. That said, very little substantive action was taken, with the vast bulk of employers engaging with the Accord. This should not be viewed as a voluntary action, though, as it was clearly undertaken to ensure that supplying the brands could continue. Second, as outlined, Bangladeshi actors also engaged in a series of activities to build capacity within the country.

The government significantly ramped up its internal labour inspectorate and a new leadership group emerged within the BGMEA, which recognised that without there being a credible worker safety programme, significant risk was being placed on the main driver of Bangladeshi economic development. Whether this was to the level required or whether the political will was there to carry this out is another matter. One issue is that arrangements – such as those established by the Accord, which, in the short term can be successful in eliminating the most egregious abuses – need, to be sustainable in the long term, to work out ways of having meaningful representation of interests such as employers and government in the countries subjected to the governance. But initiatives such as the Accord certainly pushed national actors to initiate processes they believed could be acceptable to actors such as brands, the ILO and global trade unions.

# 8 | Building Representative Structures at the Workplace Level

If workers in Rana Plaza and Tazreen Fashion Factory had more of a voice, deaths and injuries could have been prevented. (Human Rights Watch, 2015: 4)

As the quote above suggests, Rana Plaza demonstrated the need for worker participation and voice at the workplace level. However, as should be clear, the lack of worker voice and representation is a chronic problem in the Bangladesh RMG sector. For this reason, many international labour actors have focused on supporting local union organising. As well as the ILO, various union groups such as IndustriALL, the AFL-CIO Solidarity Center and the Danish trade union federation, 3F, as well as non-union labour groups such as the WRC, the ETI and the German Friedrich-Ebert Stiftung, have undertaken projects to build the capacity of trade union leaders and support fledgling trade union organising. However, these attempts proved frustratingly slow to create representation at the factory level and often faced stiff, if not outright violent, resistance from employers. For this reason, progress was seen as incommensurate to the challenge of establishing workplace representation. In this context, the question arises: How could worker representation be established at their workplace level?

Interestingly, brands starting to source from Bangladesh started asking similar questions about involving workers in monitoring workplace conditions. By the time of the Rana Plaza disaster, they had become increasingly frustrated with their predominant CSR practice – social auditing of factory compliance against predefined codes of conduct. Social auditing failed to improve labour conditions significantly in global supply chains, despite brands devoting up to 80 per cent of their ethical sourcing budget to it (ETI, 2014). Codes of conduct are implemented with little or no worker input, which reveals a significant problem with this approach: upstream actors in the supply chain are often passive recipients of regulation, with little worker participation from the level of production. As a result, workers are largely excluded from participation in CSR activities, despite being their alleged beneficiaries (Donaghey and Reinecke, 2018).

With the collapse of Rana Plaza, it became harder to ignore the signs of continuing labour rights violations in supplier factories. Local brand CSR staff would often visit their supplier factories and, for this reason, were aware of the discrepancy between social auditing results and the conditions they witnessed in the factory or heard about informally. It was increasingly clear that social auditing was failing to unveil so-called 'non-compliances', which were often hidden and concealed from auditors, and that the entire approach of social auditing was predicated on an unrealistic idea of regulating the supply chain from the top. Instead, developing worker voice at the factory level was viewed as a way for workers to be involved in identifying safety issues and also having this fed back to the brands.

Thus, there was a search from both global labour and global capital for ways of building worker representation at the 'coalface' – that is, in the places of production where labour rights violations occurred. In Chapter 3, we conceptualised the interface between different forms of representation and the level at which representation takes place – transnational level or workplace level. So far, our arguments have explored representation mainly at the transnational level. In this chapter, we turn to the question of how representative structures can be developed at the workplace level to enable the representation of workers in Bangladesh RMG factories by these workers. To do so, we researched the Joint Ethical Trading Initiatives (JETI) Social Dialogue Project in Bangladesh, as outlined in Chapter 4, and interviewed participating factory managers and brands as well as workers. We also observed manager–worker interactions in factory-level participation meetings. In the cases of the workplace dialogue we examined, representation at the workplace level was not created through union organising. Instead, it was created through input from brands and hence by capital. Nevertheless, such non-union representation structures can provide a meaningful form of voice for workers as the next-best alternative to unions (Johnstone et al., 2011; Pike, 2020). A central question of this chapter thus concerns how worker representation may be created in contexts hostile to such representation.

## 8.1 What Is Workplace Social Dialogue?

Workplace dialogue has been recognised as a mechanism for developing better workplace relations and enabling the democratic participation of workers in solving workplace issues (Wilkinson et al., 2014), particularly in the area of OSH (Quinlan, 1999; James et al., 2007). Worker participation means workers are involved in the design, structures and processes of workplace governance, which is regarded as an important activity in itself (Sobczak 2007; Dawkins, 2012) but also as a mechanism for improving labour standards (Donaghey and Reinecke, 2018; Walters and Quinlan, 2019). Worker participation does not just mean periodic involvement in negotiating universally applicable codes of conduct or standards but requires an ongoing process of worker voice in local, workplace-level decision-making and problem-solving where workers can use dialogue in pursuit of their interests: participation can aid in constraining the worst elements of managerial discretion and avoid workplace-based conflict (Streeck, 1995).

In many European countries, worker participation is embedded in a supportive framework of industrial relations that is institutionalised at three levels: the national, sectoral and workplace levels (Rogers and Streeck, 1995). The traditional form of worker representation in such processes is through the trade union, but it may also involve other forms of elected representation, such as works councils. Unlike in the European context, where workplace social dialogue is firmly embedded in public policy, with legal frameworks and/or national and sector level supporting structures, such institutional conditions for dialogue are often absent in low-cost sourcing countries. Dialogue is often challenged by the lack of legally mandated systems, immature industrial relations, low levels of adherence to the law and general antagonism between employers and employees. In the case of Bangladesh, even though – as outlined in Chapter 4 – worker participation committees are enshrined in national labour law, their implementation is, like that of many other labour laws and regulations, undermined by a lack of enforcement, weak unions and employer resistance. Scholars have argued that 'soft law', or non-mandatory processes, can provide institutional support for employee participation, particularly where the political will to use 'hard law' is lacking (Teague, 2005). This raises the question of whether, as with other governance gaps, global corporations play a role in using 'soft law' mechanisms to create conditions for participation and dialogue.

## 8.2 The Shortcomings of the Social Auditing Model

The 2013 Rana Plaza disaster had confronted brands with the failure of current CSR practice: social auditing against codes of conducts. While brands were still heavily investing in the practice, most brands admitted a growing frustration with auditing as a 'top-down, here-comes-the-buyer approach', as a CSR manager from a major international brand confirmed (Brand A.1). In addition, brand interviewees highlighted that the auditing approach could be superficial in nature to the point of being dangerous. A brand CSR manager elaborated:

So with auditing, you can put a tick in the box and pretend everything is okay . . . it's just functionally useless . . . . There's been times when we've been to factories and you see a lot of pipework on the wall and they [factory managers] say 'yes, it's a hydrant system [in case of fire]'. And if you take the trouble to trace it back you find that at the end of it there is nothing! . . . you know, that's no good to man or beast at the end of the day! (Brand A.1)

Auditing was recognised as working to encourage pretence, such as 'second sets of books' or 'cosmetic changes' to placate external auditors.

These issues around codes have been well documented in Bangladesh and beyond (LeBaron and Lister, 2015). Even those who have highlighted the positive effects of Codes of Conduct have also been well aware of their limitations (Locke, 2013). Hence, by failing to police the workplace, the problem was reframed as the need to enable workers themselves to have avenues to raise issues such as locked fire exits or refuse unsafe work. Brands started to recognise that their CSR activities would have to start promoting workers' participation. One labour consultant to a major brand explained:

If you look at Rana Plaza and the Tazreen factory fire . . . people know there is a problem, like at Tazreen the alarms were going off but workers couldn't leave [because fire exits were locked], you know, because there was no voice. (Consultant interviewee)

Instead, brands were increasingly aware that CSR had to start 'putting the worker at the centre of it because at the end of the day we're saying we want it to be a safe environment for workers. So you need to have a worker piece' (Brand D.1).

Workplace dialogue was therefore presented as 'a stop to a top-down protocol implemented across the supply chain' to make 'the old top-down system obsolete' (Brand A.1). It would place dialogue into local ownership, as a CSR manager from Bangladesh working for an international brand explained:

Workplace dialogue really is part of the solution because at the end of the day this is a topic that belongs in Bangladesh between the management and the workers. (Brand E)

Similarly, another CSR manager argued that workplace dialogue 'ultimately places ownership [over workplace issues] to where it belongs [at the workplace]' (Brand A.1). It was seen as a transfer of problem-solving discourse to the local level. Rather than seeing Bangladeshi workers as passive recipients of CSR activities, they were now seen as active contributors to problem-solving. Workers themselves would resolve workplace issues on an ongoing basis through formalised practices of dialogue with management, rendering periodic checking through external 'snapshot' audits obsolete:

You don't need to do an audit there. You can sit with the workers' representatives to discuss how these things are working. So ideally that's how it would work ... you know, the dialogue structure is there every day, representing workers all the time, dealing with these issues. (Consultant Interviewee)

Brands thus saw workplace dialogue as a way of delegating control to local actors: 'We want to partner and transfer the ownership and the accountability to the proper stakeholders' (Brand A.1).

Brands highlighted that while they did not have a mandate to establish directly worker participation, as this would be undue interference in the employment relationship, they emphasised their responsibility to create the conditions to enable dialogue:

We cannot force any factory to establish a trade union. We cannot force the workers to do that either and we cannot try to implement our own worker committees .... But what is our responsibility is to try to give the right people the keys and the resources to be able to do that together. And we want to be supportive in that sense. So it's important for us to freely say that this is important to us and that we want this dialogue to take place. (Brand E)

## 8.3 Developing Structures for Workplace Representation

It was quickly realised that creating institutional conditions for workplace dialogue in Bangladesh would be challenging. What became politically important here was that, at least on paper and as outlined in Chapter 4, Bangladesh had significant legislative requirements for representative worker voice and dialogue at the workplace level. While these were, on the whole, ignored by both management and the government, the very existence of such requirements provided a lever for projects to be commenced. However, in interviews, brand representatives and ETI staff highlighted two main challenges that emerged for workplace social dialogue that required the intervention of brands. First, employers were highly resistant to worker representation, let alone elected representation or trade unions, and hence lacked experience of conducting meaningful dialogue with their workers. Even though freedom of association constitutes one of the ILO's Core Labour Standards and typically forms a key provision in buyers' codes of conduct, efforts at unionisation faced stiff opposition from employers. Second, Bangladesh consistently features in the list of the ten worst countries in which to be a trade unionist due to physical threats to the lives, freedom and health of trade unionists with state collaboration in terms of supressing worker rights (ITUC, 2018). Local labour experts believe as few as 20 out of 4,296 garment factories registered with the BGMEA have unions that are independent and fully functional. This persistent adversarial culture not only prevents the development of mature industrial relations but also creates a vicious cycle of mistrust. Thus, it was viewed as essential that brands took an active role in developing workplace dialogue if such programmes were to become embedded.

Central to industrial democracy is the idea that worker participation at the level of the enterprise is embedded in a range of supporting institutions that provide for workers to exercise voice independent of management. For example, Freeman and Lazear (1995) argue that for works councils to act effectively, there needs to be a series of legal underpinnings, which include rights such as duties to establish a works council, access to information, protection of representatives and penalties for not meeting the legal requirements. Industrial relations scholars agree that, where possible, legal support for participation makes participation more effective as it removes negative externalities that may block cooperative behaviour between employers and workers (Freeman and Lazear, 1995; Hall and Purcell, 2012). This support is viewed as necessary, as the pluralist perspective argues that institutions must be present to ensure that recognition of divergent interests can be accommodated within the employment relationship. Traditionally, the state was seen as the key actor in terms of providing such supporting institutions. However, in the context of developing economies, the idea of the state acting as an autonomous or even partially autonomous actor is not a realistic expectation, given the dependency that many developing economies have in relation to low-cost labour standards. Recognising that 'the existing PCs did not have any meaningful existence as a worker voice and did not carry out their functions' (ETI, 2014: 7), private buyers would have to play a central role in creating enabling conditions for dialogue:

The difference is going to be driven through brands, you know, pushing for change in terms of establishing worker voice and dialogue. (Consultant interviewee)

### 8.3.1 Brand Roles in Building Representative Structures through Workplace Social Dialogue

In contrast to social auditing carried out by external auditors, the development of workplace dialogue required on-the-ground participation of brands' Dhaka-based staff and active involvement of headquarters staff. It was through activities such as these that brands took on 'state-like' characteristics to enable the development of workplace social dialogue. In our research, we identified three key roles in which brands engaged with suppliers to enable workplace dialogue: guarantors, capacity-builders and enforcers for dialogue.

#### 8.3.1.1 Brands as Guarantors of Dialogue

The first role taken on by brands was that of guarantor, which means that brands assured factories that the JETI were trusted to develop workplace dialogue in a way that would not threaten factory-level industrial peace or lead to worker unrest, which could disrupt production and jeopardise the commercial relationship. The workplace dialogue project thus required brands to establish 'buy in' from factory management, which was seen as 'the biggest single challenge by a long shot' (Brand F). Despite legal requirements for elected PCs, Bangladeshi employers were highly resistant to democratically elected worker participation due to adversarial labour relations. The JETI (ETI, 2014: 10) highlighted that 'the buyer–supplier relationship is central. Supplier buy-in will not be achieved without an intensive process of engagement by the brands'.

To engage factory management, brands presented themselves as trusted 'business partners' (Brand B.2), the interests of which were congruent in maintaining industrial peace. Brands assured managers that even though workplace dialogue was about introducing democratic worker representation, it was 'safe' to do so. It would neither threaten production nor challenge the position of management. This was a hard sell. Across the factories we visited, managers told us of their fear of worker participation because it was associated with militant trade unionism. They recounted both the decline of the once-thriving jute industry 'due to unionisation' in the 1970s, as well as more recent instances of workers 'thrashing' factory machinery. Thus, the prospect that elections may lead to effective worker participation, let alone the formation of a trade union, elicited employers' reluctance: 'The brands are coming to the supplier saying, "Please do the project." So the suppliers are saying "Aaaaah! ... you want me to let in the trade unions and the NGOs into my factory?"' (Consultant interviewee). To over-come this fear required brands 'to work very, very closely with factories to make it work' (Brand B.2) and to assure management that it was a mechanism to 'deal with the seeds of conflict at the very beginning' to prevent it escalating into unrest (ETI.2). Brands thus engaged actively with factory management to assure them that workplace dialogue would have a positive impact on workplace relations. In sum, brands sought to 'guarantee' to factories that workplace dialogue was a 'safe' practice that would neither threaten industrial peace nor the commercial rela-tionship and would instead strengthen buyer–supplier relationships.

### 8.3.1.2 Brands as Capacity-Builders for Dialogue

The second role that brands took on was that of building the capacity of workers to 'create enabling environments for dialogue between the social partners' (Brand B.2). Worker dialogue is contingent on the ability of worker representatives to communicate effectively with man-agement about key issues of concern. But in the Bangladesh garment industry, a largely disempowered and uneducated workforce from rural and economically disadvantaged areas was subjected to highly autocratic management. Rather than seeing Bangladeshi workers as passive recipients of CSR activities, brands aimed at enabling workers to take ownership of workplace issues through dialogue: 'the focus is very much on developing capacity to solve issues' (Brand B.3). In the training sessions we observed, workers were introduced to formal dialogue processes, including how meetings are structured and what constitutes an agenda. In role-playing activities, workers learnt how to raise an issue with management and discuss how it could be solved. This built confidence for workers to know 'how to sit down around a table with the management' (Brand H.1).

We attended two contrasting PC meetings in Dhaka in 2016, which were chosen due to their differing time involved in the dialogue project. In the first, at a very early stage, the meeting was typified by suppression of worker voice. Management were placed at the front of the room in very comfortable seats while worker representatives sat on wobbly plastic chairs arranged in a semi-circle around managers. Managers kept walking in and out of the meeting and answering their phones, often when in full flight of speaking to worker representatives. Workers mostly listened and spoke only when explicitly asked to do so by management. From our observations, it was clear that workers were not ready to raise issues with management, who viewed the session as an opportunity to speak to, rather than with, workers.

In contrast, we observed a PC meeting in one of the longest participating garment factories in the outskirts of Dhaka in 2016 where the thirteen elected worker representatives were confident about raising issues in front of management. Female and male worker representatives alike spoke out on issues ranging from safety to payment of wages and holiday leave. They stood up and presented their issues to management in an assertive voice. Management listened attentively and engaged with the issues raised. Workers followed up on responses from management in a lively exchange. While we cannot attribute the differences observed to participation in the dialogue programme alone, it nevertheless indicates the importance of capacity-building to make workplace dialogue meaningful.

### 8.3.1.3 Brands as Enforcers for Dialogue

Finally, while brands had an established role in enforcing codes of conduct, they also became enforcers of dialogue. Many factories failed to implement the legal requirement to have a PC or to allow workers to elect their representatives. Even though brands saw workplace dialogue as a shift away from the top-down 'here-comes-the-buyer' approach and regulation 'from above' (Brand B.1), in practice they became the de facto enforcer of Bangladeshi labour law in terms of establishing PCs. Brands were prepared to 'use our commercial leverage' (Brand A.1) to cajole reluctant factory owners into establishing democratically elected PCs. Unwilling suppliers risked losing business: 'We say fine, we don't force anyone . . . . But we cannot do business with someone who doesn't have the same vision for the industry' (Brand B.1).

In two of the participating factories, verification checks revealed that PC worker representatives had been appointed rather than elected. At a brand meeting in Dhaka, a local CSR manager explained how their headquarters intervened to ensure that elections would be held: 'At some point call from UK. You cannot back off' (Brand E.1). Factory management complied and agreed to organise elections. Brands argued that 'there is a need for strong monitoring from brands, otherwise the dialogue is not sustainable' (Brand H). Brands engaged in ongoing tracking of indicators to monitor the efficiency of dialogue: 'There are certain indicators that we track . . . . To what extent is the committee able to solve issues? Or do they just get talked about and then they pop up at the next meeting again?' (Brand B.1).

In sum, workplace dialogue brought about a significant shift in terms of how brands approached CSR 'at the coalface', requiring them to intervene in the employment relationship.

### 8.4 Confronting the Structured Antagonism of the Sourcing Relationship

Even though brands were engaged in developing workplace dialogue as a vehicle for reducing non-compliance, dialogue also revealed that the root causes of much of this non-compliance were ultimately linked to brands' purchasing practices. Thus, an inherent tension emerged between brands' interest in reducing non-compliance and their commercial interest in maintaining the conditions that led to them. Following Edwards' (1986, 2003) notion of 'structured antagonism', we term this the 'structured antagonism of the sourcing relationship'. For Edwards (2018), the dyadic employer–employee relationship was

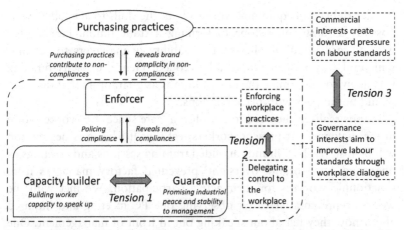

**Figure 8.1** Confronting the structured antagonism of the sourcing relationship

underpinned by an 'inevitable' conflict of interests where one party (within capitalism, the employer) had an exploitative relationship with the other party (the employee) and sought control. While the concept was developed for a two-way relationship, as will be shown below, we argue that the tripartite supply chain relationship is underpinned by analogous relationships between parties (brands–employers–workers) within a common (sourcing or employment) relationship. This structured antagonism manifested itself in a series of nested dialectical tensions that challenged brands' supply chain practices in unexpected ways. Figure 8.1 depicts the multilevel nature of these tensions, which we discuss below.

## 8.4.1 First Dialectical Tension at the Level of the Employment Relationship

As depicted in Figure 8.1, a first tension arises at the level of the workplace from the dual roles of brands seeking to endow workers with capacity for dialogue, while also presenting themselves to management as guarantors of industrial peace. The tension exposed the extent to which brands were far from neutral mediators of the employment relationship. As guarantors, brands declared themselves ready 'to stand in front of a business owner saying this [workplace dialogue] is good because they place trust in us' (Brand B.1). Yet, as a capacity builder for workers, brands declared themselves as defenders of worker rights and equipping workers with the skills to act collectively, possibly as a stepping-stone to forming a trade union. Functioning workplace dialogue implies that the ability of managers to act in a unilateral way is at least partially eroded. Hence, capacity-building was likely to undermine the role of brands as guarantors that dialogue would not impact workplace relations.

Brands realised the need to establish a 'safe space' for worker voice in the dialogue: 'At present workers feel that if I bring issues my job will be lost' (ETI.3). Brands attended training sessions and meetings as observers. Such brand 'oversight' prevented factory managers from sanctioning workers for their active participation. We met with the worker representatives after observing one PC meeting and inquired about how they felt about speaking out in front of management. One representative responded, 'We are happy because the brands are here now. We feel we can raise issues. We feel it is okay.' The observation indicates that brands provided a level of 'protection' that enhanced worker confidence that participation in dialogue would not jeopardise their position:

It's not just about getting buy-in from factory owners. It's getting the workers to trust that what we're doing is going to have a positive impact on them and it's not seen in a negative light from their management if they take part. (Brand F)

Realising the importance of providing assurance to workers, brand representatives started to visit factories to meet worker representatives and assure them that they would not be individually targeted when raising collective issues. Brand involvement even served as a mechanism for supporting union formation. In one of Brand A's participating supplier factories, the dialogue programme revealed the existence of a new union. Brand A and ETI staff worked with the fledgling union and interacted with management to bring about union recognition through registration with the Labour Department and ensure that the union was represented on the PC.

In contrast, brands realised that meaningful dialogue also required building capacity for managers and supervisors and reducing potential for conflict from aggressive management. Brands spoke of the need for change in 'management mentality' to seeing worker voice as part of a cooperative worker–management relationship: 'It's the mind-set that matters most' (Brand B.1). Senior managers in the factories we visited admitted the need to prepare supervisors for workplace dialogue: 'We're seeing across factories anywhere that workers have maximum problem with the supervisor they are dealing with. If they [managers] are not trained, it is really difficult for you to have any dialogue' (Factory A). While the JETI programme included one day of supervisor training, brands felt that this was only the starting point and that they had to invest additional resources into supervisor training. For instance, Brand A rolled out a special supervisor training programme across all its supplier factories.

In sum, the roles of guarantor for managers and capacity-builder for workers risked undermining each other and suppressing meaningful dialogue. In response, brands realised that they also had to take a more active role in ensuring a 'safe space' for workers, as well as building dialogue capacity for supervisors.

### 8.4.2 Second Dialectical Tension at the Level of the Compliance Relationship

As depicted in Figure 8.1, a second tension arose at the level of the compliance relationship. By putting a system in place that empowered workers to speak out about workplace grievances, brands claimed to shift away from top-down auditing to placing 'ownership [over workplace issues] to where it belongs' (Brand B.1): between employers and workers. But in their role as 'enforcer', brands readily admitted that they would not relinquish control to suppliers: 'We claim the right to go back to the old top-down monitoring system which is auditing' (Brand B.1). If dialogue revealed non-compliances, brands insisted on the need to intervene and that their suppliers 'need to put it right' (Brand A.1). Instead of external auditors doing periodic checks, trained worker representatives could keep watchful 'eyes and ears' inside the factory and thereby provide a more effective form of oversight.

This tension was problematic because it could ultimately undermine dialogue. Clearly, it was not in the interest of factory management to allow dialogue to expose non-compliance. Factory managers lived in fear that if 'brands know about problems they won't accept the product' (Brand D.2). If seen as a threat to the sourcing relationship, factory managers were likely to suppress dialogue, thereby impeding problem-solving. Being confronted with this tension, brands realised that they had to develop a different approach to how they exercised control over non-compliance. While social auditing had previously allowed brands to claim taking a zero-tolerance approach to non-compliance, brands admitted that it enabled 'plausible deniability' and disowning responsibility:

Zero-tolerance it's just a tool for plausible deniability so you can say, 'We have told you we have zero-tolerance, we have auditing, so we take no responsibility if things go wrong'. (Brand H.2)

Instead, brands realised that a zero-tolerance policy would constrain dialogue partners to discuss the 'real' issues and push them into hiding. Brands declared that they wanted transparency about the 'real' workplace issues going on at the factory: 'We want the actual challenges, we don't want a second set of books' (Brand B.1). At a JETI workshop in Dhaka with participating local brand representatives, this issue was discussed intensely:

ETI.2: 'The real issues are not picked up by audits, yet we know they exist. So if they come out through discussion in the PC, does this create a problem?'

Brand H.2: 'For us, we really need to understand what the root causes of these issues are and then help factories address it. Other brands they practice a zero-tolerance approach and they simply stop orders if there are problems. But that is really not helpful at all. We want to see that the system is working and that grievances are addressed.'

Moving from a 'hear no evil, see no evil' approach to wanting to know about the 'real issues' was a significant shift in approach. Previously, brands' social compliance teams were incentivised to reduce the number of non-compliances detected in their supplier factories. Now, exposure of the 'real' issues was seen as an indicator that dialogue was functioning.

As a result, rather than policing standards through top-down auditing, brands declared themselves willing to collaborate with their suppliers in addressing non-compliance: 'We see it very much as the role for our supply chain team to act as developers, not auditors' and to 'help you to solve your problems, not about simply carrying out auditing' (Brand B.3). To do so, brands emphasised management systems that would help factories address the 'root causes' of non-compliance. For instance, several brands started to train suppliers in production planning to avoid the need of workers having to work excessive overtime due to poor planning. Thus, for dialogue between management and workers to work, brands realised that they had to engage in dialogue with their suppliers:

Social Dialogue is predicated on another level of dialogue – between factory and brand. For workplace dialogue to be effective, there needs to be dialogue between brand and factory on issues such as need for flexibility regarding overtime and so on. Trust is needed and transparency. It's a cascading chain. (ETI.1, Dhaka)

In sum, rather than pursuing a zero-tolerance approach that allowed for plausible deniability by concealing non-compliances and their causes, brands realised the need to recognise their existence and engage in dialogue with their suppliers in order to solve problems.

### 8.4.3 Third Dialectical Tension at the Level of the Commercial Relationship

The final and most fundamental tension depicted in Figure 8.1 arose from brands' declared aim to improve labour standards through workplace dialogue while perpetuating many practices that were the root cause of abusive labour conditions: the relentless demands by the brands for lower prices, flexibility, short lead times and penalties for delayed deliveries. This tension was revealed through confrontation with non-compliances that could not be resolved at the workplace level. Instead, dialogue revealed that the cause for workplace conflict was often ultimately rooted in commercial pressure placed on suppliers. Almost every single factory manager or owner we met bemoaned time pressures, last-minute orders and cancellations, as well as unfair pricing:[1] 'If I don't get the fair price from the customer, how is it possible to maintain so many things?' (Factory A Managing Director).

This tension became apparent over important issues of labour compliance, such as the persistent problem of excessive overtime. We observed a supplier meeting in Dhaka, where conversations about workplace dialogue revealed the toxic relationship between overtime, low wages and brand pressure. A factory manager at the meeting shared his experience:

[1] Anner (2019) reports that the price of cotton trousers exported to the United States from Bangladesh decreased from $62.26 in 2013 to $54.29 in 2017 despite inflation and fluctuations in the price of cotton.

The reality in the factory is that workers work more than 10 hours. They work after 10pm or sometimes more. The PC members informed us, 'We cannot work like this. We have family and others.' Then, we talked with top management about PC member concerns. (Factory B)

Excessive overtime was often the result of frequent changes in order specifications and short lead times, due to unpredictable consumer demand in a fast-fashion market, coupled with high fines for delays. Time pressures drove factory managers to push workers into working overtime. Thus, helping suppliers to develop better production planning alone would ultimately not eliminate excessive overtime but instead required brands to change their own commercial practices, as one CSR manager admitted:

I think the big thing is we are a business, fabric does go late, things do happen but the question is does it have to happen 90% of the time? It's just to give yourself that thought, 'What can I do to try to mitigate that circumstance where that factory hasn't got to do excessive overtime?' ... But you know, it is a hell of a thing and I'd love to sit here and say, 'Oh, we're great, we've got no problems'. But we do! We're a commercial business. (Brand F)

In the above case, the factory was able to agree terms with its buyer that allowed it to reduce overtime. Factory management advised not keeping workers after 10 p.m. But removing overtime work revealed another problem: workers were often financially dependent on overtime pay to top up their base salary by up to a third of base pay:

So for three or four months, there was no more work after 10pm. After four months, we had a PC meeting. The PC members now complained that workers are getting small money. They cannot afford [to pay necessary expenses for] their family. (Factory B)

This example illustrates how factories struggled to resolve the source of workplace conflict through factory-level adjustment alone.

CSR managers were surprisingly reflective about the fact that resolving the grievances brought up by workers required brands to change their own commercial practices. Some brands admitted that they had to wake up 'to take responsibility as brands for the unintended consequences' created by their own purchasing practices:

For brands not to realise how they're driving unethical practices in the supply chain I think is a ... I mean, thankfully now I think people are starting to be a little bit more honest about that, about what our role has to be. (Brand I.1)

This third tension exposes the structured antagonism of the sourcing relationship most clearly. While brands aimed at resolving tensions 1 and 2 through important, yet relatively moderate changes in CSR practices, it became clear that these tensions could only be fully resolved if tension 3 was substantially addressed. However, resolving tension 3 would require a significant change in sourcing practices, threatening brands' commercial interests and potentially the business model that underpinned a brand's sourcing strategy. Not surprisingly, perhaps, most mainstream brands have not fundamentally changed their sourcing practices to alleviate this downward pressure. The attempt to promote workplace dialogue is thus likely to be undermined by commercial strategies at the headquarters level. Nevertheless, our findings indicate that brands' involvement in workplace dialogue prompted them to rethink their attitude to non-compliances and to acknowledge their own role in creating them. This brings to the fore the divergent interests and trade-offs that are required to act socially responsibly.

## 8.5 Conclusion

In this chapter, we set out to explore how brands used their CSR to enable the development of structures for worker representation in their global supply chains and how this affects the nature of democratic representation. Our empirical case focused on the role of brands in the development of workplace social dialogue in their supplier factories in the Bangladesh garment industry. What is particularly noteworthy is that brands mobilised their powerful position as lead actors in the supply chain to provide the supportive framework that industrial relations scholars have argued is needed to develop workplace dialogue but that is generally reserved for the state (Freeman and Lazear, 1995; Teague, 2005). As argued by Kabeer et al. (2020), the prospect of the Bangladeshi government taking meaningful action to improve labour standards is not promising. In this context, while far from ideal, from a pragmatic perspective, brands were the actors most likely to be able to deliver in terms of developing workplace representation in Bangladeshi factories. Brands thus acted simultaneously as guarantors, capacity-builders and enforcers of workplace dialogue based on their market power. This exemplifies a significant departure from simply 'outsourcing regulation' (O'Rourke, 2006) through reliance on top-down codes and monitoring systems towards a much more worker-driven approach to improving labour conditions that directly involves worker representatives, factories and brands. Thus, brands can play an important role in developing embryonic representation structures even in a context of highly antagonistic worker–management relations. This presents a significant improvement on traditional CSR approaches based on codes of conduct, which rarely engage meaningfully with workers themselves.

These roles taken on by the brands, while contrary to the social auditing approach of CSR, are less surprising from the perspective of the political economy of industrial relations. In this context, while taking action that did constrain a purely market-based approach to sourcing, brands were building structures over which they retained ultimate control and which actually could increase their control in some respects. While a significant advance on what had existed prior to the project, and significantly more than what would be delivered by public regulation in Bangladesh, workplace dialogue provided a valuable forum for workers to raise concerns about operational issues arising from the supply chain model.

In our case though, it did expose the brands to the fact that many of the issues raised by workers were rooted in the nature of these problems. Looking more closely at the case shows that playing this role in developing workplace social dialogue confronts brands with the structured antagonism of the supply chain relationship. Structured antagonism became manifest in the multiple dialectical tensions that emerged from the divergent interests of brands, employers and workers. Confrontation with the structured antagonism meant that brands could no longer position themselves as neutral providers of labour governance. Instead, it exposes the contradiction between brands' aim of reducing non-compliance and their commercial interest in maintaining the conditions that led to it. While the prevailing practice of social auditing has been criticised for providing the 'illusion of improvement' (Egels-Zandén and Lindholm, 2015: 37), CSR at the workplace level challenges corporate actors to confront the daily reality of affected stakeholders. As illustrated by our tensions, it also confronts brands with their own complicity in creating the underlying cause of labour rights violations. Whereas CSR at the headquarters level may conceal the structural problems arising from exploitative pricing and purchasing practices, workplace representation is likely to reveal in concrete terms the inherently conflicting interests between capital and labour: brands outsource production to places with governance gaps to exploit cheap labour costs while workers have little power to challenge brand practices. A central point about creating representative structures is that they must be built around a recognition that organisations are made up of plural and potentially divergent interests: dealing with the structured antagonism is not about findings consensus amidst parties so as to resolve these tensions but instead requires an ongoing process of political contestation between the interests and positions of managers, workers and brands. While the notion of structured antagonism implies that it can never be fully resolved, the question concerns the extent to which workplace social dialogue can achieve a more balanced approach and elevate the attention paid to the concerns of workers. For instance, if tension 1 was successfully addressed, then workplace dialogue could serve as a stepping stone towards more independent worker representation and see brands taking steps to ensure that freedom of association and the right to collective bargaining are being respected in their supplier factories, as we observed in one case above. But if it became too skewed towards managerial interests, then being a 'guarantor' to management might implicitly or explicitly frustrate the attempts of workers to mature workplace participation committees into independent trade unions.

Taken together, brands can play an important role in enabling workplace representation. Yet such structures are likely to create significant tensions for brands. First, this is a departure from brands simply outsourcing responsibility for code enforcement to external auditors because it involves corporations at the level where competing interests meet and labour rights violations arise. However, the creation of representative structures is certainly not an altruistic act by the brands – these representative structures were created with a view to maintaining control of suppliers by the brands, while taking the worst edges off labour rights violations. They certainly were not created as a mechanism to undermine the cost basis of the supply chain model. Workplace social dialogue does not fundamentally challenge the core asymmetries of power in the global supply chain and is ultimately contingent on firms' voluntary participation, their market-based strategies and corporate benevolence to promote worker engagement. Whether or not workplace social dialogue will provide a meaningful route of engaging workers will ultimately depend on the extent to which workplace dialogue can advance the interests of workers vis-à-vis those of factories and brands.

# 9 | Conclusion

## The Emergence of Transnational Industrial Democracy?

This book has been concerned with the question of how the democratic governance of global economic relations and political participation in them, particularly by workers, can be enabled in global supply chains. As the previous chapters have laid out, private economic actors have become engaged in global regulatory arenas. Powerful corporations are staking a claim to serve a social purpose and are taking over governance roles previously thought to be the realm of governments. Civil society groups who base their power on the threat of mobilising consumers are organising to demand a say into how products are produced. New forms of private political participation and deliberation have emerged in the form of multi-stakeholder initiatives and cross-sector partnerships, where brands, NGOs and trade unions open up new political arenas, with or without the state. These developments change how the democratic representation of worker interests is carried out. On the one hand, this may be a welcome development where actors with significant economic power, namely brands, are prepared to exercise their power to achieve higher labour standards. On the other hand, it also raises the question as to what type of democracy it is when private actors – corporations and consumer-oriented NGOs alongside trade unions – become involved in the political arena. Are these initiatives about democratising global markets or are they about market-driven democracy? In any case, it is a 'skewed' (Montanaro, 2012) form of democracy. Rather than being based around institutions of democracy and the political participation of people based on rights as people, these new constellations composed of largely private actors are based on the mobilisation of their economic power and are thus market-driven. Rules are created and enforced through market forces and responsive to consumers rather than citizens.

The question, then, is whether this power can be democratically harnessed, steered or even redirected? Can democratic governance be reclaimed? The challenge is not only to create a feel-good mechanism for consumers and smoke screens for brands but to create the potential for real change to the exploitative and dangerous conditions of those workers at the sharp end of global supply chains. As we have argued throughout the book, this requires workers to have a voice and to have meaningful representation of their interests within governance mechanisms. Without doubt, the global supply chain model poses significant challenges in terms of developing more democratic participation of workers. Thus, the central question that has motivated this book is whether and how – in the context of possibly one of the most advanced forms of neoliberalism, typified by increased concentration of power in the hands of large corporations (Hathaway, 2020) – more democratic and effective governance institutions can be developed that are based on the representation of worker interests? And what difference do such institutions make in transnational labour governance?

While the weakness of the existing social auditing model is widely recognised, in very few circumstances have lead actors taken the step to try to build alternatives that put worker representation at their centre. This book presents the argument that the response to Rana Plaza was qualitatively different from previous initiatives in transnational labour governance and points towards a possible new logic of governance, which we call transnational industrial democracy. The remainder of this concluding chapter focuses on the key characteristics of this new logic. It combines elements of the associative logic of industrial democracy but emerges within the context of transnational supply chains and is tied to their structural limitations and contradictions.

## 9.1 Market-Driven Democracy: Towards a New Logic of Transnational Governance

The main argument of the book has been that the representation of worker interests must and, more importantly, can play a central role in developing and maintaining transnational labour governance if highly exploitative systems of work are to be tackled. Both the Accord and JETI Social Dialogue programmes are examples of embryonic forms of transnational industrial democracy, as to their centre is the promotion of the democratic participation of workers and their representatives in supply chain governance systems at both the transnational and workplace levels. Without doubt, the Accord, which sought not just to solve the problem of unsafe factories, but also to build a system of representation to prevent such a situation arising again in the future, marked the most significant response to the Rana Plaza disaster. The analysis provided highlights that there is potential to develop more worker-centric systems of representation but that such systems generally depend on brands enforcing them, which carries with it a number of in-built contradictions. As such, the form of transnational industrial democracy presented here falls significantly short of what would generally be thought of as an ideal type of industrial democracy, being driven by strong local unions and embedded in institutional infrastructures of the state. However, as Rodrik (2008) argues, second-best institutions often are the only alternative in highly adverse conditions and are better than nothing. Thus, what we see is a combination of an associational model of industrial democracy and market-driven governance. The key features of this new logic will now be developed.

### 9.1.1 Features of Industrial Democracy at the Transnational Level

Transnational industrial democracy is based on a number of well-established core principles of industrial democracy. In Chapter 3, we outlined the logic of industrial democracy as being built upon a pluralist conception of the firm, a belief that democratic labour governance processes require worker representation and participation, a consequent focus on process rights – particularly freedom of association – and finally, the creation of credible commitments through collective agreements. Here, we identify three core features – new actor constellations, transnational codetermination and workplace representation – of how this form of transnational industrial democracy marked a significant departure from existing private, transnational labour governance initiatives, as well as more established patterns of industrial democracy.

#### 9.1.1.1 New Actor Constellations: Representative Alliances

In the transnational sphere, a new constellation of actors and new allocation of representative roles in the form of alliances of unions and labour rights NGOs has emerged to act as a restraint on the economic power of global corporations. These combine traditional vehicles of industrial democracy – the representation of workers through unions – with models of deliberative democracy, where workers are represented discursively through proxy representatives such as labour rights NGOs. Generally, the traditional model of industrial democracy sees representation in labour governance limited to 'producer groups' – that is, the representatives of capital and labour, usually in the form of employers/employer associations and unions that aggregate the interests of the members they represent. What emerges in this new form of transnational industrial democracy is that labour actors leverage different forms of power through consumption forces to regulate production, as NGOs and GUFs have greater consumption-based leverage over brands than local unions have over employers in production contexts. The workplace, as the traditional site of contestation, can become dislocated in favour of sites of consumption leading to geographical cross-representation where (more visible) representation is taking place. As a result, the brands have more to fear from their reputation being damaged than from workers disrupting production across the supply chain.

In this context, the role of representative alliances between labour actors is of crucial importance in developing worker representation: in Bangladesh, neither unions nor labour rights NGOs had strong representational bases, which would generally be expected of coherent systems of industrial democracy. To a large extent though, the mutual weakness of both created the circumstances where symbiotic cooperation between the two groups seeking to represent workers could occur. As Chapter 5 outlined, NGOs, operating under a logic of attention, and unions, operating under a logic of membership, were able to compensate partially for each other's weaknesses. NGOs, who focus their attention on consumers rather than workers, compensated for low union membership density, while unions compensated for NGOs' lack of representative structures.

While it may be argued that this was far from being a perfectly democratic system of worker interest representation, it succeeded in combining the strengths of each actor, which lay at different points in the supply chain. NGOs were more focused on channelling consumer sentiment against brand image and GUFs were more focused on institution-building and thus, with some exceptions, were generally able to operate in a way where they were not effectively competing for the same space but instead were working together to occupy a void. This shows that within the supply chain context, weaknesses at different points in the supply chain can be compensated for at other points in the chain. In this way, representative strength may arise from what Baccaro and Lim (2007) call a 'coalition of the weak'. The disadvantage, though, can be that worker representation remains dependent on the attentional dynamic in consumer countries and the extent to which the representation is a true reflection of those being represented is unclear. A key point, therefore, is that both unions and NGOs need to recognise their respective limitations in terms of developing structures of democracy.

### 9.1.1.2 Balancing Power: Transnational Co-determination by Corporate and Worker Representatives

A core institutional feature is the emergence of efforts to build an embryonic form of 'transnational co-determination', where capital and labour have joint oversight in the design and implementation of transnational labour governance regimes. It draws on the industrial democracy model as parties agree to be bound by the agreement made by those to whom they aggregate the representation of their interests. While the idea of 'co-determination' is often narrowly applied to the German works council model, it is broader in origin and, to use Müller-Jentsch's terms (2003: 40), 'the dominant theme of codetermination was labour's claim to a legitimate role in the running of companies and the economy'. This certainly was the case in the Accord, where representatives of business and workers had equal voting rights and where negotiated agreements between the groups were a central feature of the approach. The workplace social dialogue programme was less advanced, but its central rationale was the development of worker representation through workers themselves at the workplace level. Transnational co-determination thus involves the recognition and inclusion of representatives of the interests of workers at both the peak and transnational level, as well as at the workplace level. Without doubt, the model of transnational co-determination developed is far from perfect and how it would develop in the absence of transnational institutions that harness the leverage of brands over their suppliers is precarious. Regardless of this, giving workers mechanisms through which they can raise issues collectively, either in a transnational system or with brands in workplace dialogue committees, involved workers in a way that has rarely been witnessed in supply chains.

Adopting such a pluralist approach to governance is likely to lead to a greater focus on democratic institution-building. Chapter 6 provided a natural experiment in terms of comparing how a pluralist initiative based on principles of industrial democracy, the Accord, differed from a unitarist one based on voluntary CSR, in the form of the Alliance. What was particularly striking was that the corporate-driven CSR approach was based on a rather short-term, problem-solving approach, focused on remedying the 'problems' rather than tackling the underlying issues. The Alliance dissolved after five years into a traditional social auditing model rather than making an attempt to build longer-term governance capacity. In contrast, the Accord, which on occasion was frustratingly slow for actors on the ground in Bangladesh, was built upon the aspiration of building capacity for a system that could develop meaningful institutions beyond the lifetime of the Accord and saw spillover initiatives develop, as outlined in Chapter 7. Thus, the emphasis was on building democratic institutions to govern health and safety, not 'just' to fix factory safety as a one-off intervention.

### 9.1.1.3 Workplace Representation

Transnational industrial democracy involves creating workplace-level representation to complement representation at the transnational level, rather than simply taking a top-down approach. This addresses the common criticism of both NGO- (Rasche, 2011) and GUF- (Fichter and McCallum, 2015) driven transnational labour governance in that efforts are concentrated on worker representation vis-à-vis the multinational buyers at the transnational level without meaningful efforts to develop workplace representation at the coalface (Reinecke and Donaghey, 2021b). A problem here is that while independent trade unions are ideally at the heart of industrial democracy, in the supply chain context, genuine freedom of association is suppressed – whether it is through employers, as in Bangladesh, or by the state, as in China or Vietnam. Based on the reality that brands are not going to stop sourcing from countries due to their lack of truly independent worker representation or in face of the challenges that independent trade unionism faces in contexts like Bangladesh, there is a need to develop second-best alternatives on the basis that some representation is better than none.

It was in this context that both the JETI social dialogue project and the Accord's OSH Committees played a role. In both approaches, workplace-level systems were created as mechanisms through which the collective and aggregated interests of workers were represented. In the workplace social dialogue project presented in Chapter 8, while it was mostly composed of non-union worker representatives, the rationale behind such programmes is to develop systems of worker representation, not only because it provides a more effective way of protecting worker safety and worker rights but also because workers have a legitimate right to a voice in governing their workplace as a matter of principle. Workplace representation, though, is not just representation for the sake of it: it can play an important complementary role to higher level representation. As developed in Chapter 8, the workplace dialogue brought into focus the role of brands in creating downwards pressures on factories and workers that would not have been evident in broader, more principle-based representation. Because of this, a core contradiction emerges: the actor whose purchasing practices are the root cause of many labour abuses in supply chains, the brand, also becomes the regulator. Despite this contradiction, in the current context, this is probably as effective a mechanism as can be established.

## 9.1.2 Market-Driven Features of Transnational Industrial Democracy

A core distinction of the emerging form of transnational industrial democracy is that it is market driven. Rather than being driven by the regulatory power of the state, enforcement is driven by the economic power of global capital. As observed in our research, private governance can become stricter than public regulation, since host countries act as 'competition states' and neo-liberal trade ideologies prevent effective cross border regulation. However, oversight of worker rights and representation is also contingent on private actors and on the supply chain relationship continuing. Here we outline three factors that typify this more market-driven approach to democracy: enforcement through brands, leverage of consumer pressure against brands and built around, not challenging, the supply chain model.

### 9.1.2.1 Enforcement through the Economic Power of Brands
The model of transnational industrial democracy presented is based upon participation rights not as citizens of a particular economy, as when guaranteed through government regulation, but the economic

position and power of the brands and their commercial contracts. The core area of divergence from both deliberative and associational ideals of democracy, as outlined in Chapter 3, is that the enforcement mechanism that was witnessed in both the Accord and the workplace social dialogue programme was that of the economic and market power of global brands: brands use their economic power to impose constraints on their suppliers, the employers/factory owners, based on contractual market relations. While contractual relations are typically assumed to take place between consenting parties, the economic power of brands in developing country contexts means that producers are not just price-takers but also governance-takers. Another effect of market-driven governance is that efforts to create regulation often lead to competition between private regulators and even 'markets' for standards (Reinecke et al., 2012). Competitive regulation enables brands to set up initiatives on terms more favourable to their business interests, as occurred when mainly North American brands created the Bangladesh Alliance as a more business-friendly alternative to the Accord.

In contrast to most existing regimes of social auditing and certification-based governance, a key differentiating feature that emerged within the Accord (and to some extent the Alliance) was the collective approach adopted by the brands. While one brand has relatively little leverage through its purchasing power, over 200 brands sourcing from the same country combined had substantial leverage over their suppliers. This is because the fragmented nature of supply chains denudes much of the economic power of individual brands against suppliers who supply up to ten or more brands. Nevertheless, the important point here was that by removing price competition over health and safety between brands enabled the exercise of collective leverage to implement change. Similarly, in the workplace dialogue programme, the fact that it was seen as a collective approach by brands encouraged employers to participate based on their supplier relationship. What occurred here was, to put it bluntly, employers being subjected to a governance regime due to the collective economic power generated through the market-based, short-term contracts in supply chain relationships.

### 9.1.2.2 Leverage of Consumer Pressure against Brands
Linked to the previous point, the very nature of the supply chain model seeks production regimes that have low levels of regulation and

ineffective governance. Due to the low standards and poor implementation where standards do exist, neither employers nor brands were threatened in their production processes by legal regulation or worker organisation in Bangladesh. The changed nature of 'brands', however, has created the key pressure point in the industry around which action can coalesce. Brands have emerged as little more than a hollow shell at the production end: they often employ few, if any, production workers. By escalating the 'brand' of their product, reputational issues become key to manage. While the actual effect of negative imaging is far from proven, in the age of rapid mainstream media and social media, brands have become highly cautious about exposure of their name to negative publicity.

The potential exposure of brands to negative publicity essentially arises from the risks of the supply chain model: by taking a low-cost route and also reducing legal risk by having legally independent contractors manufacture their goods in low-cost and poor labour standard contexts, brands effectively increase their risk of reputational exposure. In the case of Rana Plaza, this was amplified by an abrupt and sudden backlash by consumers, particularly through social media. This response was marshalled through many activist groups to push brands to make commitments beyond those they had undertaken before as a means of demonstrating their response to the disaster. The epitome of this effect was the case of Fruit of the Loom, which, after signing the Alliance, also joined the Accord due to the pressures it was facing from student activist group on campus. Labour actors were able to identify that employer recalcitrance could be overcome through exerting pressure on brands, which in turn exerted pressure on employers. Thus, combining these first two market-based characteristics creates a chain of pressure from the potential of consumer dissatisfaction towards brands and subsequently from brands onto the employers in their supply chain.

### 9.1.2.3 Built Around, Not Challenging, the Supply Chain Model

Institutions established under this new model of transnational industrial democracy are built around and work within the supply chain model, rather than specifically confronting it. Thus, they are built on the power asymmetries of this model and on the fragmented and often short-term economic relationships between supply chain actors who have little to no mutual commitment towards each other beyond their contractual obligations. Even though the COVID-19 pandemic has demonstrated the fragility of supply chains and dismantled the myth of hyper-flexible sources of supply, in principle brands can still move on to other suppliers or even production countries. Similarly, the transnational labour actors on whose pressure the governance model depends, GUFs and NGOs, could decide to focus their attention and limited resources on other pressing issues. Thus, the model is precarious as it is reliant on the continuation of the supply chain. This, however, will be unsurprising to scholars of industrial relations: as Willy Brown (1973) pointed out nearly half a century ago, the institutions of industrial relations follow the product markets in which they are set.

Yet, while initiatives responding to the Rana Plaza disaster may be criticised for failing to challenge supply chain capitalism (e.g., Alamgir and Banerjee, 2018), the question is whether the aim is to end the supply chain model altogether. It is important to remember that initiatives that challenge the model itself are also challenging the method by which millions of workers try to alleviate themselves from poverty on a daily basis: through factory work. As such, labour actors had as their goal the amelioration of conditions within the supply chain context rather than the ending of the model itself. This approach reflects the reality of building institutions for the representation of workers' interests within supply chains: workers are dependent on the supply chain model in terms of furthering their economic interests. In addition, while the conditions themselves may be significantly worse than manufacturing conditions in more developed economies, they are often viewed as superior to alternatives in primary industries. This point has been made by Naila Kabeer (2017) in relation to Bangladeshi garment workers: in a highly patriarchal society such as Bangladesh, the garment sector has provided a way for the advancement of women in that society, even if the model itself is highly exploitative. This should not be surprising as the very idea of industrial democracy as put forward by Webb and Webb (1987) was one of Fabian-inspired reformism in the context of capitalism, rather than one of radical social revolution. The expectation was that trade unions played their role in advancing democratically the interests of workers and that the interests of employers in the form of economic efficiency also had to be recognised in the capitalist system. When applied to the supply chain context, the implication is that mechanisms of industrial democracy are not viewed as challenging the model but rather concerned with bringing about a better balance of the respective interests of capital and labour.

## 9.2 Structural Limitations

The system of transnational industrial democracy presented here falls significantly short of what generally would be thought of as an ideal type of industrial democracy, due to a series of underlying structural issues that inhibited what might be considered a more solid foundation to the attempts to develop meaningful worker representation. This presents part of the conundrum of 'second-best institutions': to paraphrase Voltaire, should the perfect become the enemy of the better? While the achievements in improving safety within the RMG sector in Bangladesh were significant, there are inherent structural limitations and these need to be recognised. In particular, the external imposition of voice, the exclusion of national actors and the disaster-driven nature of the response highlight that while important lessons can be drawn, the emerging system does have a number of structural weaknesses.

### 9.2.1 *External Actors' Imposition of Voice*

The first structural limitation is that worker representation emerged at the behest of brands, which exerted their economic power as lead actors in the supply chain over their supplier factories. Low union density and the lack of public supporting institutional infrastructure have placed significant limits on the scope and force of the democratic representation of supply chain workers. Thus, the central role that brands, actors of global capital, have played in the design and enforcement of systems of worker representation is contrary to what could be considered as the pluralist norm.

Scholars have long criticised the representation of workers as disproportionately skewed towards business interests or the agendas of Western activists (Siddiqi, 2009; Tanjeem, 2017). In both the Accord and the workplace social dialogue programme, in different ways, the representation of worker interests emerged through downwards pressure from transnational actors, rather than being generated directly by the workers themselves. In the Accord, while a central feature was the establishment of OSH committees, the representation of worker interests occurred primarily at the transnational level. In contrast, while the workplace dialogue process examined in Chapter 8 was focused on developing factory-level dialogue, participation of employers was driven by the need to satisfy the brands and their desire to reduce non-compliance with their codes of conduct. Thus, brands became guarantors, enforcers and capacity-builders both of and for systems of workplace representation. This structural weakness has emerged across other transnational labour governance initiatives. IFAs, for example, have been criticised by Fichter and McCallum (2015) for adopting a top down 'social partnership' approach between brands and GUFs rather than an activist-oriented approach based on adversarial agitation. That said, while union organising at the grassroots level is important, it is also crucial not to fetishise it. In economies like the United Kingdom and United States, where shopfloor organisation has been the focus of the labour movement, dismantling union power has been relatively easy. In contrast, in economies such as Sweden and Belgium, where union density, coverage and power have remained important, the model is based on top-down provision of collective goods rather than an organising model. This is not arguing that union membership is not important but, in the context of power asymmetries of global supply chains, the ideal of achieving meaningful level of bottom-up unionisation is far from the reality. What is important, though, is that mechanisms are developed to incentivise low-paid workers to see a purpose in collectivising. The real challenge is not the inability to take industrial action – for example, wildcat strikes have been a feature in supply chain relationships throughout apparel producing economies (Anner, 2018). What is important is that workers have independent and democratic means for aggregating their collective voice. Without this, there is the potential for worker voice to be truncated, focused on the peak level with little meaningful interaction with the workers who unions are purporting to represent.

### 9.2.2 Lack of Inclusion of National Actors and Institutions

In the traditional model of industrial democracy, the state devolves governance power to private actors. In the market-driven scenario, private actors denude the host country state and assume quasi-regulatory power by acting as the enforcers of private governance regimes. As a result, generally key subjects of regulation, employers, were excluded from participating in governance. This points to the second structural weakness: while powerful in mobilising private transnational actors, this approach to transnational industrial democracy is less successful in mobilising national actors – especially public regulatory bodies and employers against whom many of the rules are aimed. In both the Accord and the workplace social dialogue programme, Bangladeshi employers and the government of Bangladesh had very little input into the actual design of the programmes. Their exclusion also runs contrary to established forms of both associative and deliberative governance, where the objects of governance participate in the governance structures. As developed in Chapter 7, this became the Accord's Achilles heel. The exclusion of both the government of Bangladesh and the employers resulted in sustained resistance and hostility towards the Accord, which ultimately prevented the Accord model from being extended beyond its term. It also undermined the ultimate goal of the Accord to establish sustainable institutions that could become self-reinforcing. Excluding two such important actors created a scenario where the extent to which cooperation could be developed between parties was highly constrained.

It is, however, important to highlight that in both the Accord and the JETI social dialogue programme, the central feature was creating institutions to implement the legal requirements of domestic Bangladeshi laws. In the Accord, standards generally corresponded to the Bangladeshi building code. Similarly, the workplace social dialogue programme was little more than implementing to the letter the amended Bangladeshi law on worker participation committees. It could thus be argued that these transnational initiatives reinforced, rather than displaced, domestic labour market institutions and that, more generally, they have the potential to make state institutions more relevant (Amengual and Chirot, 2016). However, the explicit exclusion of Bangladeshi actors from the design and creation of institutions, even where they were simply implementing domestic regulations, created significant resentment with the government and employers. This reality however was drowned out by the rhetoric of exclusion and neo-imperialism as mobilised against the institutions. Thus, legal reality was replaced by political posturing as a mechanism used to undermine the transnational model.

### 9.2.3 Disaster-Driven

Governance innovations are, like other institutional innovations and adaptations, shaped by the context within which they are set (Streeck and Thelen, 2005). Without doubt, the model of transnational industrial democracy that emerged was a product of the sheer scale of the Rana Plaza disaster. As the pictures of a building collapse that killed over 1,100 workers reverberated across the world, the Rana Plaza disaster became a 'focusing event' (Schuessler et al., 2019) that acted as a catalyst to accelerate a shift in thinking in relation to OSH in Bangladesh. For example, as outlined in Chapter 5, literally weeks before the disaster, the MoU in response to the death of 112 in Tazreen, which ultimately was mainly adopted to form the Accord, could not get four brands to commit to it. But once Rana Plaza happened, brands quickly came on board.

The focusing event, though, acted as a double-edged sword. On the one hand, it helped get parties to set aside their differences to establish an agreed path forward on the specific actions needed to prevent similar disaster happening again. This clear focus facilitated a collective approach. On the other hand, a drawback of being so closely linked to a 'focusing event' is that the response was tightly tied to solving the problem associated with that event, which meant wider issues of low wages and worker exploitation fell outside the remit of many of the initiatives that were taken. Moreover, it raises questions about whether and to what extent the development of institutional innovations is contingent on disasters like Rana Plaza. Does it really mark a significant departure across the model? Without doubt, the urgency of responding to Rana Plaza precipitated a significant move. Nevertheless, developing more worker-centric forms of transnational labour governance has emerged in a number of related areas since the Rana Plaza disaster; however, it remains to be seen how these will evolve. Take, for example, the 'Action. Collaboration. Transformation' (ACT) initiative that emerged directly as a spillover from the Accord (Ashwin et al, 2020). This seeks to develop a system of sectorally, bargained living wages in up to eight garment manufacturing economies across Asia between IndustriALL and brands. In addition, the Bangladesh experience has also changed the way individual firms carry out their business. For example, H&M is seeking to eliminate the use of social auditing and replacing it with workplace social dialogue across its entire supply chain. British fast fashion retailer ASOS has negotiated an IFA with IndustriALL – the first online retailer to take this step. While these are small steps in a vast global industry, they may indicate the direction industry leaders are taking: towards recognising the role of worker representation and trade unions as legitimate partners in transnational labour governance.

These structural weaknesses are far from isolated in a world where labour rights are continually under attack. In addition, while far from ideal, the exercise of brand power in this area is better than simply decrying the system as being imperfect. As Kabeer and colleagues (2020) highlight, the Bangladesh government is highly unlikely to take steps to improve labour rights in the short term. The same is likely in the case of other states who are competing for production contracts. One of the balancing acts thus is to achieve genuine reforms that will improve the lives of workers without endangering the jobs available to those workers.

## 9.3 Towards Transnational Industrial Democracy?

The emerging bricolage of transnational labour governance described in this book cannot be viewed as even close to a perfect system of transnational industrial democracy. What is important, however, is that the core features of the institutional design were based around key principles of industrial democracy but transposed to the context of the current globalised neoliberal environment: inclusion of independent representatives of workers' interests and the recognition of the need for compromise between the interests of workers and those of business, implemented through the power of brands. While easy arguments could be made to highlight how these systems do not live up to normative yardsticks of industrial democracy, the very achievements of these initiatives are probably as promising as any initiative focused on workers to have emerged in the transnational sphere. In a highly hostile environment for worker representation, institutions were established that placed workers at the centre of the governance approach. These institutions went on not only to change significantly the safety of factories from which brands were sourcing but also to force the government of Bangladesh and the employers to engage more seriously with OSH.

In supply chain contexts such as apparel, where labour is weak and brands have significant discretion to regime shop, the prospects of achieving robust forms of labour governance are not high. Models of private governance rarely reach the levels of those who call for higher levels of public regulation (Stroehle, 2017; Frenkel and Schuessler, 2021; Morris et al., 2021). It is clear that market-driven transnational industrial democracy in itself is not enough to protect labour rights in global supply chains. Supportive regulatory frameworks are also needed whether from buyer states or through the form of brands. But the very system places host states in the invidious position of choosing to raise labour standards and lose their attractiveness or to allow standards to spiral downwards as a pathway to economic development. Nevertheless, greater legislative movement has occurred in buyer countries. The publication of the UN Guiding Principles on Business and Human Rights (UNGPs), which established that governments have a duty to protect human rights and companies have a responsibility to respect human rights, has set off a wider legislative trend in EU and US economies. However, this trend has largely focused on human rights reporting requirements by companies – for example, the UK Modern Slavery Act 2015 (Gutierrez-Huerter et al., 2021) – or mandatory human rights due diligence – for example, the US Dodd Frank Act's section 1502 on conflict minerals (Reinecke and Ansari, 2016) or the French Duty of Vigilance Act 2017 (Evans, 2020) or the upcoming EU Mandatory Human Rights Due Diligence Directive. Human rights due diligence, the process by which companies 'identify, prevent, mitigate and account for how they address impacts on human rights', is a welcome development. However, there is no mandatory participation role for the potential and actual victims of human and labour rights abuses to have a say in how companies address adverse human rights impacts or what taking appropriate action would look like. It once again focuses on unilateral corporate action without mandatory democratic input. Thus, while initiatives like those outlined in this book are not enough in themselves to protect labour rights in global supply chains, neither are corporate reporting or due diligence mechanisms in the absence of democratic input.

As we were finalising this book, global supply chains were in crisis. The reliance of developed nations on receiving cheap produce through the supply chain model has been exposed by two years of the COVID-19 pandemic. Nationalist and populist tendencies, seen manifest in Brexit and Trump, have emphasised a politics of wealthy economies feeding off the poor when it is to their advantage but drawing down the shutters to stop the poor advancing economically. And finally, what some viewed as the unimaginable event of a return to large-scale wars in Europe is reviving ideas of self-sufficiency. Thus, while global supply chains are still the dominant mode of production and trade in the global economy, the unfettered advance of the neoliberal global trade model seems to have hit a roadblock. However, these tendencies do not reverse the negative effects of the global supply chain model but instead exacerbate them. While COVID-19, for example, has meant that Western consumers found empty supermarket shelves and long waiting lists for the first time in many people's living memory, workers in developing economies lost their jobs as factories saw their orders cancelled. Indeed, the initial response of many Western brands was to try to walk away without paying from contracts into which many suppliers had already invested significant resources (see Anner, 2021). While a significant campaign emerged that led to many buyers honouring their contractual commitments, these contracts were generally short term and involved little to no investment from the brands. The current nature of footloose capital places huge power in the hands of brands, with workers suffering the consequences even more in times of crisis. Now more than ever we need more meaningful initiatives, in both qualitative and quantitative terms, in transnational industrial democracy to counter the worst effects of the global supply chain model. We hope this book helps to clarify lessons from the response to the Rana Plaza disaster in terms of building the institutions for transnational industrial democracy.

# Appendix 1

## The Practical and Political Issues of Studying Transnational Labour Representation

### A1.1 Introduction

In this appendix, we offer a reflection on the practical and political aspects of studying labour representation in a transnational context. First, to the extent that any research account is influenced by the particular process of doing research, we will reflect on the 'lived experience' of being in the field and how it shaped our perspective. Second, writing a book about transnational representation raises some difficult meta-level questions about 'who can represent whom?' Representation is an inherently political issue and not only in labour movements: it is also an epistemological question concerning academic research and writing more generally. Thus, we will offer some reflections and raise questions about the 'academic' politics of representation.

### A1.2 Experiencing the Research Context in Bangladesh

Engaging in ongoing fieldwork is often described as a matter of 'getting your hands dirty' in the mud of the field. Certainly our feet got dusty on the streets of Dhaka! Table A1.1 provides an overview of our data sources in Bangladesh and in other countries.

Since much of this book has dealt with the question of the political representation of the interests of Bangladeshi workers, fieldwork helped us get a sense of the world that was to be represented – the world of Bangladeshi employment relations. It allowed us to meet in person with the different actors constituting this world, both from Bangladesh and from its buying countries: workers and union leaders, factory owners and factory management, brand staff, Accord staff, Bangladeshi and international NGO workers and so on. By no means does this allow us to 'represent' this world in terms of a faithful portrayal or speak on behalf of anyone, but it helped us to understand

Table A1.1. *Data sources*

| Method | Respondents | N | Bangladesh or transnationally based | Further details |
|---|---|---|---|---|
| Interviews | International trade unionists | 20 | 10 Bangladesh based | 12 initial |
| | | | 10 internationally based | 8 follow up |
| | Bangladeshi trade unionists-IndustriAll | 14 | All Bangladesh based | 11 initial |
| | | | | 3 follow up |
| | Bangladesh trade unionists- non-IndustriAll | 3 | All Bangladesh based | 3 initial |
| | International NGOs | 9 | 3 Bangladesh based | 7 Initial |
| | | | 6 internationally based | 2 follow up |
| | Locally based NGO | 1 | Bangladesh based | 1 initial |
| | Accord staff | 13 | 8 Bangladesh based | 7 initial |
| | | | 5 internationally based | 6 follow up |
| | Brands | 33 | 18 Bangladesh based | 25 initial |
| | | | 15 internationally based | 8 follow up |
| | Factory management | 4 | All Bangladesh based | 3 Initial |
| | | | | 1 follow up |
| | Bangladesh Garments Manufacturers and Exporters Association (BGMEA) | 7 | All Bangladesh based | 5 Initial |
| | | | | 2 Follow up In addition, 3 interviewees under factory management held BGMEA office |
| | International Labour Organization | 10 | 5 Bangladesh based | 7 initial |
| | | | 5 internationally based | 3 follow up |

Table A1.1. (*cont.*)

| Method | Respondents | N | Bangladesh or transnationally based | Further details |
|---|---|---|---|---|
| | Joint Ethical Trading Initiatives | 11 | 5 Bangladesh based 6 Internationally based | 8 initial 3 follow up |
| | Alliance/Nirapon | 5 | 4 Bangladesh based 1 Internationally based | 4 initial |
| | Governments | 4 | All Bangladesh based | 4 initial |
| | BD based labour experts | 3 | All Bangladesh based | |
| | Total interviews | 140 | | 107 initial 33 follow up |
| Group meetings | Management | 8 | All Bangladesh based | Meetings during 8 factory visits 16 managers in total |
| | Workers | 6 | All Bangladesh based | 3 facilitated by unions 3 facilitated by management |
| Observations | Observations of representative training | 4 | All Bangladesh based | |
| | ETI Bangladesh category group meetings | 5 | London | Involving MNCs, unions and staff from the 3 Ethical Trading Initiatives |
| | Dhaka Apparel Summit | 1 | Dhaka | Brand representatives |
| | ETI social dialogue stakeholder meetings | 3 | Dhaka | Factory representatives Worker representatives |

the practical challenges, the multiple viewpoints and political complexities not in the abstract or from the far-away comfort of our offices but instead through our first-hand observations and experiences of the lived realities of Bangladesh. In these days of Zoom, Teams, Skype and myriad other online tools, the temptation exists to carry out interviews without visiting the site of the research. For us, seeing and experiencing the physical reality of Bangladesh was an important step in the research process. For brief moments, it allowed us to 'be there' – feeling the hot tropical air in the factory halls or listening to the regular hum of the sewing machines. Doing research in an unfamiliar territory made us perceptive to the differences of a world that we were seeing for the first time. This counteracted our Western naivety. Even though tragedies such as the 2017 Grenfell Tower fire in London remind us that building and fire safety is a precarious accomplishment anywhere, in Bangladesh the lack of building and fire safety was noticeable straight away. In our own hotel, we were glad to detect a fire exit staircase, but it was frequently blocked by potentially flammable laundry bags. In one of our rooms, the smoke detector was covered in adhesive tape, which left its utility redundant. When we notified reception, we were told that the smoke detector had annoyed previous guests who smoked in their rooms. Opposite the hotel, a thirteen-storey building was being erected. On its unfinished rooftop, construction workers walked around pulling heavy cement bags literally to the very edge, where there were no safety railings that would prevent them from falling off the building. Dhaka's cityscapes were characterised by wild tangles of 'spaghetti sky' – an amalgamation of overhead electrical cables, TV, telephone and internet wiring, all strung from the same concrete poles. When walking the streets, we often had to navigate some of the cables that had fallen off. Road safety in Dhaka traffic was another reality check. We rode local rickshaws that more than once went in the opposite direction of the traffic on main roads on which the lanes were already shared by big buses, cars, trucks, rickshaws and CNGs, all criss-crossing each other. The iconic images where railway travellers sit on top of the running train are not an exaggeration either. When we drove through Dhaka, local contacts would point out many residential units that had been converted into makeshift factories, often engaged in subcontracting, to take advantage of the relatively 'quick money' to be made in the sector in Bangladesh. They were recognisable at night from having strip lighting illuminating the storeys. Being on the upper floors of buildings, up winding alleyways, often on streets not wide enough for an ambulance or fire engine to gain access, there would be little hope of extinguishing any serious fire that broke out in any of these factories.

Doing fieldwork in Bangladesh was a stimulating experience, but it was not without its challenges. During our second visit, shortly after the contested general election in January 2015, a month-long *hartal*, or general strike, had been declared by the opposition party. During this period, we had to undertake additional clearances to be allowed to travel by our university employers. The *hartal* made carrying out interviews difficult – particularly with brand interviewees as, for example, one day saw meetings and interviews cancelled because a petrol bomb was thrown at a building nearby. Locals expressed shock to us about the petrol bomb. For one of us, who had lived in a Western city where many petrol bombs were thrown fairly often, it raised the reality that Western researchers carrying out work in Western cities with much more violent contexts often faced many fewer restrictions on travel than they did to less-violent developing nations.

Seeking to economise, we booked a much cheaper hotel in accordance with our university's approved rates of hotels for Dhaka (under £40 a night, whereas most 'Western-style' hotels were charging London rates). We arrived late at night from a 20+ hour journey via Doha, Qatar, and did not think much of it when the safe did not work in one of the rooms. The next day, the passport in that room was missing. We had to present ourselves at the local police station in Gulshan. Our local Bangladeshi contacts had all warned us about any dealings with the local police and none were willing to accompany us to the police. Would we have to pay a bribe as we observed all Bangladeshi nationals doing in the police station?[1] Might they interrogate us about the nature of our work? Had our entry visa been sponsored by the BGMEA or a foreign embassy, as for most Western visitors, we would have been less worried. However, we had entered on a tourist visa (as had most NGO workers and researchers we met), as research visas were notoriously difficult to receive, particularly for those engaged in critical social science–based research. Luckily, the

---

[1] It is important to say here that seeing police being handed money by citizens for simply doing their job is not just a phenomenon in Bangladesh and, for one of us, growing up seeing this occur in our home country was not unusual either.

embassy had arranged for us to meet a senior member of the diplomatic police official upon arrival at the police station. When he arrived,
he handled our case with efficiency and professionalism, sparing us the
awkward experience of figuring out whether we had to pay bribes to
local officers.

While we had walked freely around the streets of Dhaka and travelled by bicycle-drawn rickshaws on our initial visits, the changing
security situation during our later trips confined us to chauffeur-driven
cars, hotels and the expat clubs, where the city's foreigners would meet
to socialise. Especially after the brutal July 2016 attack on the Holey
Artisan Bakery (which we had visited two months previously while in
Dhaka), where twenty-nine people were killed, we were advised not to
walk around any longer. When entering a hotel, a café or any public
premises, we had to pass airport-style security checks observed by
heavily armed security guards. Our university policy also prevented
us from visiting certain places, such as Dhaka University, which was
identified as a hotbed for political protest. The extent to which the
danger to us was real was unclear, however, the restrictions placed
upon us isolated us from daily Dhaka life.

These experiences of Dhaka life allowed us to appreciate the massive
change it would take to establish a safety culture in the RMG sector.
The challenge was not just to put in fire doors but to ensure they would
not get locked the next day. It was not enough to have fire exits but to
have factories where emergency services could reach unimpeded and
quickly. It was not enough to renew electrical systems, but it was also
necessary to ensure their regular maintenance. It was not enough to fix
existing factories; it was also vital to ensure that the managers and
workers inside the factories were able to identify and address ongoing
safety issues. Thus, we got a much clearer sense of the level of challenge
as well as achievement and personal sacrifice that all the different
actors experienced who worked relentlessly to establish factory safety
in Bangladesh.

## A1.3  Confronting Privilege: The Researcher's Politics of Representation

In a book about transnational representation, a pertinent question is:
Who can represent whom in a research account? The question of writing
across racial, class and gender boundaries is one that has occupied

literary theory, feminist scholarship and other areas for some time, but it is also one we confronted both in our fieldwork and in academic writing. To clarify, we do not claim to represent the workers or speak for them. Throughout the book, we have refrained from taking the perspective of the workers – there are some significant accounts of researchers who have done so (Siddiqi, 2009, 2020; Tanjeem, 2019). Instead, our book is an account of how the workers are represented by others. It is also important to remember that our research, while having much of its empirical context set in Bangladesh, was not specific to Bangladesh: it involved examining how modern capitalism has developed to be transnational in nature and how actors combine across the transnational realm to develop instruments of governance.

Nevertheless, in the context of historical imperialism and the hierarchies of global value chains, it is an important political question to ask whether scholars from one particular end of the supply chain can legitimately write about issues regarding workers at the other end of the global supply chain? In this book, we have argued that is it important for workers to be represented by representatives independent of employers and brands. Neither the factory owner nor the brand can speak for workers because they are implicated in the interests that constrain the worker. One can also not claim for oneself a lived experience that one has never known and a struggle in which one has played no part. But what this means in practice is a difficult question. Would this mean that to write about workers in global supply chains one has to come from the same social class as the workers – the working class? Or be the same gender, female, as most Bangladeshi garment workers are? Or that one has to share the same ethnic origin – an ethnic Bangladeshi? And what is more important – class, race or gender? Is it more legitimate for Bangladeshi scholars from a more privileged class background to write about Bangladeshi garment workers? Or is it more legitimate for non-Bangladeshi scholars from a working-class background to write about Bangladeshi workers? And can male scholars write about issues concerning workers who are predominantly female? These questions all raise important issues that require critical awareness and giving voice to a diversity of research perspectives, but they should not be barriers that exclude researchers on the basis of their class, race or gender.

We were confronted with privilege, difference, gender and often a sense of guilt during our fieldwork in Bangladesh. Despite not being from an elite background in our home countries, within the Bangladesh context we were primarily perceived as both white English-speaking academic researchers with posts at prestigious Western universities from the 'colonising' Britain and with an ability to shape knowledge and therefore representation of what was going on in the post-colonial south. Our physical presence alone – being white, tall, in Juliane's case red-haired, and dressed in Western style – stood out remarkably. At Dhaka airport, staff at airport shops such as the mobile phone SIM-card sellers immediately recognised us from previous trips. There were rickshaw drivers who would pull over and greet us after having been away for several months in different parts of Dhaka, a city of about 16 million people. Thus, we clearly stood out from afar as foreigners. It is likely that our physical appearance suggested an even greater economic and political importance than our actual position as academic researchers. The few Westerners who were visible in Bangladesh were typically buyers from Western brands, business investors, diplomats and foreign embassy staff or foreign government officials – thus all potential sources of some form of inward investment into the country. The default assumption was that we had to be of some similar 'importance'. Thus, white privilege in a post-colonial setting was likely reinforced by the power asymmetries of global supply chains and our assumed position within them.

These are the basic characteristics that we brought to our research and that affected how we were perceived and received in the field. It offered us an advantageous position in the context of historical imperialism and the hierarchies of global value chains. In the Bangladeshi context, this shaped our ability to gain access to certain sites and people – it facilitated access to elite actors while complicating access to the workers. We were surprised to learn that some Bangladeshi research students at Western universities had difficulty gaining access to companies – brands and employers – compared with Western researchers, or upper-class Bangladeshi students and researchers.

On our first visit to Dhaka in 2014, we arrived at the RMG Apparel Summit at the Bangabandhu International Conference Center in a run-down car that was presented to us as a 'taxi'. The majority of local attendees arrived in air-conditioned, chauffeur-driven cars. But when we entered the auditorium, we were handed VIP tickets and ushered to sit in the first row, where we found ourselves surrounded by the RMG business elite. We were extremely embarrassed by having

turned up in simple jeans and striped t-shirts when everyone else was
wearing dark suits and ties, and the few Bangladeshi women in
attendance wore beautiful silk saris. Exchanging business cards, which
we learnt is as common a greeting as a handshake is in Western
contexts, we realised that we were seated next to the Head of the
Industrial Police, the top union-busting government official. During
the breaks, we were approached by local factory managers who
assumed that we must be buyers. We struggled to convince them that
we were 'merely' researchers rather than potential clients. As our
research progressed over the years, we met several academics who
were also garment factory owners.

Nevertheless, these assumptions may have played a role when local
actors readily agreed to interviews with us. We were invited to visit
factories, which typically started with a tour of the factory premises. At
one visit to a large factory, the factory showed off its private fire
brigade, which staged a fire drill just when we passed the factory-
owned fire pond. Then multiple members of the senior management
team, if not the owner himself (yes typically a him), would meet us in
the main showroom/conference room where buyers and other important visitors were hosted. The visit was typically concluded with a
catered lunch.

As with much qualitative research, this type of interview situation
was a complex social event characterised by impression management,
political action and cultural scripts (Alvesson, 2003). Our hosts and
respondents took great care to manage our impression of their factory
and used the interview as an opportunity to convey certain selective
and favourable 'truths' to us. For instance, factory owners typically
constructed themselves as the victims of exploitative Western brands,
whose purchasing practices and low prices meant they made losses that
prevented them from investing in making their factory safe, let alone
paying workers higher wages. There is no doubt that brands, as we
discuss in Chapter 8 in particular, do squeeze local producers.
However, at the same time, some of the factory owners were likely to
be more economically and politically privileged than we were – or, for
that matter, many of the representative of the brands or CSR staff who
they usually hosted in those conference rooms. They often wielded
political power in Bangladeshi elite circles and displayed signs of
personal wealth such as expensive watches or cars. Once, we witnessed
a black Ferrari, identified as the car of a factory owner who lived

nearby, driving down Road 96 in Gulshan, Dhaka, seemingly oblivious to the damage being inflicted on his expensive car by this unsealed, heavily potholed road. Many of those factory owners we met also commuted between Dhaka and their UK, US or Canadian homes, to where they had relocated their families.

Thus, the version of reality we encountered was one that was skilfully adapted by politically aware actors in ways that reflected our position as Western academics able to shape the representation of Bangladeshi factories in the Western world. At times, we were guilty of channelling our bewilderment of the contradictions we encountered into the construction of a generalised image of the Bangladeshi factory owner as a skilled impression manager who exploited workers despite his personal wealth. But we also encountered other factory owners who ran small-scale subcontracting operations out of upper floors of retail buildings. They seemed to be genuinely struggling with the demands of safety upgrades. Thus, we had to take care to balance our accounts against the structural and political forces that shaped our encounters and recognise the multiplicity of situations and experiences that resisted our construction of 'the' Bangladeshi factory owner.

Another privilege of being Westerners was that we could move between worlds. We could speak to the ILO or the Accord or embassy staff or brands. The fact that we had met with either their head office staff or possibly themselves in Western settings, if not the airport, positioned us within a shared world. Moreover, the 'expat' clubs – notably the German Club on Road 104 in Gulshan-2, where our cravings for German beer (for one of us) and pizza drove us – allowed us to become part of a shared expat world. Here, we would serendipitously meet many of these foreigners (staff from buying companies, foreign organisations) who in the Bangladeshi context were construed as the Western elite. Many were related to the RMG industry. We could thus informally chat over drinks and food and learn the types of views and experiences that are usually not shared in formalised interview situations.

As much as our privileged outsider position helped us to access elite actors, it represented an obstacle when it came to speaking to workers. The obvious barriers of culture and language aside, we quickly realised that we could not access the perspectives of workers in the factories we visited. When we negotiated to meet workers on site, the meetings were typically arranged with what we suspected were handpicked workers who were likely to be briefed before the meeting to make a good

impression. Moreover, the only Westerners who typically visited factories were the all-important buyers or their CSR staff from brand
headquarters. We too were perceived as aligned with these positions
and interests. Out on factory premises, the answers that workers would
give seemed carefully staged to please management: 'What is good in
the factory?' – 'Yes, everything is good.'

We tried to mitigate this by joining meetings of workers at the offices
of trade union federations. At trade union offices, we could meet
workers in a more trusted environment away from the controlling gaze
of their supervisors and the general controls and constraints imposed
by conducting interviews within the workplace. Being union members
ourselves in the United Kingdom, namely of the University and College
Union (UCU), was extremely helpful for establishing credentials and
common ground with Bangladeshi unionists. While hardly anyone had
reacted to the emails we had sent off two weeks before our first visit,
leaving us worried that nobody would speak to us, we learnt that
planning in Bangladesh was generally a last-minute thing and local
labour actors spontaneously agreed to interviews with us when meeting them in person. On our second night, we had been invited by the
UK's Ethical Trading Initiative (ETI) to attend the opening of its new
joint office with Danish union 3F. While there, we realised that nearly
all our key targeted informants from the labour side were there and we
promptly signed them up for interviews. For one of our first visits to a
union office, to the NGWF, Google Maps indicated a half-hour travel-
ling time for a distance of 5.5 kilometres from our hotel. We left an
hour before the meeting. It became apparent that this was not enough
and two hours into the journey, having travelled about 2 kilometres,
we contacted the union to say we didn't know how long it would take
and we should cancel. The General Secretary assured us that we should
keep coming – he would wait. Eventually, after four hours in the car,
we got there to be overwhelmed: about twenty-five female trade unionists who had walked off the job at a factory earlier that day were
waiting to meet us and to talk to us about their experience. We also
presented ourselves as engaged union members in our home countries
and expressed solidarity with the workers. This demonstration of
empathy with the workers' cause helped to establish trust.

However, it also confronted us with some uncomfortable questions.
First, while to us as academics, writing academic outputs based on our
research is an end in itself, we were left with the impression that many

interviewees – particularly those unfamiliar with the details of the academic world – attributed to us and our potential work greater agency than we felt we had. The question inevitably became 'For whom are you writing this report?' with the expectation that our work would directly inform policy actors or that we would reach out to brands to achieve a direct intervention. We felt a sense of guilt that our work did little, at least in the immediate time frame, to ameliorate the current condition and confront the particular injustices that these workers had endured. This is not saying that our research did not have a central aim of impact: it did, and we participated in many working groups and presented our research to unions, NGOs and corporate members of the ETI on several occasions, in the hope that it would be impactful. Nevertheless, we were aware that the knowledge that we were about to produce would not immediately contribute to improve safety in their factory, giving them higher salaries or more secure jobs.

Second, could the NGO activist or trade unionist be doing something more useful with their time than meeting an umpteenth researcher asking the same questions? As academic researchers, our work is dependent on others giving us access to their domain and to their time. But while to the individual researcher getting a one-hour interview with a key actor may not seem like much, to often over-stretched interviewees these one-hour interviews quickly add up. As we read research by other authors on the response to Rana Plaza, we deduced that many of the same interviewees were interviewed by a multitude of research teams.

Finally, we were also confronted with gender relations in our field-work and encountered how complex layers of gender and White privilege shaped field interactions. When entering a restaurant together as a mixed-gender research team, the greeting 'Good evening, Sir' was an immediate reminder of the subordinate position of a woman in the Bangladeshi context – that is, Juliane's position. Yet when Juliane entered a restaurant with a local Bangladeshi man, the greeting changed to 'Good evening, Madam' – suggesting that White privilege trumped male privilege in this context. When organising a project event in Dhaka with Bangladeshi partners from a Western university, Juliane's name and role were quietly eliminated from the agenda and programme despite her and Jimmy being of equal rank and her being the university's Principal Investigator on the project. Jimmy's intervention reinstated her position but still reminded Juliane of her gendered self. While being a mixed-gender research team had many advantages, the co-presence of another White male in the field setting likely had the effect that gender relations came to dominate field interactions. This was also visible when we conducted our interviews jointly but rotated who took the lead in asking our questions. When Juliane led the interview, responses were typically directed at Jimmy. Male Bangladeshi respondents also typically avoided eye contact with Juliane. This was in line with Muslim etiquette, whereby people of the opposite sex who have no relation with each other (non-*mahram*) must not gaze directly into their eyes (while Jimmy might have inadvertently offended Bangladeshi women). Even if culturally appropriate in this context, for Juliane this refusal to interact with her felt like a denial of her agency and presence as an autonomous person, which made interviewing an often uncomfortable and alienating experience.

Our privileged ability to move across stakeholder lines allowed us access to a wide range of perspectives and enabled us to appreciate the multiplicity of interpretations. This was important because it allowed us to consider the same situation or issue from multiple viewpoints and appreciate the complexity of it, which was rarely black or white. As reported above, Bangladeshi unions were aligned both with the labour interests in securing worker safety and with those of employers in sharing a sense of national pride in defending the interests of their industry at large. We got a sense of the radically different worlds and realities inhabited by the actors whose interactions we examined: the reality of a Bangladeshi union leader radically differs from brands' CSR staff in London. It also confronted us with discrepancies between the different accounts. For instance, while Bangladeshi employers shared their frustration over brands forcing them to implement rigid and strict safety standards while not paying them higher prices for goods, Western brands shared their frustration over employers refusing to ensure basic safety standards while squandering income on expensive lifestyles and squeezing their workers to the bone. Rather than seeking to reconcile conflicting accounts, being in the field helped us appreciate the validity of different accounts from the perspective of different actors.

## A1.4 Conclusion and Final Reflection

Conducting fieldwork at the intersection of local and global power relations prompted us to reflect on how these dynamics invariably shaped the phenomena of representation and transnational institution-building that we set out to study. Being confronted with privilege and gender made us realise that we did not bring neutral bodies to the field with our physical presence but that our own 'being there' was intimately inscribed into the power relations that shaped the research context. On the personal side, visiting Bangladesh on numerous occasions came to mean a lot to us personally. The research has become more to us than simply trying to apply or develop an abstract academic theory to an empirical context in a far away and foreign land – as long as people associate us with being 'Rana Plaza' researchers, it means that the devastation of Rana Plaza to workers and their families has not been forgotten.

# Appendix 2

## When CSR Meets Industrial Relations: Reflections on Doing Interdisciplinary Scholarship

Theoretically, this research emerged at the intersection between industrial relations and organisation theory–based CSR scholarship. It was driven by a desire to understand the interface between consumer-driven and labour-driven dynamics and the democratic consequences in conceptual terms. Practically, this book is what happens when an industrial relations and an organisation theory scholar meet and engage in a series of at times heated conversations and arguments about whether 'old school' trade unionism or the 'new wave' of social movement activism is better placed to drive change in global supply chains. Here, we offer a reflection on doing interdisciplinary work that, in our case, was central to developing the ideas presented in this book.

### A2.1 How Our Collaboration Began

Doing interdisciplinary work is often hailed as the holy grail for innovative research, but it is also extremely difficult to realise because, on one level, theoretical paradigms are often incommensurable. Interdisciplinarity is relative, of course. We did not come from opposite ends of the university. Our collaboration began in 2012 when we worked in the same department, the Industrial Relations and Organisational Behaviour group at the University of Warwick, having joined it on the same day in September 2010 – Juliane on the organisational and Jimmy on the industrial relations side. This meant we came from opposite ends when looking at the world of global supply chains. Jimmy's approach was concerned with the ways in which governance structures could affect the ways in which workers and their representatives influence how employment and the workplace are governed. Juliane's research, in contrast, focused on the role of organisations and consumer movements in driving sustainable practices in global supply chains.

We soon realised that we were both teaching about labour standards in global supply chains but that the literatures to which each of us referred had little overlap and rarely acknowledged the other's existence. With few exceptions (Egels-Zandén and Hyllman, 2011; Williams et al., 2017), most scholarship had either focused on the role of unions or on the role of civil society actors in attempts at taming corporate power, with little conversation between the two approaches. CSR scholars tend to ignore the existence of trade unions or view them as simply 'another' part of civil society, whereas industrial relations scholars often ignore the role of consumer activists and voluntary CSR due to their lack of being grounded in the interests of workers (Reinecke and Donaghey, 2015; Donaghey and Reinecke, 2018). In fact, these two literatures also seem outright opposed to each other in terms of their theoretical assumptions and ideological orientation. One focuses on the role of discourse, meaning and framing, the other on the role of structures and interests. But maybe they could also inform each other? Can labour and consumer power be complementary to develop transnational governance?

We started to explore this question by conceptualising both the differences and complementary opportunities for how employment relations and consumption relations were mobilised in global labour governance. At a June 2013 meeting in London with Polly Jones, who had a background in both international trade unionism (formerly international officer at Unison) and NGOs campaigning (as a board member of War on Want), she pointed out that the emerging Bangladesh Accord was an emerging example of cooperation between unions and NGOs in negotiating the Accord. All of a sudden, our 'academic' questions had become real overnight.

## A2.2 How Our Different Backgrounds Informed Our Intellectual Outlook

The researcher's own pre-understanding – the stock of prior accumulated knowledge, disciplinary training, experiences inside and outside academia, beliefs and interests – is rarely acknowledged, even if it informs the research process. When reflecting back on our research journey, our own experiences in and outside academia have significantly informed our investigation. Jimmy had always been actively involved in union work since joining academia, holding branch officer positions in UCU at local and national level as well as laterally becoming University of South Australia National Tertiary Education Union Branch Secretary. Being an 'insider' to the labour movement was extremely helpful for establishing credentials and common ground with respondents, particularly unionists. Moreover, this experience shaped his intellectual outlook. Being heavily involved in negotiations and seeing their reality, Jimmy was accepting that one does not always have to look for the ideal type. One has to satisfice.

Juliane's research was focused on how social movements and activist campaigns worked to convert consumers' purchasing power into market-driven governance interventions, such as Fairtrade or other sustainability standards (Reinecke, 2010; Reinecke et al., 2012; Levy et al., 2017). Her intellectual outlook was shaped by her observations of the emergence of new power relationships in global value chains (GVCs) and the role of civil society actors in exerting power on lead actors by shaping meanings and frames regarding responsible behaviour. This illustrates the power of consumption relations to exert pressure on globally sourcing brands to improve labour and environmental standards in their supply chain.

## A2.3 How Industrial Relations and Organisation Theory Can Complement Each Other

There are some 'historical' precedents for cross-fertilisation: Kelly (1998) drew on insights from social movement theory, most often associated with organisation studies, to develop a theory of worker mobilisation in industrial relations. In the opposite direction, much of critical management studies found its roots in the more industrial relations-oriented labour process theory.

One source of complementarity was to bring consumption relations, and the dynamics affecting this approach, to industrial relations. Whereas the employment relationship is the central unit of analysis in industrial relations theory, the global production context requires expanding the focus to include other actors who are central to affecting the employment relationship: the brand emerges as the lead actor. Indeed, the greatest threat to the pursuit of profits by a brand might not be disruption of production due to industrial action of supply chain workers. Thus, the most important strategy for improving workplace conditions might not to be negotiating with employers but rather putting pressure on brands to disrupt consumption. Here, organisation theory brought understanding of the role and dynamics of CSR and consumer movements as driver of global labour governance.

On the flipside, our focus on industrial democracy brought to organisation studies research a focus on structural issues of worker representation. In contrast to CSR research, industrial relations insists on the particular role of workers and their elected representative in labour governance, arguing that labour interests can only be effectively represented vis-à-vis capital at different points in the supply chain by labour itself. Within CSR research, much focus has been placed on discourse, meaning and framing. However, for CSR to be anything more than an attempt at placating Northern consumer audiences, those who suffer the consequences of global capital and attempts at governing it must be involved.

## A2.4 What We Learnt from Each Other's Perspective

Without doubt, there is a tendency in both industrial relations and organisation studies to sneer at much of the empirical work carried out by the other discipline. Consumer-oriented activism and union organising are based on different ideologies, methods and cultures of effecting change, which are reflected in different academic communities. This scepticism was illustrated when one editor in chief of a leading industrial relations journal desk rejected our first empirical journal article, describing worker health and safety as a 'motherhood and apple pie issue'.

In the industrial relations tradition, researchers often have a normative disposition to showing that collective bargaining is the right way of organising work (Kochan, 1999). Jimmy, too, was highly sceptical of NGOs and social movement activists, who often seemed to be campaigning for the sake of making noise while unions were investing in negotiations to get the best outcome for members. In the worst case, NGOs could undermine union negotiations. Now the world has become a patchwork of black and white. This feeds into the interpretation of what happens in the field – for instance, when looking at the role of NGOs in the Accord. Even if they are not elected worker representatives, their ability to put pressure on brands by making noise is useful in a context where workers do not have the power to put pressure on their employers.

In contrast, like many organisation theory but also some political science scholars, Juliane saw unions as just another type of civil society actor, alongside NGOs. Juliane did not pay much attention to the specific relevance of unions in protecting worker rights in global supply chains. From her perspective and research, unions were active in national employment relations but, apart from some solidarity campaigns and backing of private governance initiatives, they did not seem to play a big role in moving private governance forward. While NGOs are built on visibility and gaining attention, the unions' behind-the-scenes negotiations are easily overlooked unless one is involved.

## A2.5 Drawing Lessons: Sustaining an Interdisciplinary Approach

A core feature that enabled our interdisciplinary lens was the sheer magnitude of the Rana Plaza disaster, which focused our attention on the issue over theoretical commitments. Thus, we both shared a problem-driven approach to our research, which has long been central to industrial relations research (Kochan et al., 1999). The problem-oriented approach means that researchers are generally flexible in terms of methods and theories as long as it provides a means to investigate the problem at the centre of the research. Without doubt, this shared orientation to problem-driven research played a key role in facilitating our joint efforts because it did not tie us to any particular perspective but rather encouraged us to use lenses from across our perspectives to shed light on the problem of how to govern worker safety in global supply chains.

A second, related feature that enabled our cross-disciplinary stance was commitment to our data and willingness to be led by what we saw in the field. For instance, our fieldwork made us realise that there are limited avenues for the ideal-type democratic representation of workers through unions in Bangladesh, as outlined in Chapter 2. This calls for greater openness towards alternative routes of representation. Thus, Rodrik's (2008) work on second-best institutions really appealed to us. Rodrik encourages scholars not to search for the ideal solutions that often cannot achieve the perfect world but to search for an acceptable compromise that can be achieved – even if it is only second-best. The Accord is not perfect for the many reasons we discussed in this book, but we saw how fire doors and exit staircases were installed in factory buildings where previously there were none. We saw how concrete pillars were fortified to prevent the buildings from collapse. We saw that the Bangladeshi Building Code was applied to new factory buildings, that safety committees were being formed and that factory owners had started to boast about how safe their factories were. For all the faults that still exist, there are significantly fewer deaths in the industry compared with previously. We thus feel the responsibility as academic scholars to acknowledge the accomplishments of all parties involved, even if it is about acknowledging the positive role of the Alliance, a corporate-driven governance model with no say for unions. If it brings benefits for workers, it should not be dismissed right away even if the underlying model is problematic.

In sum, this book is the result of a conversation between two related yet also different disciplines and our chosen field of research. Without doubt, it has drawn very explicitly on established approaches from respective fields. Yet what we believe is somewhat new in our approach is that we have integrated these approaches to shed light on an emergent context with which neither existing approach alone could adequately engage.

# References

Alam, Q., and Teicher, J. (2012). The state of governance in Bangladesh: The capture of state institutions. *South Asia: Journal of South Asian Studies*, 35(4): 858–884.

Alamgir, F., and Banerjee, S. (2019). Contested compliance regimes in global production networks: Insights from the Bangladesh garment industry. *Human Relations*, 72(2): 272–297.

Alliance (2015). *Worker Helpline. Available at* www.bangladeshworkersafety .org/programs/worker-helpline (accessed 20 May 2015).

Amable, B. (2003). *The Diversity of Modern Capitalism*. Oxford: Oxford University Press.

Amengual, M., and Chirot, L. (2016). Reinforcing the state: Transnational and state labor regulation in Indonesia. *Industrial & Labor Relations Review*, 69(5): 1056–1080.

Amengual, M., Distelhorst, G., and Tobin, D. (2020). Global purchasing as labor regulation: The missing middle. *Industrial & Labor Relations Review*, 73(4): 817–840.

Anner, M. (2012). Corporate social responsibility and freedom of association rights: The precarious quest for legitimacy and control in global supply chains. *Politics & Society*, 40(4): 609–644.

(2015). Labor control regimes and worker resistance in global supply chains. *Labor History*, 56(3): 292–307

(2018). CSR participation committees, wildcat strikes and the sourcing squeeze in global supply chains. *British Journal of Industrial Relations*, 56(1): 75–98.

(2019). Squeezing workers' rights in global supply chains: Purchasing practices in the Bangladesh garment export sector in comparative perspective. *Review of International Political Economy*, 27(2): 320–347.

Anner, M., Greer, I., Hauptmeier, M., Lillie, N., and Winchester, N. (2006). The industrial determinants of transnational solidarity: Global interunion politics in three sectors. *European Journal of Industrial Relations*, 12(1): 7–27.

Ashwin, S., Oka, C., Schuessler, E., Alexander, R., and Lohmeyer, N. (2020). Spillover effects across transnational industrial relations agreements: The potential and limits of collective action in global supply chains. *Industrial & Labor Relations Review*, 73(4): 995–1020.

Atkinson, M. M., and Coleman, W. D. (1985). Corporatism and industrial policy. In A. Cawson (ed.), *Organized Interests and the State*. London: Sage, pp. 22–44.

Baccaro, L. (2006). Civil society meets the state: Towards associational democracy? *Socio-Economic Review*, 42(1): 185–208.

Baccaro, L., and Lim, S. H. (2007). Social pacts as coalitions of the weak and moderate: Ireland, Italy and South Korea in comparative perspective. *European Journal of Industrial Relations*, 13(1): 27–46.

Baccaro, L., and Mele, V. (2012). Pathology of path dependency? The ILO and the challenge of new governance. *Industrial & Labor Relations Review*, 65(2): 195–224.

Baccaro, L., and Pontusson, J. (2016). Rethinking comparative political economy: The growth model perspective. *Politics & Society*, 44(2): 175–207.

Banerjee, S. B. (2008). Corporate social responsibility: The good, the bad and the ugly. *Critical Sociology*, 34(1): 51–79.

(2018). Transnational power and translocal governance: The politics of corporate responsibility. *Human Relations*, 71(6): 796–821.

Bangladesh Garment Manufacturers and Exporters Association (BGMEA). (2020). Sustainability Report 2020. Available at http://download .bgmea.com.bd/BGMEA%20Sustainability%20Report%202020.pdf (accessed 11 June 2021).

Bansal, P., and Roth, K. (2000). Why companies go green: A model of ecological responsiveness. *Academy of Management Journal*, 43(4): 717–736.

Barnett, C., Clarke, N., Cloke, P., and Malpass, A. (2005). The political ethics of consumerism. *Consumer Policy Review*, 15(2): 45–51.

Barrientos, S., and Smith, S. (2007). Do workers benefit from ethical trade? Assessing codes of labour practice in global production systems. *Third World Quarterly*, 28(4): 713–729.

Bartley, T. (2007). Institutional emergence in an era of globalization: The rise of transnational private regulation of labor and environmental conditions. *American Journal of Sociology*, 113(2): 297–351.

(2018). *Rules without Rights: Land, Labor, and Private Authority in the Global Economy*. Oxford: Oxford University Press.

Bartley, T., and Egels-Zandén, N. (2016). Beyond decoupling: Unions and the leveraging of corporate social responsibility in Indonesia. *Socio-Economic Review*, 14(2): 231–255.

Baur, D., and Palazzo, G. (2011). The moral legitimacy of NGOs as partners of corporations. *Business Ethics Quarterly*, 21(4): 579–604.

Bendell, J. (2005). In whose name? The accountability of corporate social responsibility. *Development in Practice*, 15(3–4): 362–374.

Benhabib, S. (ed.). (1996). *Democracy and Difference: Contesting the Boundaries of the Political*. Princeton, NJ: Princeton University Press.

Beynon, H. (1973). *Working for Ford*. London: Allen Lane.

Bohman, J. (2012). Representation in the deliberative system. In. J. Parkinson and J. Mansbridge (eds.), *Deliberative Systems: Deliberative Democracy at the Large Scale*. Cambridge: Cambridge University Press, pp. 72–94.

Boyer, R. (2001). The diversity and future of capitalisms: A 'régulationist' analysis. In G. Hodgson, M. Itoh and N. Yokokawa (eds.), *Capitalism in Evolution: Global Contentions – East and West*. Aldershot: Edward Elgar, pp. 100–121.

Braverman, H. (1974). *Labor and Monopoly Capital: The Degradation of Work in the Twentieth Century*. New York: New York University Press.

Brinkerhoff, D. W., and Brinkerhoff, J. M. (2002). Governance reforms and failed states: Challenges and implications. *International Review of Administrative Sciences*, 68(4): 511–531.

Brown, W. (1973). *Piecework Bargaining*. London: Heinemann.

Bryde, O. (2011). Transnational democracy. In U. Fastenrath, R. Geiger, D. Khan, A. Paulus, S. von Schorlemer and C. Vedde (eds.), *From Bilateralism to Community Interest: Essays in Honour of Bruno Simma*. Oxford: Oxford University Press, pp. 211–223.

Budd, J. W. (2004). *Employment with a Human Face: Balancing Efficiency, Equity, and Voice*. Ithaca, NY: Cornell University Press.

Carroll, A. B. (1999). Corporate social responsibility evolution of a definitional construct. *Business & Society*, 38(2): 268–295.

Cerny, P. G. (1995). Globalization and the changing logic of collective action. *International Organization*, 49(4): 595–625.

(1997). Paradoxes of the competition state: The dynamics of political globalization. *Government and Opposition*, 32(2): 251–274.

Clark, G. L., and Wrigley, N. (1997). Exit, the firm and sunk costs: Reconceptualizing the corporate geography of disinvestment and plant closure. *Progress in Human Geography*, 21(3): 338–358.

Clarke, S. (1992). What in the f—'s name is Fordism? In N. Gilbert, R. Burrows and A. Pollertt (eds.), *Fordism and Flexibility*. London: Palgrave Macmillan, pp. 13–30.

Clean Clothes Campaign, International Labor Rights Forum, Maquila Solidarity Network and Worker Rights Consortium. (2019). Bangladesh Government's safety inspection agencies not ready to take over Accord's work. Available at https://laborrights.org/sites/default/files/publications/RCC%20report%204-1_3.pdf (accessed 7 November 2021).

Clegg, H. (1951). *Industrial Democracy and Nationalization: A Study Prepared for the Fabian Society.* Oxford: Blackwell.

Cohen, J. (1989). The economic basis of deliberative democracy. *Social Philosophy and Policy,* 6(2): 25–50.

Cohen, J., and Rogers, J. (1992). Secondary associations and democratic governance. *Politics & Society,* 20(4): 393–472.

Commons, J. R. (1919). *Industrial Goodwill.* New York: McGraw-Hill.

Compa, L. (2004). Trade unions, NGOs, and corporate codes of conduct. *Development in Practice,* 14: 210–215.

Conroy, M. E. (2007). *Branded! How the 'Certification Revolution' Is Transforming Global Corporations.* New York: New Society.

Crane, A., Matten, D., and Moon, J. (2008). *Corporations and Citizenship.* Cambridge: Cambridge University Press.

Crouch, C. (2009). Privatised Keynesianism: An unacknowledged policy regime. *The British Journal of Politics and International Relations,* 11(3): 382–399.

Croucher, R., and Cotton, E. (2008). *Global Unions, Global Business: Global Union Federations and International Business.* New York: Libri.

Cullinane, N., and Dundon, T. (2014). Unitarism and employer resistance to trade unionism. *The International Journal of Human Resource Management,* 25(18): 2573–2590.

*Daily Star* (2018) Tofail blasts Accord. *The Daily Star.* Available at www .thedailystar.net/business/news/tofail-blasts-accord-1659820 (accessed 20 September 2021).

Dawkins, C. E. (2012). Labored relations: Corporate citizenship, labor unions, and freedom of association. *Business Ethics Quarterly,* 22(3): 473–500.

(2019). A normative argument for independent voice and labor unions. *Journal of Business Ethics,* 155(4): 1153–1165.

Den Hond, F., and De Bakker, F. G. (2007). Ideologically motivated activism: How activist groups influence corporate social change activities. *Academy of Management Review,* 32(3): 901–924.

Department of Inspection for Factories and Establishments (DIFE). (2020). Gender roadmap, 2020–2030. Available at www.ilo.org/wcmsp5/ groups/public/—asia/—ro-bangkok/—ilo-dhaka/documents/publication/ wcms_753443.pdf (accessed 17 April 2021).

Dingwerth, K., and Pattberg, P. (2009). World politics and organizational fields: The case of transnational sustainability governance. *European Journal of International Relations,* 15(4): 707–743.

Disch, L. (2011). Toward a mobilization conception of democratic representation. *American Political Science Review,* 105(1): 100–114.

(2012). Democratic representation and the constituency paradox. *Perspectives on Politics*, 10(3): 599–616.

(2015). The 'constructivist turn' in democratic representation: A normative dead-end? *Constellations*, 22(4): 487–499.

Djelic, M. L., and Sahlin-Andersson, K. (eds.). (2006). *Transnational Governance: Institutional Dynamics of Regulation*. Cambridge: Cambridge University Press.

Dobbin, F., and Sutton, J. R. (1998). The strength of a weak state: The rights revolution and the rise of human resources management divisions. *American Journal of Sociology*, 104(2): 441–476.

Doellgast, V. (2012). *Disintegrating Democracy at Work*. New York: Cornell University Press.

Dolan, C., and Humphrey, J. (2004). Changing governance patterns in the trade in fresh vegetables between Africa and the United Kingdom. *Environment and Planning A*, 36(3): 491–509.

Donaghey, J., and Reinecke, J. (2018). When industrial democracy meets corporate social responsibility: A comparison of the Bangladesh Accord and Alliance as responses to the Rana Plaza disaster. *British Journal of Industrial Relations*, 56(1): 14–42.

Donaghey, J., Reinecke, J., Niforou, C., and Lawson, B. (2014). From employment relations to consumption relations: Balancing labor governance in global supply chains. *Human Resource Management*, 53(2): 229–252.

Dryzek, J. S. (1999). Transnational democracy. *Journal of Political Philosophy*, 7(1): 30–51.

(2010). *Foundations and Frontiers of Deliberative Governance*. Oxford: Oxford University Press.

Dryzek, J. S., and Niemeyer, S. (2008). Discursive representation. *American Political Science Review*, 102(4): 481–493.

Edwards, P. (1986) *Conflict at Work: A Materialist Analysis of Workplace Relations*. Oxford: Basil Blackwell.

(2003). The employment relationship and the field of industrial relations. In P. Edwards (ed.), *Industrial relations*, 2nd ed. Oxford: Basil Blackwell, pp. 434–460.

Edwards, P. K. (2018). *Conflict in the Workplace: The Concept of Structured Antagonism Reconsidered*. Coventry: University of Warwick.

Egels-Zandén, N. (2009). Transnational governance of workers' rights: Outlining a research agenda. *Journal of Business Ethics*, 87: 169–188.

Egels-Zandén, N., and Hyllman, P. (2006). Exploring the effects of union–NGO relationships on corporate responsibility: The case of the Swedish clean clothes campaign. *Journal of Business Ethics*, 64(3): 303–316.

(2011). Differences in organizing between unions and NGOs: Conflict and cooperation among Swedish unions and NGOs. *Journal of Business Ethics*, 101(2): 249–261.

Egels-Zandén, N., and Lindholm, H. (2015). Do codes of conduct improve worker rights in supply chains? A study of Fair Wear Foundation. *Journal of Cleaner Production*, 107: 31–40.

Egels-Zandén, N., and Merk, J. (2014). Private regulation and trade union rights: Why codes of conduct have limited impact on trade union rights. *Journal of Business Ethics*, 123(3): 461–473.

Ehrnström-Fuentes, M. (2016). Delinking legitimacies: A pluriversal perspective on political CSR. *Journal of Management Studies*, 53(3): 433–462.

Engman, M., Onodera, O., and Pinali, E. (2007). Export processing zones: Past and future role in trade and development. *OECD Trade Policy Papers*, No. 53. Paris: OECD.

Erixon, L. (2008). The Swedish third way: An assessment of the performance and validity of the Rehn-Meidner model. *Cambridge Journal of Economics*, 32(3): 367–393.

(2010). The Rehn-Meidner model in Sweden: Its rise, challenges and survival. *Journal of Economic Issues*, 44(3): 677–715.

Ethical Trading Initiative (ETI). (2014). *Auditing working conditions*. Available at www.ethicaltrade.org/in-action/issues/auditing-working-conditions (accessed 15 February 2019).

European Commission. (2018). *Implementation of the Bangladesh Compact: Technical status report*. Available at https://trade.ec.europa.eu/doclib/docs/2018/september/tradoc_157426.pdf (accessed 8 November 2021).

Eurostat (2020). Where do our clothes come from? Available at https://ec.europa.eu/eurostat/web/products-eurostat-news/-/edn-20200424-1 (accessed 8 November 2021).

Evans, A. (2020). Overcoming the global despondency trap: Strengthening corporate accountability in supply chains. *Review of International Political Economy*, 27(3): 658–685.

Feuerstein, P. (2013). Patterns of work reorganization in the course of the IT industry's internationalization. *Competition & Change*, 17(1): 24–40.

Fichter, M., and McCallum, J. K. (2015). Implementing global framework agreements: The limits of social partnership. *Global Networks*, 15(s1): S65–S85.

Ford, M., and Gillan, M. (2015). The global union federations in international industrial relations: A critical review. *Journal of Industrial Relations*, 57(3), 456–475.

Fox, A. (1974). *Beyond Contract: Work, Power and Trust Relations.* London: Faber & Faber.

  (1975). Collective bargaining, Flanders, and the Webbs. *British Journal of Industrial Relations*, 13(2): 151–174.

Fransen, L. (2012). Multi-stakeholder governance and voluntary programme interactions: Legitimation politics in the institutional design of corporate social responsibility. *Socio-Economic Review*, 10(1): 163–192.

Fransen, L., and Burgoon, B. (2015). Global labour-standards advocacy by European civil society organizations: Trends and developments. *British Journal of Industrial Relations*, 53(2): 204–230.

Frenkel, S., and Schuessler, E. (2021) From Rana Plaza to COVID-19: Deficiencies and opportunities for a new labour governance system in garment global supply chains. *International Labour Review* 160(4): 591–609.

Freeman, R., and Lazear, E. (1995). An economic analysis of works councils. In J. Rogers and W. Streeck (eds.), *Works Councils: Consultation, Representation and Cooperation in Industrial Relations.* Chicago: Chicago University Press, pp. 27–52.

Gereffi, G. (1994). The organization of buyer-driven global commodity chains: How US retailers shape overseas production networks. In G. Gereffi and M. Korzeniewicz (eds.), *Commodity chains and global capitalism.* Westport, CT: Praeger, pp. 95–122.

Gereffi, G., Humphrey, J., and Timothy, S. (2005). The governance of global value chains. *Review of International Political Economy*, 12(1): 78–104.

Gilbert, D. U., and Rasche, A. (2007). Discourse ethics and social accountability: The ethics of SA 8000. *Business Ethics Quarterly*, 17(2): 187–216.

Global Justice Now. (2016). 10 biggest corporations make more money than most countries in the world combined. Available at www.globaljustice .org.uk/news/2016/sep/12/10-biggest-corporations-make-more-money-most-countries-world-combined (accessed 5 May 2021).

Goodin, R. E. (2007). Enfranchising all affected interests, and its alternatives. *Philosophy & Public Affairs*, 35(1): 40–68.

Greer, I., and Hauptmeier, M. (2012). Identity work: Sustaining transnational collective action at General Motors Europe. *Industrial Relations: A Journal of Economy and Society*, 51(2): 275–299.

Gunningham, N. (2008). Occupational health and safety, worker participation and the mining industry in a changing world of work. *Economic and Industrial Democracy*, 29(3): 336–361.

Gutierrez-Huerter, O. G., Gold, S., and Trautrims, A. (2021). Change in rhetoric but not in action? Framing of the ethical issue of modern slavery in a UK sector at high risk of labor exploitation. *Journal of Business Ethics*. Available at https://link.springer.com/article/10.1007/s10551-021-05013-w (accessed 2 March 2022).

H&M. (2014). Sustainability report. Available at https://about.hm.com/content/dam/hmgroup/groupsite/documents/en/CSR/reports/Conscious%20Actions%20Sustainability%20Report%202014_en.pdf (accessed 17 January 2015).

H&M. (n.d.). Production. Available at https://career.hm.com/content/hmcareer/en_au/workingathm/what-can-you-do-here/corporate/production.html (accessed 6 June 2021).

Habermas, J. (1989). *The Structural Transformation of the Public Sphere: An Inquiry into a Category of Bourgeois Society*. Cambridge, MA: MIT Press.

Hahn, R., and Weidtmann, C. (2016). Transnational governance, deliberative democracy, and the legitimacy of ISO 26000: Analyzing the case of a global multistakeholder process. *Business & Society*, 55(1): 90–129.

Haidinger, B., Schönauer, A., Flecker, J., and Holtgrewe, U. (2014). Value chains and networks in services: Crossing borders, crossing sectors, crossing regimes. In M. Hauptmeier and M. Vidal (eds.), *Comparative Political Economy of Work*. Basingstoke: Palgrave Macmillan, pp. 98–118.

Hall, M., and Purcell, J. (2012). *Consultation at Work: Regulation and Practice*. Oxford: Oxford University Press

Hammer, N. (2005). International framework agreements: Global industrial relations between rights and bargaining. *Transfer: European Review of Labour and Research*, 11(4): 511–530.

Hammer, N., and Plugor, R (2016). Near-sourcing UK apparel: Value chain restructuring, productivity and the informal economy. *Industrial Relations Journal*, 47(5–6): 402–416.

Hammer, N., and Plugor, R. (2019). Disconnecting labour? The labour process in the UK fast fashion value chain. *Work, Employment & Society*, 33(6): 913–928.

Hammer, N., Plugor, R., Nolan, P., and Clark, I. (2015). New industry on a skewed playing field: Supply chain relations and working conditions in UK garment manufacturing. Focus area – Leicester and the East Midlands. Leicester: University of Leicester. Available at https://hdl.handle.net/2381/31720 (accessed 20 November 2021).

Hasan, R., Moore, M., and Handfield, R. (2020). Addressing social issues in commodity markets: Using cost modeling as an enabler of public policy in the Bangladeshi apparel industry. *Journal of Supply Chain Management*, 56(4): 25–44.

Hassel, A. (2008). The evolution of a global labor governance regime. *Governance*, 21(2): 231–251.

Hathaway, T. (2020). Neoliberalism as corporate power. *Competition & Change*, 24(3–4): 315–337.

Heery, E. (1993). Industrial relations and the customer. *Industrial Relations Journal*, 24(4): 284–295.

Hirschman, A. O. (1970). *Exit, Voice, and Loyalty: Responses to Decline in Firms, Organizations, and States*. Cambridge, MA: Harvard University Press.

Hobbes, T. (1651). *Leviathan*, with selected variants from the Latin edition of 1668 (E. Curley ed.) Indianapolis, IN: HackettThomas.

Human Rights Watch. (2015). Whoever raises their head, suffers the most: Workers' rights in Bangladesh Garment factories. Available at www.hrw.org/node/278009/printable/print (accessed 15 March 2019).

Hyman, R. (2001). *Understanding European Trade Unionism: Between Market, Class and Society*. Thousand Oaks, CA: Sage.

IndustriALL. (2012). Tchibo joins agreement on garment factory safety in Bangladesh. Available at www.industriall-union.org/tchibo-joins-agreement-on-garment-factory-safety-in-bangladesh (accessed 20 November 2021).

(2013a). IndustriALL leading the struggle for Bangladesh Garment workers. Available at www.industriall-union.org/report-industriall-leading-the-struggle-for-bangladeshi-garment-workers (accessed 20 November 2021).

(2013b). We made it! Global breakthrough as retail brands sign up to Bangladesh factory safety deal. Available at www.industriall-union.org/we-made-it-global-breakthrough-as-retail-brands-sign-up-to-bangladesh-factory-safety-deal (accessed 20 November 2021).

International Labour Organization (ILO). (2015). Rana Plaza two years on: Progress made & challenges ahead for the Bangladesh RMG sector. Available at www.ilo.org/wcmsp5/groups/public/—asia/—ro-bangkok/—ilo-dhaka/documents/publication/wcms_317816.pdf (accessed 20 November 2021).

(2018). International framework agreements in the food retail, garment and chemicals sector. Available at www.ilo.org/wcmsp5/groups/public/—ed_dialogue/—sector/documents/publication/wcms_631043.pdf (accessed 20 November 2021).

(2022). Social Dialogue Report 2022. Available at https://www.ilo.org/wcmsp5/groups/public/—dgreports/—dcomm/—publ/documents/publication/wcms_842807.pdf (accessed 19 May 2022).

International Labor Rights Forum (ILRF). (2015). *Our voices, our safety: Bangladeshi garment workers speak out*. Washington, DC:

International Labour Rights Forum. Available at: http://laborrights.org/ sites/default/files/publications/Our%20Voices,%20Our%20Safety%20 Online_1.pdf (accessed 1 May 2017).

International Trade Union Confederation (ITUC). (2018). *ITUC Global Rights Index 2018*. Available at www.ituc-csi.org/ituc-global-rights-index-2018 (accessed 23 October 2017).

(2019). *ITUC Global Rights Index 2019*. Available at www.ituc-csi.org/ IMG/pdf/2019-06-ituc-global-rights-index-2019-report-en-2.pdf (accessed 23 October 2020).

(2020). *ITUC Global Rights Index 2020*. Available at www.ituc-csi.org/ ituc-global-rights-index-2020 (Accessed 17 November 2019).

Iversen, T., and Soskice, D. (2020). Response to Carles Boix's review of *Democracy and Prosperity: Reinventing Capitalism through a Turbulent Century. Perspectives on Politics*, 18(2): 547–548.

James, P., Johnstone, R., Quinlan, M., and Walters, D. (2007). Regulating supply chains to improve health and safety. *Industrial Law Journal*, 36(2): 163–187.

Jenkins, J., and Blyton, P. (2017). In debt to the time-bank: The manipulation of working time in Indian garment factories and 'working dead horse'. *Work, Employment and Society* 31(1): 90–105.

Jessop, B. (2002). Liberalism, neoliberalism, and urban governance: A state–theoretical perspective. *Antipode*, 34(3): 452–472.

(2011). Rethinking the diversity and variability of capitalism. In G. Wood and C. Lane (eds.), *Capitalist Diversity and Diversity within Capitalism*. London: Routledge, pp. 151–209.

Johnstone, S., Wilkinson, A., and Ackers, P. (2011). Applying Budd's model to partnership. *Economic and Industrial Democracy*, 32(2): 307–328.

Kabeer, N. (2017). Economic pathways to women's empowerment and active citizenship: What does the evidence from Bangladesh tell us? *The Journal of Development Studies*, 53(5): 649–663.

Kabeer, N., Huq, L., and Sulaiman, M. (2020). Paradigm shift or business as usual? Workers' views on multi-stakeholder initiatives in Bangladesh. *Development and Change*, 51(5): 1360–1398.

Kaldor, M. (2003). The idea of global civil society. *International Affairs*, 79(3): 583–593.

Kang, Y. (2021). The rise, demise, and replacement of the Bangladesh experiment in transnational labour regulation. *International Labour Review*, 160(3): 407–430.

Kaufman, B. E. (2004). *The Global Evolution of Industrial Relations: Events, Ideas and the IIRA*. Geneva: ILO.

Kelly, J. (1998). *Rethinking Industrial Relations: Mobilisation, Collectivism and Long Waves*. London: Routledge.

Keohane, R. 2003. Global governance and democratic accountability. In D. Held and M. Koenig-Archibugi (eds.), *Taming Globalization: Frontiers of Governance*. Bristol: Polity Press, pp. 130–159.

Kessler, I., and Bach, S. (2011). The citizen-consumer as industrial relations actor: New ways of working and the end-user in social care. *British Journal of Industrial Relations*, 49(1): 80–102.

Khan, F. R., Munir, K. A., and Willmott, H. (2007). A dark side of institutional entrepreneurship: Soccer balls, child labour and postcolonial impoverishment. *Organization Studies*, 28(6): 1055–1077.

King, B. G., and Pearce, N. A. (2010). The contentiousness of markets: Politics, social movements, and institutional change in markets. *Annual Review of Sociology*, 36: 249–267.

Knudsen, J. S., and Moon, J. (2017). *Visible Hands: Government Regulation and International Business Responsibility*. Cambridge: Cambridge University Press.

Kochan, F., Jackson, B., and Duke, D. (1999). *A Thousand Voices from the Firing Line: A Study of Educational Leaders, Their Jobs, and the Problems They Face*. Columbia, MO: University Council for Educational Administration.

Koenig-Archibugi, M., and MacDonald, K. (2013). Accountability-by-proxy in transnational non-state governance. *Governance*, 26(3): 499–522.

Krasner, S. (1999). *Organized Hypocrisy*, Princeton, NJ: Princeton University Press.

Labowitz, S., and Baumann-Pauly, D. (2014). *Business as Usual Is Not an Option. Supply Chains and Sourcing after Rana Plaza*. New York: Stern Center for Business and Human Rights, New York University.

Laclau, E. (2005). *On Populist Reason*. London: Verso.

Lange, D., and Washburn, N. T. (2012). Understanding attributions of corporate social irresponsibility. *Academy of Management Review*, 37(2): 300–326.

LeBaron, G., and Lister, J. (2015). Benchmarking global supply chains: The power of the 'ethical audit' regime. *Review of International Studies*, 41(5): 905–924.

LeBaron, G., Lister, J., and Dauvergne, P. (2017). Governing global supply chain sustainability through the ethical audit regime. *Globalizations*, 14(6): 958–975.

Levi, M., Adolph, C., Berliner, D., Erlich, A., Greenleaf, A., Lake, M., and Noveck, J. (2013). Aligning rights and interests: Why, when and how to uphold labor standards. Background Paper for the World Development Report, 8258024-1320950747192.

Lim, A., and Tsutsui, K. (2012). Globalization and commitment in corporate social responsibility: Cross-national analyses of institutional and political-economy effects. *American Sociological Review*, 77(1): 69–98.

Lipset, S. M. (1952). Democracy in private government: A case study of the International Typographical Union. *The British Journal of Sociology* 3(1): 47–58.

Locke, R. M. (2013). *The Promise and Limits of Private Power: Promoting Labor Standards in a Global Economy.* Cambridge: Cambridge University Press.

Locke, R. M., Amengual, M., and Mangla, A. (2009). Virtue out of necessity? Compliance, commitment, and the improvement of labor conditions in global supply chains. *Politics & Society*, 37(3): 319–351.

Locke, R. M., Rissing, B. A., and Pal, T. (2013). Complements or substitutes? Private codes, state regulation and the enforcement of labour standards in global supply chains. *British Journal of Industrial Relations*, 51(3): 519–552.

Lund-Thomsen, P. (2008). The global sourcing and codes of conduct debate: Five myths and five recommendations. *Development and Change*, 39(6): 1005–1018.

Lury, C. (2004). *Brands: The Logos of the Global Economy.* London: Routledge.

Lynch, L. M. (1994). *Training and the Private Sector. International Comparisons NBEC.* Chicago: University of Chicago Press.

Maeckelbergh, M. (2011). The road to democracy: The political legacy of '1968'. *International Review of Social History*, 56(2): 301–332.

Mansbridge, J. (2003). Rethinking representation. *American Political Science Review*, 97(4): 515–528.

(2009). A 'selection model' of political representation. *Journal of Political Philosophy*, 17(4): 369–398.

(2011). Clarifying the concept of representation. *American Political Science Review*, 105(3): 621–630.

(2012). On the importance of getting things done. *PS: Political Science & Politics*, 45(1): 1–8.

Marchington, M., Willmott, H., Grimshaw, D., and Rubery, J. (2005). *Fragmenting Work: Blurring Organizational Boundaries and Disordering Hierarchies.* Oxford: Oxford University Press.

Marshall, T. H. (1950). *Citizenship and Social Class.* Cambridge: Cambridge University Press.

Martin, R. (1968). Union democracy: An explanatory framework. *Sociology*, 2 (2): 205–220.

Matten, D., and Crane, A. (2005). Corporate citizenship: Towards an extended theoretical conceptualization. *Academy of Management Review*, 30(1): 166–179.

McCallum, J. (2017). *Global Unions, Local Power: The New Spirit of Transnational Labor Organizing.* Ithaca, NY: Cornell University Press.

Miller, D. (2011). Global social relations and corporate social responsibility in outsourced apparel supply chains: The Inditex Global Framework Agreement. In K. Papadakis (ed.), *Shaping Global Industrial Relations*. London: Palgrave Macmillan, pp. 179–198.

Mintzberg, H. (1983). The case for corporate social responsibility. *Journal of Business Strategy*, 4: 3–15.

Montanaro, L. (2012). The democratic legitimacy of self-appointed representatives. *The Journal of Politics*, 74(4): 1094–1107.

Morelli, C. (2021). Regulating the post-independence textile trade: Anglo-Indian tariff negotiations from independence to the Multi-Fibre Arrangement. *Business History*, 63(1), 38–51.

Morris, J., Jenkins, J., and Donaghey, J. (2021). Uneven development, uneven response: The relentless search for meaningful regulation of GVCs. *British Journal of Industrial Relations*, 59(1), 3–24.

Müller-Jentsch, W. (1976). *Zum Verhältnis von Staat und Gewerkschaften*. Frankfurt: Rahmenbedingungen und Schranken staatlichen Handelns.

(2003). Re-assessing co-determination. In H. Weitbrecht and W. Muller-Jentsch (eds.), *The Changing Contours of German Industrial Relations*. Munich: Rainer Hampp Verlag, pp. 39–56.

Nanz, P., and Steffek, J. (2004). Global governance, participation and the public sphere. *Government and Opposition*, 39(2): 314–335.

Nicholls, A., and Opal, C. (2005). *Fair Trade: Market-Driven Ethical Consumption*. Thousand Oaks, CA: Sage.

Nienhüser, W. (2020). Works councils. In A. Wilkinson, J. Donaghey, T. Dundon and R. Freeman (eds.) *Handbook of Research on Employee Voice*. Cheltenham: Edward Elgar, pp. 250–276.

Niforou, C. (2012). International framework agreements and industrial relations governance: Global rhetoric versus local realities. *British Journal of Industrial Relations*, 50(2): 352–373.

(2014). International framework agreements and the democratic deficit of global labour governance. *Economic and Industrial Democracy*, 35(2): 367–386.

O'Rourke, D. (2006). Multi-stakeholder regulation: Privatizing or socializing global labor standards? *World Development*, 34(5): 899–918.

Olson, M. (1965). *The Logic of Collective Action*. Cambridge, MA: Harvard University Press.

Permanent Court of Arbitration. (2018). Bangladesh Accord Arbitrations. Available at https://pca-cpa.org/en/cases/152 (accessed 17 January 2021).

Petit, P. (1999). Structural forms and growth regimes of the post-Fordist era. *Review of Social Economy*, 57(2): 220–243.

Pike, K. (2020). Voice in supply chains: Does the Better Work Program lead to improvements in labor standards compliance? *Industrial & Labor Relations Review*, 73(4): 913–938.

Piketty, T. (2014). *Capital in the Twenty-First Century*. Cambridge, MA: Harvard University Press.

Pitkin, H. F. (1967). *The Concept of Representation*. Berkeley: University of California Press.

(2004). Representation and democracy: Uneasy alliance. *Scandinavian Political Studies*, 27(3): 335–342.

Preuss, L., Gold, M., and Rees, C. (2015). The rise of corporate social responsibility as a challenge for trade unions. In L. Preuss, M. Rees and C. Gold (eds.), *Corporate Social Responsibility and Trade Unions*. London: Routledge, pp. 1–25.

Preuss, L., Haunschild, A., and Matten, D. (2009). The rise of CSR: Implications for HRM and employee representation. *International Journal of Human Resource Management*, 20(4): 953–973.

Quan, K. (2008). Use of global value chains by labor organizers. *Competition & Change*, 12(1): 89–104.

Quinlan, M. (1999). The implications of labour market restructuring in industrialized societies for occupational health and safety. *Economic and Industrial Democracy*, 20(3): 427–460.

Rahim, M. M., and Islam, S. S. (2020). Freedom of association in the Bangladeshi garment industry: A policy schizophrenia in labour regulation. *International Labour Review*, 159(3): 423–446.

Rahman, Z., and Langford, T. (2014). International solidarity or renewed trade union imperialism? The AFL–CIO and garment workers in Bangladesh. *WorkingUSA*, 17(2): 169–186.

Rainnie, A., Herod, A., and Champ, S. M. (2007). Spatialising industrial relations. *Industrial Relations Journal*, 38(2): 102–118.

Rasche, A. (2010). The limits of corporate responsibility standards. *Business Ethics: A European Review*, 19(3): 280–291.

Ravallion, M. (2014). Income inequality in the developing world. *Science*, 344(6186): 851–855.

Razsa, M., and Kurnik, A. (2012). The Occupy Movement in Žižek's hometown: Direct democracy and a politics of becoming. *American Ethnologist*, 39(2): 238–258.

Regini, M. (2000). Between deregulation and social pacts: The responses of European economies to globalization. *Politics & Society*, 28(1), 5–33.

Rehfeld, A. (2006). Towards a general theory of political representation. *The Journal of Politics*, 68(1): 1–21.

Reinecke, J. (2018). Social movements and prefigurative organizing: Confronting entrenched inequalities in Occupy London. *Organization Studies*, 39(9): 1299–1321.

Reinecke, J., and Ansari, S. (2015). What is a 'fair' price? Ethics as sense-making. *Organization Science*, 26(3): 867–888.

(2016). Taming wicked problems: The role of framing in the construction of corporate social responsibility. *Journal of Management Studies*, 53(3): 299–329.

Reinecke, J., and Donaghey, J. (2015). After Rana Plaza: Building coalitional power for labour rights between unions and (consumption-based) social movement organisations. *Organization*, 22(5): 720–740.

(2021a). Political CSR at the coalface: The roles and contradictions of multinational corporations in developing workplace dialogue. *Journal of Management Studies*, 58(2): 457–486.

(2021b). Towards worker-driven supply chain governance: Developing decent work through democratic worker participation. *Journal of Supply Chain Management*, 57(2): 14–28.

Reinecke, J., Donaghey, J., Bocken, N., and Lauriano, L. (2019). *Business Models and Labour Standards: Making the Connection*. London: Ethical Trading Initiative.

Reinecke, J., Donaghey, J., Wilkinson, A., and Wood, G. (2018). Global supply chains and social relations at work: Brokering across boundaries. *Human Relations* 71(4): 459–480.

Reinecke, J., Manning, S., and Von Hagen, O. (2012). The emergence of a standards market: Multiplicity of sustainability standards in the global coffee industry. *Organization Studies*, 33(5–6), 791–814.

Riisgaard, L., and Hammer, N. (2011). Prospects for labour in global value chains: Labour standards in the cut flower and banana industries. *British Journal of Industrial Relations*, 49(1): 168–190.

Risse, T. (2004). Global governance and communicative action. *Government and Opposition*, 39(2): 288–313.

(2006). Transnational governance and legitimacy. In A. Benz and I. Papadopolous (eds.), *Governance and Democracy: Comparing National, European and International Experiences*. London: Routledge, pp. 179–199.

Rodrik, D. (2008). Second-best institutions. *American Economic Review*, 98 (2): 100–104.

(2013). *The Globalization Paradox: Democracy and the Future of the World Economy*. New York: W.W. Norton.

Rogers, J., and Streeck, W. (1995). The study of works councils: Concepts and problems. In J. Rogers and W. Streeck (eds.), *Works Councils*. Chicago: University of Chicago Press, pp. 3–26.

Rueda, D., and Pontusson, J. (2000). Wage inequality and varieties of capitalism. *World Politics*, 52(3): 350–383.

Ruggie, J. G. (2018). Multinationals as global institution: Power, authority and relative autonomy. *Regulation & Governance*, 12(3): 317–333.

Rugman, A. M. (2010). Globalization, regional multinationals and Asian economic development. *Asian Business & Management*, 9(3): 299–317.

Ryder, G. (2015). The International Labour Organization: The next 100 years. *Journal of Industrial Relations*, 57(5): 748–757.

Safi, M. (2018). Bangladesh to eject safety inspectors brought in after Rana Plaza disaster. *The Guardian* (28 November). Available at www .theguardian.com/world/2018/nov/28/international-inspectors-to-leave-bangladesh-after-factory-fire (accessed 29 November 2021).

Sanches, W., and Hoffman, C. (2017). 2018 Accord on Fire and Building Safety in Bangladesh: May 2018. Available at https://bangladesh .wpengine.com/wp-content/uploads/2020/11/2018-Accord.pdf (accessed 29 November 2021).

Saward, M. (2008). Representation and democracy: Revisions and possibilities. *Sociology Compass*, 2(3): 1000–1013.

(2010). *The Representative Claim*. Oxford: Oxford University Press.

Scharpf, F. W. (1997). Economic integration, democracy and the welfare state. *Journal of European Public Policy*, 4(1): 18–36.

Scherer, A. G., and Palazzo, G. (2007). Toward a political conception of corporate responsibility: Business and society seen from a Habermasian perspective. *Academy of Management Review*, 32(4): 1096–1120.

(2011). The new political role of business in a globalized world: A review of a new perspective on CSR and its implications for the firm, governance, and democracy. *Journal of Management Studies*, 48(4): 899–931.

Scherer, A. G., Palazzo, G., and Baumann, D. (2006). Global rules and private actors: Toward a new role of the transnational corporation in global governance. *Business Ethics Quarterly*, 16(4): 505–532.

Scherer, A. G., Rasche, A., Palazzo, G., and Spicer, A. (2016). Managing for political corporate social responsibility: New challenges and directions for PCSR 2.0. *Journal of Management Studies*, 53(3): 273–298.

Schmelzer, M. (2010). Marketing morals, moralizing markets: Assessing the effectiveness of fair trade as a form of boycott. *Management & Organizational History*, 5(2): 221–250.

Schmitter, P. C. (1974). Still the century of corporatism? *The Review of Politics*, 36(1): 85–131.

(1983). Democratic theory and neocorporatist practice. *Social Research*, 50(4): 885–928.

Schmitter, P. C., and Streeck, W. (1981). The organization of business interests: A research design to study the associative action of business in the advanced industrial societies of Western Europe. Discussion Papers IIMV/Arbeitsmarktpolitik – IIM/Labour Market Policy. Available at http://hdl.handle.net/11858/00-001M-0000-0012-5BAB-5 (accessed 29 November 2021).

Scholte, J. A. (2008). From government to governance: Transition to a new diplomacy. In W. Malet (ed.), *Global Governance and Diplomacy*. London: Palgrave Macmillan, pp. 39–60.

Schormair, M. J. L., and Gilbert, D. U. (2021). Creating value by sharing values: Managing stakeholder value conflict in the face of pluralism through discursive justification. *Business Ethics Quarterly*, 31(1): 1–36.

Schrempf-Stirling, J., and Palazzo, G. (2016). Upstream corporate social responsibility: The evolution from contract responsibility to full producer responsibility. *Business & Society*, 55(4): 491–527.

Schuessler, E., Frenkel, S. J., and Wright, C. F. (2019). Governance of labor standards in Australian and German garment supply chains: The impact of Rana Plaza. *Industrial & Labor Relations Review*, 72(3): 552–579.

Severs, E. (2012). Substantive representation through a claims-making lens: A strategy for the identification and analysis of substantive claims. *Representation*, 48(2): 169–181.

Siddiqi, D. M. (2009). Do Bangladeshi factory workers need saving? Sisterhood in the post-sweatshop era. *Feminist Review*, 91(1): 154–174.

   (2015) Starving for justice: Bangladeshi garment workers in a 'post-Rana Plaza' world. *International Labor and Working-Class History*, 87: 165–173.

   (2017). Before Rana Plaza: Toward a history of labor organizing in Bangladesh's garment industry. In V. Crinis and A. Vickers (eds.), *Labour in the Clothing Industry in the Asia Pacific*. London: Routledge, pp. 60–79.

   (2020). Logics of sedition: Re-signifying insurgent labour in Bangladesh's garment factories. *Journal of South Asian Development*, 15(3): 371–397.

Sobczak, A. (2007). Legal dimensions of international framework agreements in the field of corporate social responsibility. *Relations Industrielles/Industrial Relations*, 62(3): 466–491.

Soule, S. A. (1997). The student divestment movement in the United States and tactical diffusion: The shantytown protest. *Social Forces*, 75(3): 855–882.

Spooner, D. (2004). Trade unions and NGOs: The need for cooperation. *Development in Practice*, 14(1–2): 19–33.

Standing, G. (1997). Globalization, labour flexibility and insecurity: The era of market regulation. *European Journal of Industrial Relations*, 3(1): 7–37.

(2008). The ILO: An agency for globalization? *Development and Change*, 39(3): 355–384.

Starkey, K., and McKinlay, A. (1989). Beyond Fordism? Strategic choice and labour relations in Ford UK. *Industrial Relations Journal*, 20(2): 93–100.

Stone, D. A. (1989). Causal stories and the formation of policy agendas. *Political Science Quarterly*, 104(2): 281–300.

Streeck, W. (1992). *Social Institutions and Economic Performance: Studies of Industrial Relations in Advanced Capitalist Economies*. London: Sage.

(1995). Works councils in Western Europe: From consultation to participation. In J. Rogers and W. Streeck (eds.), *Works Councils: Consultation, Representation, and Cooperation in Industrial Relations*. Chicago: University of Chicago Press.

(1997a). Industrial citizenship under regime competition: The case of the European works councils. *Journal of European Public Policy*, 4(4): 643–664.

(1997b). Beneficial constraints: On the economic limits of rational voluntarism. In R. Boyer and J. R. Hollingsworth (eds.), *Contemporary Capitalism: The Embeddedness of Institutions*. Cambridge: Cambridge University Press, pp. 197–219.

(2016). *How Will Capitalism End? Essays on a Failing System*. New York: Verso.

Streeck, W., and Kentworthy, L. (2003). Theories and practices of neocorporatism. In T. Janoski, R. R. Alford, A. M. Hicks and M. A. Schwartz (eds.), *The Handbook of Political Sociology*. Cambridge: Cambridge University Press.

Streeck, W., and Schmitter, P. C. (1985). Community, market, state-and associations? The prospective contribution of interest governance to social order. *European Sociological Review*, 1(2): 119–138.

Streeck, W., and Thelen, K. A. (2005). *Beyond Continuity: Institutional Change in Advanced Political Economies*. Oxford: Oxford University Press.

Stroehle, J. C. (2017). The enforcement of diverse labour standards through private governance: An assessment. *Transfer: European Review of Labour and Research*, 23(4): 475–493.

SumOfUs. (2013). How many more Bangladeshi workers need to die? Available at https://actions.sumofus.org/a/asda-bangladesh-accord (accessed 12 March 2014).

Sumon, M. H., Shifa, N., and Gulrukh, S. (2017). Discourses of compensation and the normalization of negligence: The experience of the Tazreen factory fire. In R. Prentice and G. De Neve (eds.), *Unmaking the Global Sweatshop: Health and Safety of the World's Garment Workers*. Philadelphia: University of Pennsylvania Press, pp. 147–172.

Tanjeem, N. (2017). *Can Workers of the World Unite? A Multi-sited Ethnography of Transnational Labor Organizing across the Apparel Commodity Network*. New Brunswick, NJ: Rutgers University Press.

Taylor, P., Newsome, K., and Rainnie, A. (2013). 'Putting labour in its place': Global value chains and labour process analysis. *Competition & Change*, 17(1): 1–5.

Teague, P. (2005). What is enterprise partnership? *Organization*, 12(4): 567–589.

Terlaak, A. (2007). Order without law? The role of certified management standards in shaping socially desired firm behaviors. *Academy of Management Review*, 32(3): 968–985.

Textilbuendis. (2018). Letter to Sheikh Hasina, Prime Minister of Bangladesh. Available at www.textilbuendnis.com/wp-content/uploads/2018/08/2018-08-28_Letter_Bangladesh-Accord.pdf (accessed 15 November 2021).

Thelen, K. (2003). The paradox of globalization: Labor relations in Germany and beyond. *Comparative Political Studies*, 36(8): 859–880.

(2007). Contemporary challenges to the German vocational training system. *Regulation & Governance*, 1(3): 247–260.

Thomas, H., and Turnbull, P. (2018). From horizontal to vertical labour governance: The International Labour Organization (ILO) and decent work in global supply chains. *Human Relations*, 71(4): 536–559.

Thomas, M. P. (2011). Global industrial relations? Framework agreements and the regulation of international labor standards. *Labor Studies Journal*, 36(2): 269–287.

Thompson, D. F. (2001) Political representation. In N. J. Smelser and P. B. Baltes (eds.), *International Encyclopedia of Social & Behavioral Science*. Amsterdam: Elsevier, pp. 11696–11698.

Towers, B. (1997). *The Representation Gap: Change and Reform in the British and American Workplace*. Oxford: Oxford University Press.

Traxler, F. (1999). The state in industrial relations: A cross-national analysis of developments and socioeconomic effects. *European Journal of Political Research*, 36(1): 55–85.

Traxler, F., Brandl, B., Glassner, V., and Ludvig, A. (2008). Can cross-border bargaining coordination work? Analytical reflections and evidence from the metal industry in Germany and Austria. *European Journal of Industrial Relations*, 14(2): 217–237.

UK Environmental Audit Committee. (2019). *Fixing Fashion: Clothing Consumption and Sustainability*. London: UK Parliament. Available at https://publications.parliament.uk/pa/cm201719/cmselect/cmenvaud/1952/full-report.html#footnote-260 (accessed 22 November 2021).

UNCTAD. (2016). World Investment Report 2016. Available at http://unctad.org/en/pages/PublicationWebflyer.aspx?publicationid=1555 (accessed 5 June 2016).

(2018). World Investment Report 2018. Available at https://unctad.org/webflyer/world-investment-report-2018 (accessed 5 June 2016).

Urbinati, N., and Warren, M. E. (2008). The concept of representation in contemporary democratic theory. *Annual Review Political Science*, 11: 387–412.

US Government Publishing Office. (2020). Seven years after Rana Plaza, significant challenges remain. Available at www.govinfo.gov/content/pkg/CPRT-116SPRT39906/html/CPRT-116SPRT39906.htm (accessed 12 March 2021).

Van Buren, H. J., Greenwood, M., Donaghey, J., & Reinecke, J. (2021). Agonising over industrial relations: Bringing agonism and dissensus to the pluralist frames of reference. *Journal of Industrial Relations*, 63(2), 177–203.

Van Maanen, J. (1995). An end to innocence: the ethnography of ethnography. In J. Van Maanen (ed.), *Representation in Ethnography*. Thousand Oaks, CA: Sage, pp. 1–35.

Vartiainen, J. (1998). Understanding Swedish social democracy: Victims of success? *Oxford Review of Economic Policy*, 14(1): 19–39.

Vidal, M. (2015). *Fordism and the golden age of Atlantic capitalism*. In S. Edgell, H. Gottfried and E. Ganter (eds.), *The Sage Handbook of the Sociology of Work and Employment*. London: Sage, pp. 283–305.

Vogel, D. (2008). Private global business regulation. *Annual Review of Political Science*, 11(1): 261–282.

Walters, D., and Quinlan, M. (2019). Voice and resistance: Coalminers' struggles to represent their health and safety interests in Australia and New Zealand 1871–1925. *The Economic and Labour Relations Review*, 30(4): 513–531.

Watson, D. (2019). Fordism: A review essay. *Labor History*, 60(2): 144–159.

Webb, S., and Webb, B. (1897). *Industrial Democracy* (vol. 2). London: Longmans, Green and Company.

Welford, R., and Frost, S. (2006). Corporate social responsibility in Asian supply chains. *Corporate Social Responsibility and Environmental Management*, 13(3): 166–176.

Wells, D. (2007). Too weak for the job: Corporate codes of conduct, non-governmental organizations and the regulation of international labour standards. *Global Social Policy*, 7(1): 51–74.

(2009). Local worker struggles in the Global South: Reconsidering Northern impacts on international labour standards. *Third World Quarterly*, 30(3): 567–579.

Werhane, P. (1985). *Person, Rights and Cooperation*. Englewood Cliffs, NJ: Prentice Hall.

Whittle, A., and Mueller, F. (2011). The language of interests: The contribution of discursive psychology. *Human Relations*, 64(3): 415–435.

Wilkinson, A., Dundon, T., Donaghey, J., and Freeman, R. (2014). Employee voice: Charting new terrain. In A. Wilkinson, J. Donaghey, T. Dundon and R. Freeman (eds.), *The Handbook of Research on Employee Voice*. Cheltenham: Edward Elgar, pp. 1–16.

Williams, S., Abbott, B., and Heery, E. (2017). Civil governance in work and employment relations: How civil society organizations contribute to systems of labour governance. *Journal of Business Ethics*, 144(1): 103–119.

Wills, J. (2002). Bargaining for the space to organize in the global economy: A review of the Accord–IUF trade union rights agreement. *Review of International Political Economy*, 9(4): 675–700.

Wright, C. F. (2016). Leveraging reputational risk: Sustainable sourcing campaigns for improving labour standards in production networks. *Journal of Business Ethics*, 137(1): 195–210.

Wright, E. O. (2000). Working-class power, capitalist-class interests, and class compromise. *American Journal of Sociology*, 105(4): 957–1002.

(2010). *Envisioning Real Utopias*. New York: Verso.

Yang, Y., and Mlachila, M. (2007). The end of textiles quotas: A case study of the impact on Bangladesh. *The Journal of Development Studies*, 43(4): 675–699.

Young, I. M. (2001). Activist challenges to deliberative democracy. *Political Theory*, 29(5): 670–690.

(2006). Responsibility and global justice: A social connection model. *Social Philosophy and Policy*, 23(1): 102–130.

Zajak, S. (2017). International allies, institutional layering and power in the making of labour in Bangladesh. *Development and Change*, 48(5): 1007–1030.

Zhu, J., and Morgan, G. (2018). Global supply chains, institutional constraints and firm level adaptations: A comparative study of Chinese service outsourcing firms. *Human Relations*, 71(4): 510–535

Zhu, S., and He, C. (2013). Geographical dynamics and industrial relocation: Spatial strategies of apparel firms in Ningbo, China. *Eurasian Geography and Economics*, 54(3): 342–362.

# Index

3F (Danish union), 173, 220

Accor hotel chain, 38
Accord on Fire and Building Safety in
    Bangladesh (Accord), 18, 20,
    80–85, 87, 89, 111, 116, 159–162,
    194. *See also* International Accord;
    Labour Caucus; Transition Accord
  brand commitment, 81
  capacity-building emphasis,
    130–138, 143–145, 198
  co-emergence with Alliance, 121–123
  complaints mechanism, 134,
    136–138
  contested authority, 81, 150
  credible commitments, 126
  dominance of brands, 151, 155–159,
    168, 170–172
  exclusion of employers, 81, 150–159,
    162–164, 170–172, 204–205
  exclusion of state, 81, 159, 162–164,
    170–172, 204–205
  factory closures, 132, 156
  focused approach, 84
  governance structure, 123–125, 143,
    170
  implementation and operation, 126,
    130–138, 147–149
  including affected constituency, 105
  input legitimacy, 127–129
  jurisdiction challenged in court,
    166–170
  labour-negotiation approach,
    132–134
  legacy, 139–141
  legally enforceable commitment, 82,
    126
  legitimacy, 167
  leverage through collective action,
    83, 96, 98–99, 106, 199
  member-based presence, 106
  mobilising companies to sign up,
    96–99
  negotiating the Accord, 94–96
  OSH committees, 84, 86, 88,
    130–131, 136, 140, 198, 204
  pooling of resources, 83
  principles of industrial democracy,
    143
  programme activities, 80
  remediation rates under, 81
  replacement structures, 139–141,
    162–164
  representation of labour, 99–100,
    116–121, 124–125
  representative alliances in, 90–103
  representative gaps, 118
  role of NGOs and campaign groups,
    94, 100–103, 108, 112
  safety monitoring, 83–84, 129,
    156–159
  signatories, 90, 98–100
  success indicators, 81
  tensions, 101–103
  termination and replacement by RSC,
    167–170
  transnational co-determination, 81,
    197
  worker voice, 84, 130–131, 136–138
  workers' compensation, 132–134
Accord on Fire and Building Safety in
    Bangladesh (Accord) Steering
    Committee, 81, 94, 99, 125, 133
  BGMEA lack of seat, 128, 153–154
  ILO as chair, 96, 107, 125
accountability to constituency,
    113–116
  attention based, 115–116
  deliberative, 115
  membership-based, 113–115

251

Printed in the United States
by Baker & Taylor Publisher Services